Flower Knitting

Hiroko Ibuki

100 CUTE FLOWER AND FRUIT MOTIFS

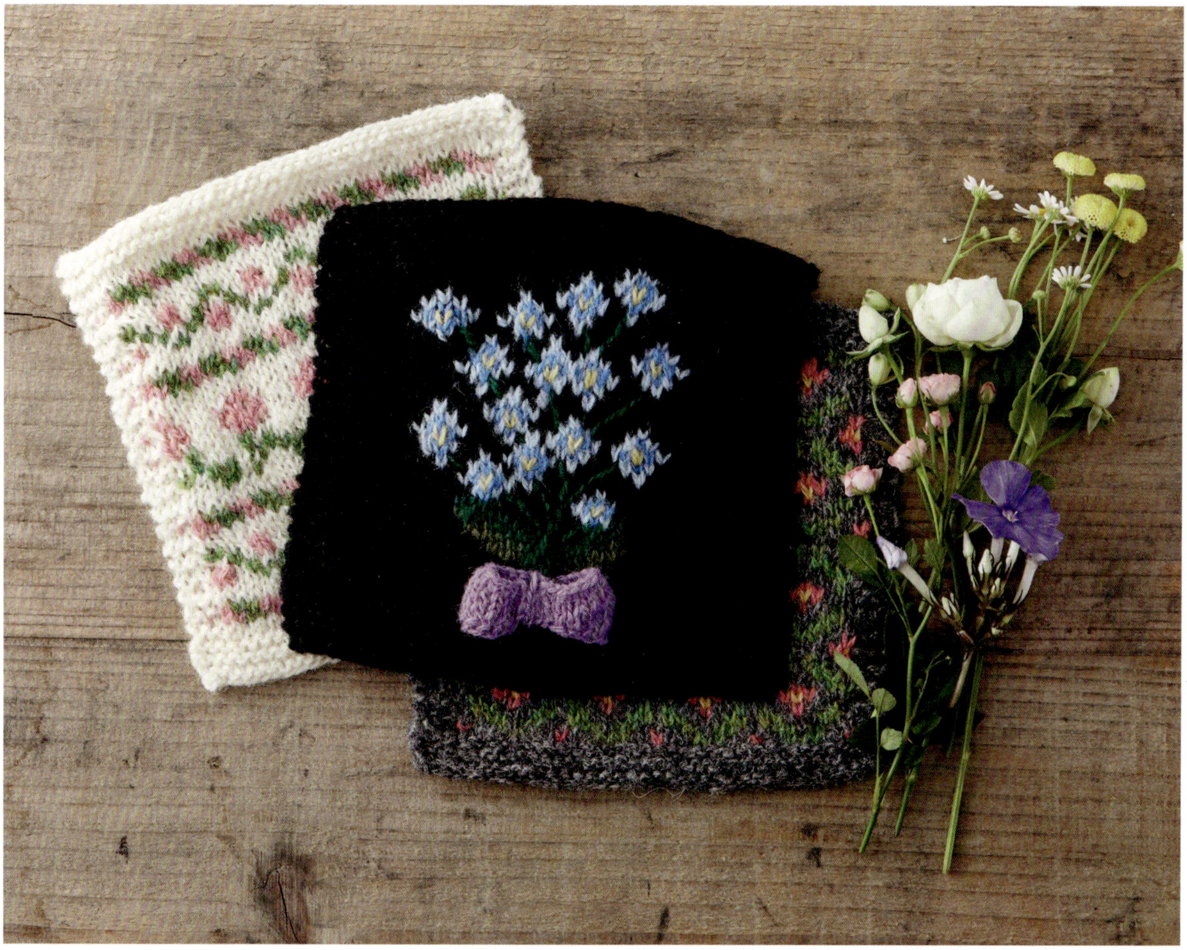

Preface

When I was asked to create a collection of colorwork knitting patterns, featuring flowers as the motif, the first thing that came to mind was my family. My grandmother, who always painted flowers, in a glass-walled room that felt like a greenhouse; my father, who loved gardening and taught me to 'pick flowers from the garden and arrange them in a vase to enjoy them in your room; and my mother, who would visit nurseries, find rare seedlings, and eagerly plant them in her garden. Growing up in such a family, it's no surprise that I, too, love flowers. And my way of expressing that love is through knitting.

When I look at the colors and shapes of plants in the photos I've taken, none of them are flowers you'd find in a flower shop. They're all ordinary flowers, the kind you see while taking a walk. But if you look closely, you'll notice their geometric patterns, exquisite color gradients, and the variety of shapes in their leaves and petals. How fun! As I kept working with my hands, I ended up creating one hundred swatches!

You could knit one of these small swatches, frame it, and display it, or you could choose your favorite swatch to knit into a garment or a scarf. "Look," "think," "work with your hands" – it's simple but a never-ending challenge.

Now, I'm off for a walk again today, to find inspiration to make the 101st swatch!

Hiroko Ibuki

Rosebud

Forget-Me-Not

Mushrooms and Moss

Poppy

Lilly of the Valley

Redcurrant

About This Book

This book features one hundred patterns that showcase a variety of techniques. Included are sequential patterns of small flowers, enlarged bloom close-ups, rows of small motifs, traditional designs with a modern twist, and patterns enhanced with embroidery.

I've also knitted sample projects using the patterns to illustrate, "For example, you can create something like this." I've chosen yarn and colors that I personally love, but what will you choose?

Feel free to mix and match the patterns and knit them in colors that reflect your personal style. To make customization easier, most garments are constructed by connecting simple rectangular shapes. Additionally, the collection includes many easy-to-make items that can bring brightness and joy to your everyday life.

About the Swatch Pages

• Charts are displayed on the opposite page from the swatch photo. Each swatch features a garter stitch along the edges to prevent curling, but the chart does not include these edge stitches.
• For repeating patterns, we have provided either a partial chart or an enlarged chart that clearly illustrates the repeat.
• The recommended length of the yarn strand is a guideline and may vary depending on the type of yarn. Try knitting a sample, unraveling it, measuring the length, and determining what works best for you (see page 39).
• In the charts, every 10 stitches and 10 rows are marked with a bold line for reference.
• For swatches knitted in different colors using the same pattern, only the yarn color numbers are listed.
• Please refer to the step-by-step photo instructions for techniques on pages 6, 27, 44, 70, and 122.

Contents

Preface *2*
About This Book *3*
Tools and Materials *6*
Lesson 1 Basic Techniques for Knitting with Multiple Colors *8*

Small Flowers

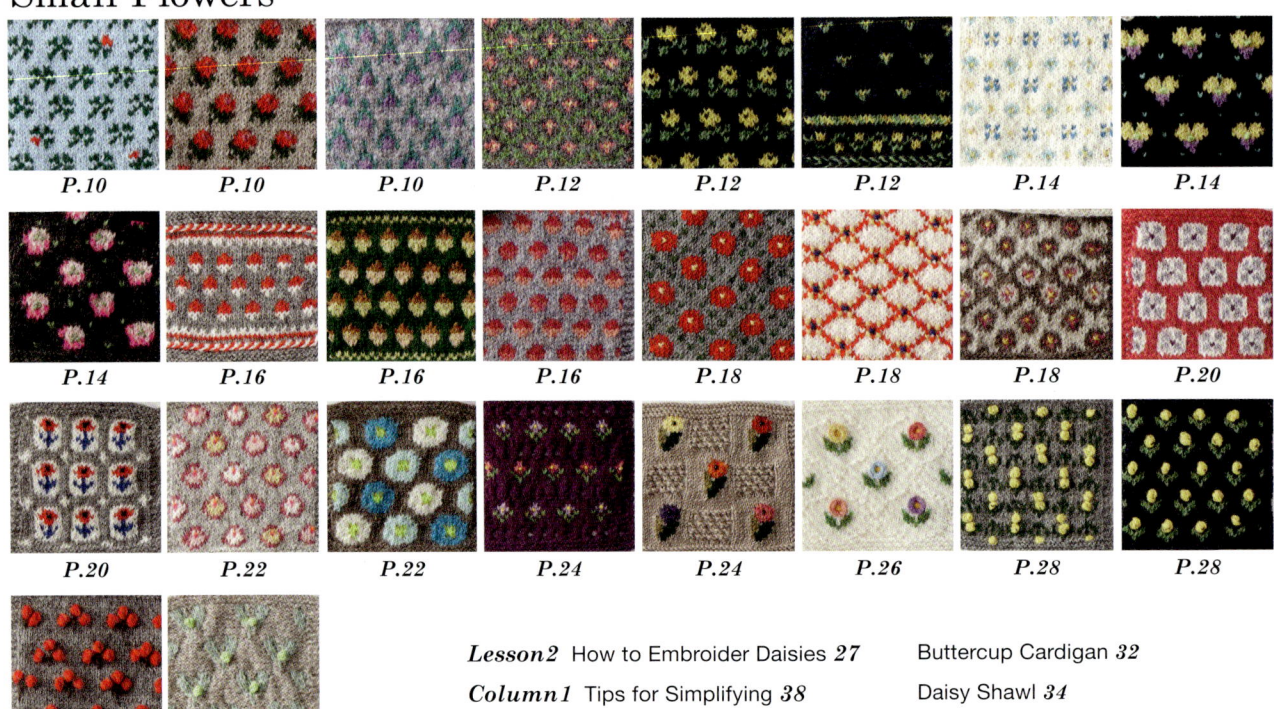

P.10 P.10 P.10 P.12 P.12 P.12 P.14 P.14
P.14 P.16 P.16 P.16 P.18 P.18 P.18 P.20
P.20 P.22 P.22 P.24 P.24 P.26 P.28 P.28
P.30 P.30

Lesson 2 How to Embroider Daisies *27*
Column 1 Tips for Simplifying *38*

Buttercup Cardigan *32*
Daisy Shawl *34*
Mistletoe Cowl *36*

Large Flowers

P.40 P.40 P.42 P.42 P.46 P.46 P.48 P.48
P.50 P.50 P.52 P.52 P.54 P.54 P.54 P.56
P.56 P.56 P.58 P.58 P.60 P.60

Lesson 3 How to Knit a Ribbon *44*
Column 2 Choosing Yarn and Creating an Image *64*

Thistle Bolero *62*

Fruits

P.66　P.66　P.68　P.68　P.72　P.72　P.72　P.74
P.74　P.76　P.76

Lesson 4 How to Knit Cherries *70*

Column 3 Adjusting to Your Own Size *79*

Cherries Bag *78*

Borders

P.82　P.82　P.82　P.84　P.84　P.86　P.86　P.88
P.88　P.90　P.90　P.92　P.92　P.94　P.94　P.96
P.96

Tea Cozy and Coaster *98*
Wrist Warmer *99*

Solid Color Patterns

P.100　P.100　P.102　P.102　P.104　P.104　P.106　P.106
P.108　P.108　P.110　P.110　P.112　P.112

Hand Warmers *114*

Lily of the Valley Hooded Shawl *115*

Lady's Mantle *116*

Things You Can Make with Swatches

Brooches, Coasters *118*

Pin Cushions, Mini-frames *119*

Patchwork Bag *120*

Patchwork Shawl *121*

Lesson 5 How to Knit Bobble Stitch *122*

Lesson 6 How to Knit Latvian Braid *124*

Lesson 7 How to Knit Trinity Stitch *125*

Lesson 8 How to Knit Smocking Stitch and Knot Stitch *126*

Lesson 9 How to Make Duplicate Stitch (Embroidery) *127*

Lesson 10 Joining Swatches *128*

Instructions *129*

Tools

This section introduces the essential tools used throughout the book.

1. **Circular Needles:** Needles connected by a cord, primarily used for knitting in the round. They can also be used for flat knitting. Choose longer cords for larger projects like garments and shorter ones for smaller items like hand warmers, based on the number of stitches required.
2. **Straight Needles:** Used for flat knitting. They are available in various materials, so choose the ones that feel most comfortable for you.
3. **Tapestry Needle:** A needle with a large eye for threading yarn. It is used for seaming or joining knitted pieces and for binding off.
4. **Pincushion, Pins, and Sewing Needles:** Pins are used to hold knitted pieces in place, while sewing needles are used for attaching felt, beads, and finishing details.
5. **Cable Needle:** Used for knitting crossing patterns (cables). Transfer stitches onto a cable needle then knit to make desired cross.
6. **Stitch Markers:** Used as markers for stitch counts, placed on the needles.
7. **Measuring Tape, Ruler:** Used to measure gauge and the knitted work.
8. **Crochet Hook:** With a hook at the tip to pull yarn through loops, it's used for seaming pieces together or for creating bobble stitches.
9. **Stitch Holders:** Used to hold stitches in place until a later stage. Yarn or other alternatives can also be used.
10. **Scissors:** Small scissors are sufficient for cutting yarn. For cutting fabric like linings for a bag, use fabric scissors.

In addition, it's good to have an iron and ironing board handy.

How to Steam Block

Always steam block your work after finishing. It will even out the stitches and create a neat look.

1 Lay the piece flat on an ironing board with the wrong side up, shape it, and pin it in place.

2 Hover a steam iron over the piece without touching and steam the surface. Let the piece cool in place.

3 The piece is complete. The stitches will be even, and the pattern will appear clearly. Measure your gauge in this state.

Materials

This section introduces the yarns used in this book. They can be purchased at craft stores or online shops. For inquiries, see page 192.

Puppy
1. Puppy New 2PLY
2. ALBA
3. Monarca
4. Kid Mohair Fine
5. Shetland
6. British Fine
7. Chaska

ROWAN
8. Felted Tweed
9. Kidsilk Haze

Jamieson's
10. Shetland Spindrift

For the swatches, the main yarns used are British Fine (top) and Shetland Spindrift (bottom). Both are British yarns and have similar texture and appearance. The fibers of Spindrift intertwine when wet blocked.

How to Wet Block

After finishing your knitting, check the instructions on the back of the yarn label and wet block the piece. Wet blocking removes oils and dirt while softening the fabric.

1 Soak the piece in lukewarm water. If you want to felt it, gently rub the piece. For garments, gently press and wash without rubbing.

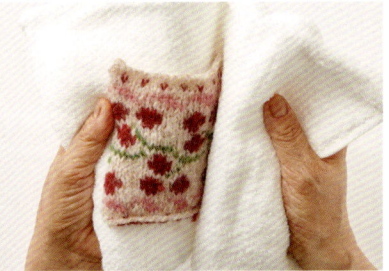

2 Pat the piece with a dry towel. Press it gently between towels to absorb the moisture. Then, lay the piece flat and dry it in the shade.

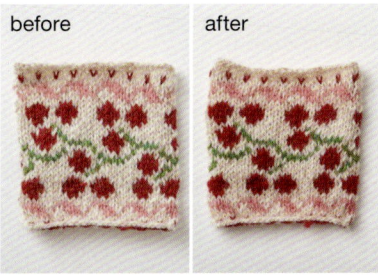

3 The piece will become soft and the stitches will even out.

Lesson 1: Basic Techniques for Knitting with Multiple Colors

There are methods for carrying the yarn horizontally and vertically. In both cases, be sure to maintain consistent tension to prevent the yarn on the back from becoming too tight or loose. When carrying the yarn over a long distance (more than 5 cm - 2"), secure it in the middle.

Weaving

1 Knit the leaf part of the small red rose from page 10. Knit up until one stitch before you need to change color.

2 The next stitch is green. Cross the green yarn with the background color (gray), keeping the green yarn underneath the gray.

3 Following the chart, knit two stitches in green, knit one stitch in gray, and knit one stitch in green. Always keep the background color yarn on top and the motif color yarn underneath.

Holding Yarn

1 Purl the section where the flower color yarn is carried across. Since there are six stitches until the next color change, after purling three stitches in the background color, cross the background color with the flower color yarn before purling the next stitch.

2 Continue to work on the purl side according to the chart. Securing the yarn in this way helps maintain even tension and prevents the yarn from getting accidentally caught on something.

Stranding

1 Stranding is demonstrated using the stem of the pink daisy from page 54. Knit up to one stitch before the stem section.

2 At the back, cross the background color (light blue) with the stem color (green), with the background color underneath and the stem color on top.

3 Since the next stitch is still in the background color, continue knitting with the background color.

4 Pick up the stem color (green) and knit one stitch. On the purl side of your work, the background color yarn will be on top of the stem color yarn.

5 Pick up the background color yarn (light blue), bringing it under the stem color yarn. Continue working with the background color yarn to the end of the row.

6 At the back, the yarn will be carried like this. Instead of carrying the yarn straight across, remember to cross it one stitch before the color change.

Tidying the Ends of Yarn
After finishing knitting, secure the yarn ends by weaving them in the back so they don't come undone.

1. Thread the tail into an embroidery needle.
2. Weave it into the same color yarn. Instead of threading it underneath, split the yarn and thread it between each strand.
3. Finally, pull the yarn tight with your fingers and then press it down slightly. This will make the stitches on the front even out. Cut off any excess yarn.

Point

In this book, some colorwork patterns require you to cut the yarn to the necessary length in advance. While this method involves the extra step of cutting and managing the yarn, it reduces the amount of carried yarn, simplifies knitting, and helps prevent tangling. For more details, refer to page 39.

List of Symbols
This is a list of symbols used for the charts presented in this book.
For instructions on how to knit, please refer to the step-by-step instructions and diagrams.

Knitting

- Knit
- Purl
- Yarn over
- Through back loop
- Purl through back loop
- Standard bind off
- Backwards loop increase
- Knit 3 together
- Slip, knit 2 together, pass slipped stitch over
- Slip 2, knit 1, pass 2 slipped stitches over
- Knit 2 together
- Slip, knit, pass
- Slip, slip, knit slipped stiches together
- Slip 4, knit 1, pass slipped stitches over
- Slip 6, knit 1, pass slipped stitches over
- Smocking stitch: worked over 7 sts, wrap yarn twice
- Smocking stitch: worked over 6 sts, wrap yarn 5 times
- Smocking stitch: worked over 5 sts, wrap yarn 3 times
- Knot stitch
- 1/1 right cross
- 1/1 left cross
- 2/1 right cross (2nd stitch purl)
- 3/3 left cross
- 3/3 right cross
- 3/1 left cross
- 3/1 right cross
- 1/3 right cross
- 1/3 left cross
- 2/2 left cross
- 1/1 right purl cross
- 1/1 left purl cross

= Increases

Bobble stitch

Pull through with crochet hook
Chain 1
Slip 4, knit 1, pass slipped stitches over
= Increases
Slip stitch into the increase

Crochet

- Chain stitch
- 2 half double crochet cluster
- 3 half double crochet cluster
- 2 double crochet cluster

Trinity stitch

Knit 3 together and knit, purl, knit into 1 stitch

* There are two methods for knitting the bobble stitch. The first method, illustrated in the chart on the left, involves turning your work, securing the bobble with a crochet hook, and then returning to knit with your needles (this counts as one row on the chart). The second method, used for the cherries pattern on pages 67 and 69, is worked over several rows.

Small Flowers

These patterns feature small, repeating flowers.
Their charm lies in the petite, delicate design, making them easy to pair with anything.

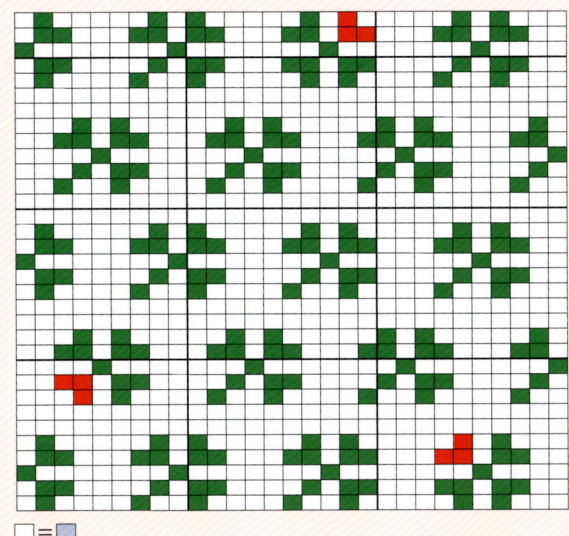

Clovers

Yarn Used:
Jamieson's Spindrift
■ #655 China Blue ■ #800 Tartan ■ #500 Scarlet
Knitting Needles: Straight Needles Size 4 (3.25 mm, UK Size 10)
Panel: 33 stitches × 40 rows
Gauge (10 cm - 4" square): 28 stitches, 28 rows

Difficulty: ★☆☆

Small Red Roses

Yarn Used:
Puppy British Fine
■ #024 Charcoal Gray ■ #055 Green ■ #006 Red
■ #068 Rose Pink
Knitting Needles: Straight Needles Size 4 (3.25 mm, UK Size 10)
Panel: 36 stitches × 40 rows
Gauge (10 cm - 4" square): 28 stitches, 32 rows

Difficulty: ★☆☆

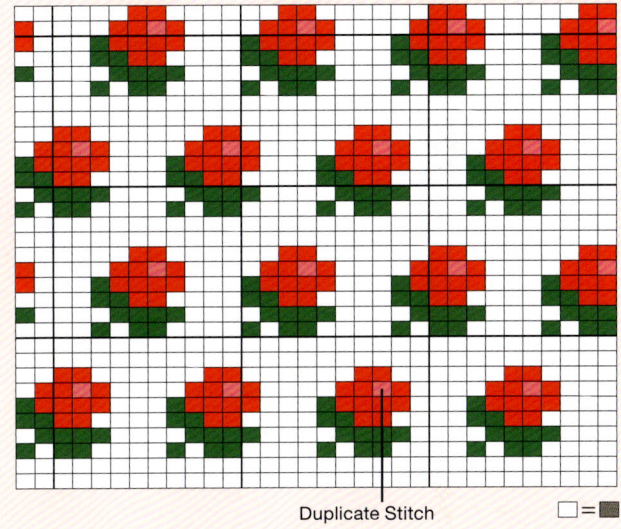

Duplicate Stitch

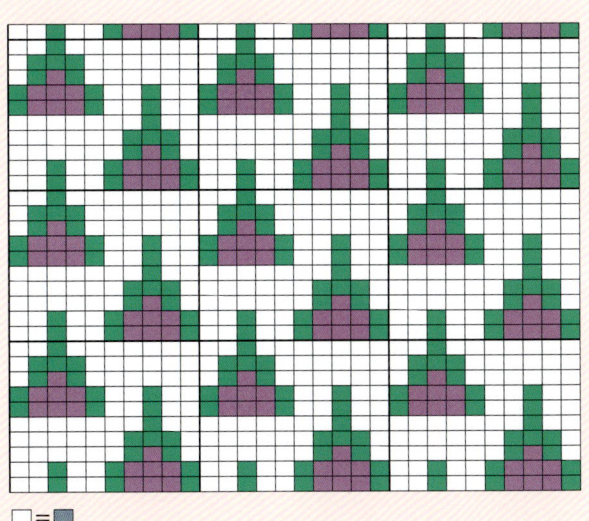

Allium siculum (Sicilian Honey Lily)

Yarn Used:
Jamieson's Spindrift
■ #180 Mist ■ #772 Verdigris ■ #616 Anemone
Knitting Needles: Straight Needles Size 5 (3.50 mm)
Panel: 35 stitches × 41 rows
Gauge (10 cm - 4" square): 28 stitches, 32 rows

Difficulty: ★☆☆

Tiny Garden

Yarn Used:
Jamieson's Spindrift
■ #315 Heron ☐ #390 Daffodil ■ #188 Sherbet
■ #259 Leprechaun
Knitting Needles: Straight Needles Size 5 (3.50 mm)
Panel: 33 stitches × 38 rows
Gauge (10 cm - 4" square): 28 stitches, 30 rows

Difficulty: ★★☆

Point
Intricate horizontal patterns don't offer much stretch, making them unsuitable for garments, but perfect for small items!

☐ = ■

Buttercups

Yarn Used:
Puppy British Fine
■ #003 Navy Blue ☐ #066 Yellow ■ #080 Yellow Green
Knitting Needles: Straight Needles Size 5 (3.50 mm)
Panel: 34 stitches × 38 rows
Gauge (10 cm - 4" square): 26 stitches, 30 rows

Difficulty: ★☆☆

☐ = ■

Buttercup Border

Yarn Used:
Puppy British Fine
■ #003 Navy Blue ☐ #066 Yellow ■ #080 Yellow Green
Knitting Needles: Straight Needles Size 5 (3.50 mm)
Panel: 30 stitches × 34 rows
Gauge (10 cm - 4" square): 28 stitches, 30 rows

Difficulty: ★☆☆

Double Latvian Braid (Refer to page 124)

☐ = ■

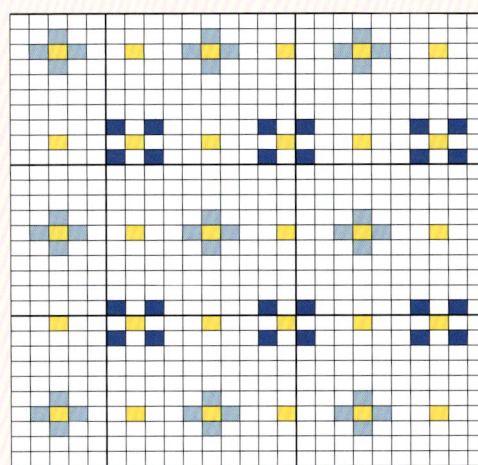

Forget-Me-Nots

Yarn Used:
Jamieson's Spindrift
☐ #104 Natural White   ☐ #390 Daffodil   ■ #676 Sapphire
☐ #929 Aqua
Knitting Needles: Straight Needles Size 4 (3.25 mm, UK Size 10)
Panel: 33 stitches × 42 rows
Gauge (10 cm - 4" square): 28 stitches, 32 rows

Difficulty: ★☆☆

Violets

Yarn Used:
Jamieson's Spindrift
■ #999 Black   ■ #616 Anemone   ☐ #785 Apple
☐ #400 Mimosa   ☐ #770 Mint
Knitting Needles: Needles: Straight Needles Size 4 (3.25 mm, UK Size 10)
Panel: 35 stitches × 42 rows
Gauge (10 cm - 4" square): 28 stitches, 34 rows

Difficulty: ★☆☆

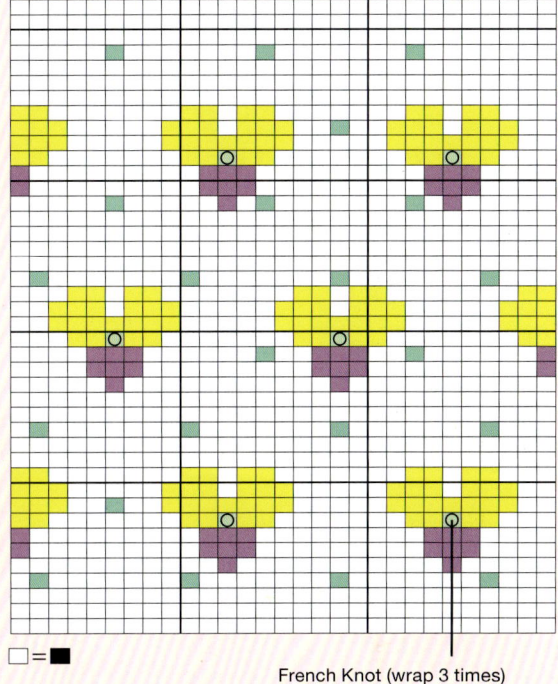

☐ = ■

French Knot (wrap 3 times)

Plums

Yarn Used:
Puppy British Fine
■ #012 Ink Black   ■ #085 Neon Pink   ■ #080 Yellow Green
☐ #031 Pink
Knitting Needles: Straight Needles Size 4 (3.25 mm, UK Size 10)
Panel: 34 stitches × 42 rows
Gauge (10 cm - 4" square): 30 stitches, 34 rows

Difficulty: ★☆☆

French Knot (wrap once)

☐ = ■

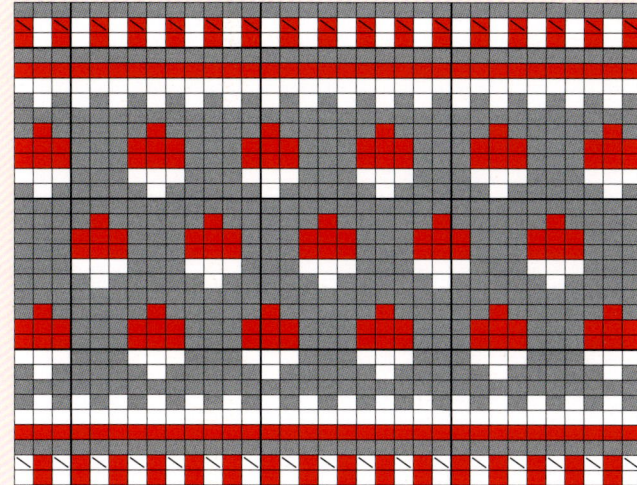

Mushrooms

Yarn Used:
Puppy British Fine
■ #009 Gray ☐ #001 White ■ #006 Red
Knitting Needles: Straight Needles Size 4 (3.25 mm, UK Size 10)
Panel: 33 stitches × 33 rows
Gauge (10 cm - 4" square): 28 stitches, 36 rows

Difficulty: ★☆☆

Latvian Braid (Refer to page 124)

Acorns

Yarn Used:
Jamieson's Spindrift
■ #788 Leaf ■ #342 Cashew
■ #1190 Burnt Umber ☐ #365 Chartreuse
Knitting Needles: Straight Needles Size 4
(3.25 mm, UK Size 10)
Panel: 34 stitches × 39 rows
Gauge (10 cm - 4" square): 26 stitches, 32 rows

Difficulty: ★☆☆

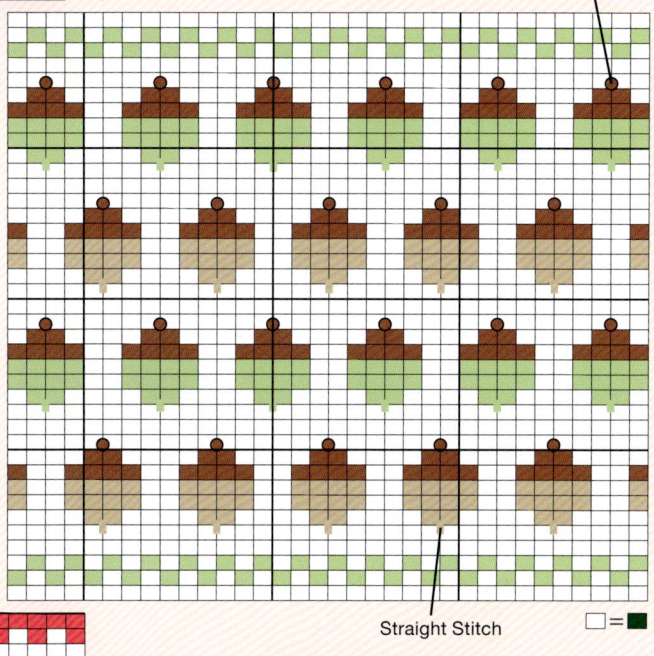

French Knot (wrap twice)

Straight Stitch

☐ = ■

Point
A pattern with a similar appearance can create a completely different effect depending on the number of rows or the type of embroidery used!

Lingonberries

Yarn Used:
Jamieson's Spindrift
■ #180 Mist ■ #540 Coral ■ #585 Plum
■ #188 Sherbet
Knitting Needles: Straight Needles Size 4
(3.25 mm UK Size 10)
Panel: 34 stitches × 40 rows
Gauge (10 cm - 4" square): 27 stitches, 30 rows

Difficulty: ★☆☆

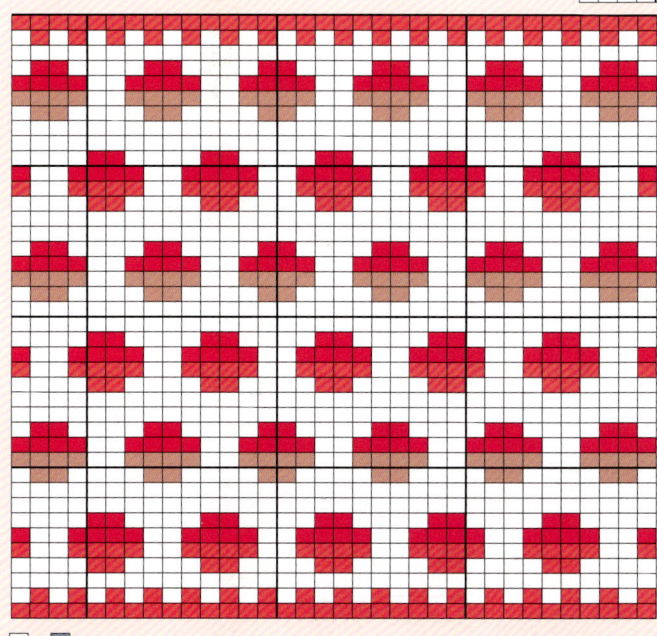

☐ = ■

Duplicate Stitch Cross Stitch

Camellias

Yarn Used:
Puppy ALBA
■ #1094 Dark Gray ■ #5139 Red
Puppy British Fine
■ #035 Mustard ■ #055 Green
Knitting Needles: Straight Needles Size 6 (3.75 mm, UK Size 9)
Panel: 33 stitches × 36 rows
Gauge (10 cm - 4" square): 26 stitches, 30 rows

Difficulty: ★☆☆

Latvian Lattice

Yarn Used:
Jamieson's Spindrift
□ #104 Natural White □ #390 Daffodil
■ #500 Scarlet ■ #710 Gentian
Knitting Needles: Straight Needles Size 5 (3.50 mm)
Panel: 33 stitches × 40 rows
Gauge (10 cm - 4" square): 28 stitches, 28 rows

Difficulty: ★☆☆

Cross Stitch

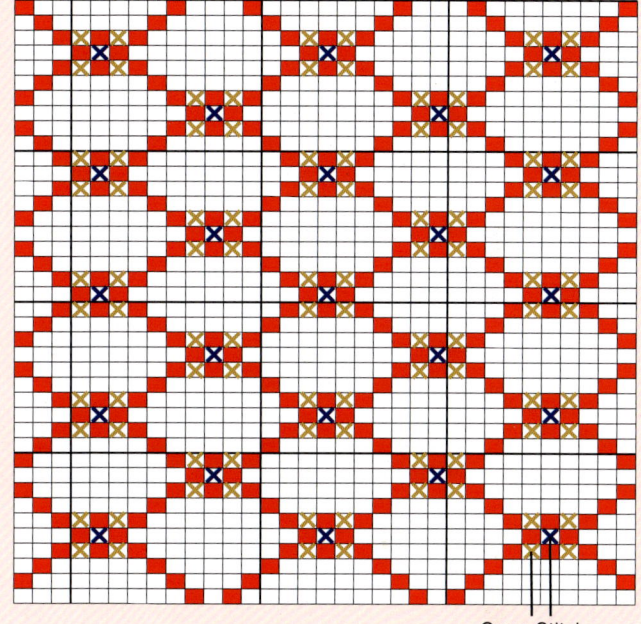

Cross Stitch

Point
For a swatch that will have embroidery added, securely fasten the yarn tails and steam block the piece beforehand to ensure a neat finish.

Zigzags and Small Flowers

Yarn Used:
Puppy British Fine
□ #040 Beige □ #066 Yellow ■ #024 Charcoal Gray
■ #068 Rose Pink
Knitting Needles: Straight Needles Size 4 (3.25 mm, UK Size 10)
Panel: 35 stitches × 40 rows
Gauge (10 cm - 4" square): 30 stitches, 32 rows

Difficulty: ★★☆

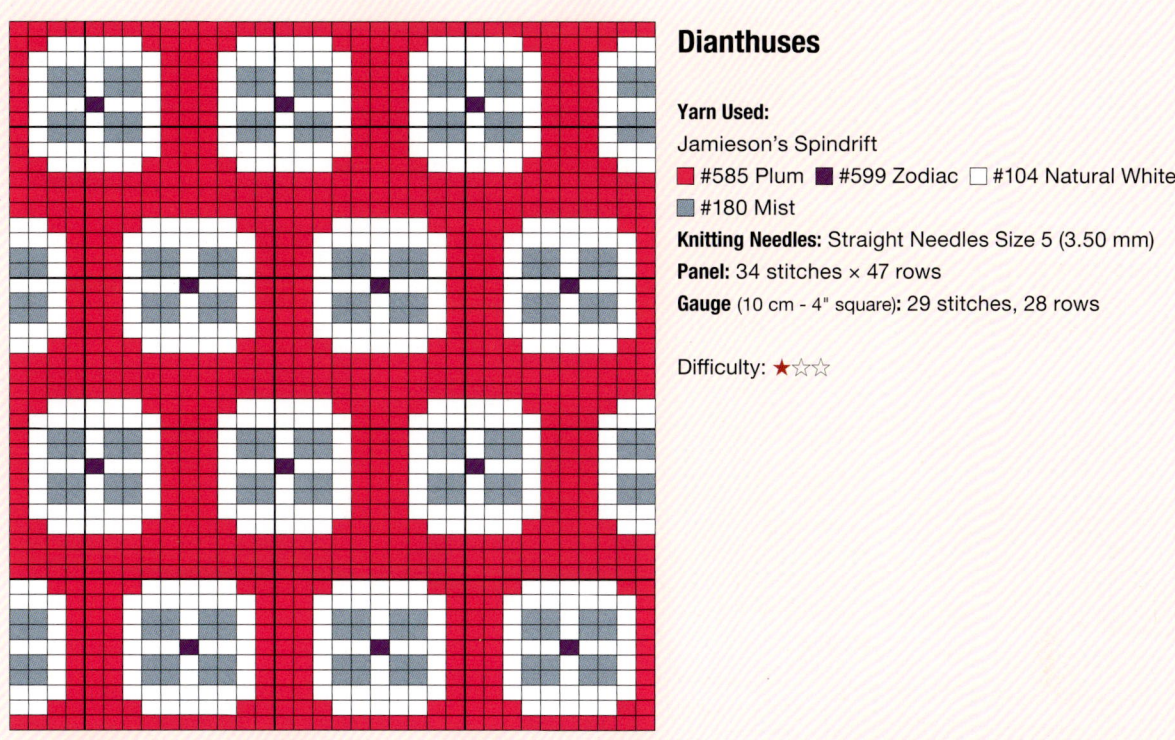

Dianthuses

Yarn Used:
Jamieson's Spindrift
- #585 Plum ■ #599 Zodiac □ #104 Natural White
- #180 Mist

Knitting Needles: Straight Needles Size 5 (3.50 mm)
Panel: 34 stitches × 47 rows
Gauge (10 cm - 4" square)**:** 29 stitches, 28 rows

Difficulty: ★☆☆

Small Poppies

Yarn Used:
Puppy British Fine
- #009 Gray ■ #006 Red □ #001 White ■ #008 Black
- #007 Ultramarine

Knitting Needles: Straight Needles Size 5 (3.50 mm)
Panel: 33 stitches × 36 rows
Gauge (10 cm - 4" square)**:** 30 stitches, 30 rows

Difficulty: ★☆☆

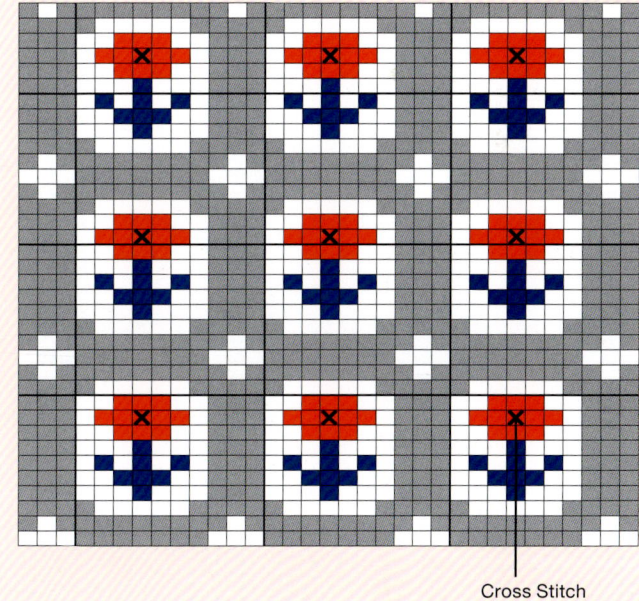

Cross Stitch

a
b

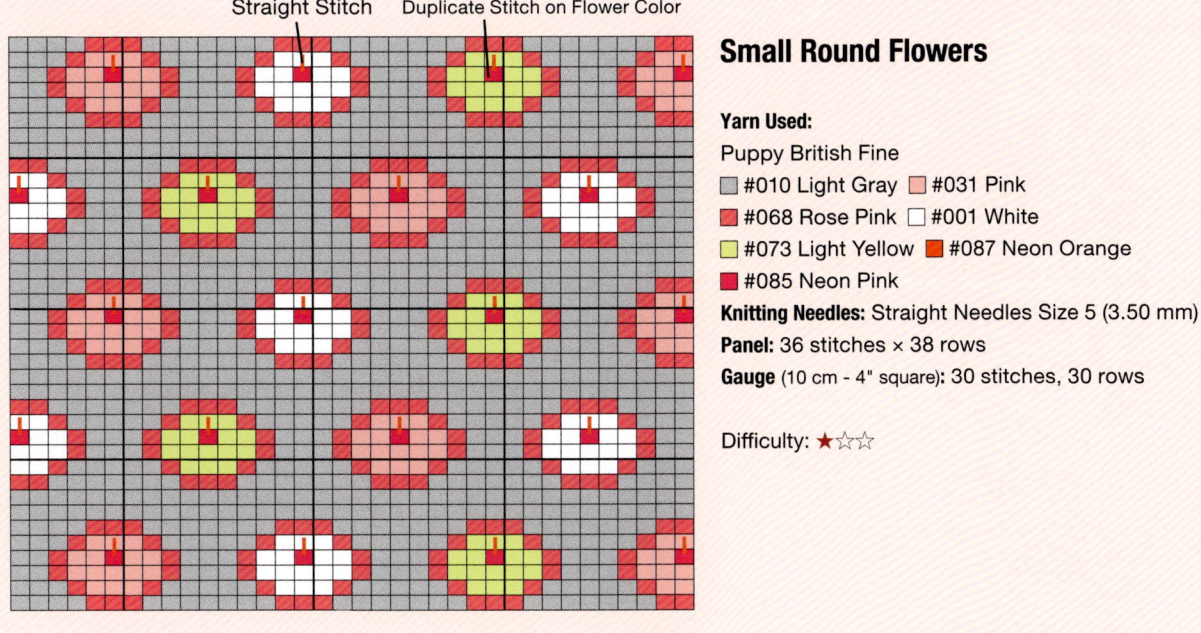

Straight Stitch   Duplicate Stitch on Flower Color

Small Round Flowers

Yarn Used:
Puppy British Fine
- #010 Light Gray
- #031 Pink
- #068 Rose Pink
- #001 White
- #073 Light Yellow
- #087 Neon Orange
- #085 Neon Pink

Knitting Needles: Straight Needles Size 5 (3.50 mm)
Panel: 36 stitches × 38 rows
Gauge (10 cm - 4" square): 30 stitches, 30 rows

Difficulty: ★☆☆

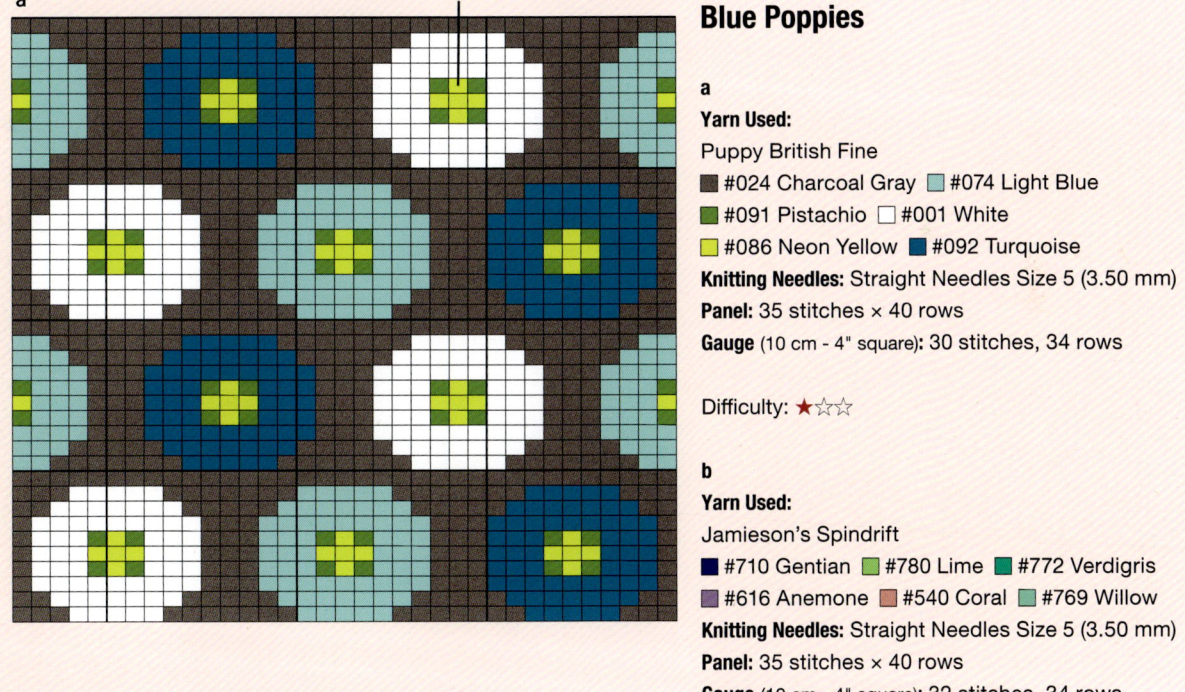

Duplicate Stitch on Flower Color

Blue Poppies

a

Yarn Used:
Puppy British Fine
- #024 Charcoal Gray
- #074 Light Blue
- #091 Pistachio
- #001 White
- #086 Neon Yellow
- #092 Turquoise

Knitting Needles: Straight Needles Size 5 (3.50 mm)
Panel: 35 stitches × 40 rows
Gauge (10 cm - 4" square): 30 stitches, 34 rows

Difficulty: ★☆☆

b

Yarn Used:
Jamieson's Spindrift
- #710 Gentian
- #780 Lime
- #772 Verdigris
- #616 Anemone
- #540 Coral
- #769 Willow

Knitting Needles: Straight Needles Size 5 (3.50 mm)
Panel: 35 stitches × 40 rows
Gauge (10 cm - 4" square): 32 stitches, 34 rows

Difficulty: ★☆☆

* Preparing the yarn for colorwork:
  Flower center: 35 cm - 13¾" long pieces
  Petals: 125 cm - 49¼" long pieces

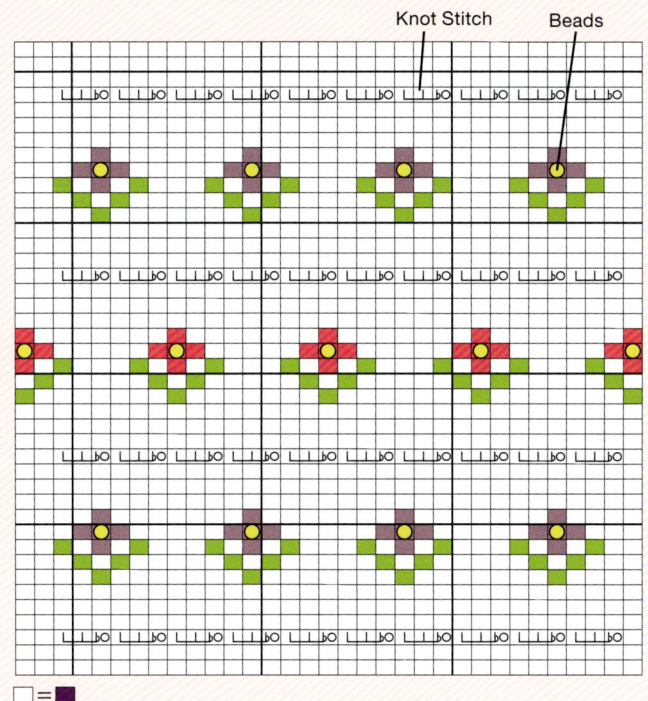

Small Flowers and Knot Stitches

Yarn Used:
Jamieson's Spindrift
■ #599 Zodiac ■ #259 Leprechaun ■ #188 Sherbet
■ #617 Lavender

Other Materials:
Beads: TOHO 8/0 Round Seed Beads No. 42
Knitting Needles: Straight Needles Size 4 (3.25 mm, UK Size 10)
Panel: 33 stitches × 42 rows
Gauge (10 cm - 4" square)**:** 28 stitches, 32 rows

Difficulty: ★☆☆

* For the Knot Stitch, refer to page 127.

Point
Dispose of the yarn and steam block to shape the swatch first, then securely sew the beads on with sewing thread.

Small Flowers and Openwork Stitches

Yarn Used:
Puppy ALBA
■ #1087 Beige ■ #1109 Yellow ■ #5139 Red
■ #1265 Orange ■ #1170 Pink ■ #1215 Purple
■ #1110 Moss Green ■ #1185 Green

Other Materials:
Beads: MIYUKI Drop Beads DP401
Knitting Needles: Straight Needles Size 6 (3.75 mm, UK Size 9)
Panel: 34 stitches × 42 rows
Gauge (10 cm - 4" square)**:** 26 stitches, 34 rows

Difficulty: ★☆☆

* Preparing the yarn for colorwork:
  Flower, Leaf (green): 60 cm - 23⅝" long pieces
  Leaf (yellow green): 55 cm - 21⅝" long pieces

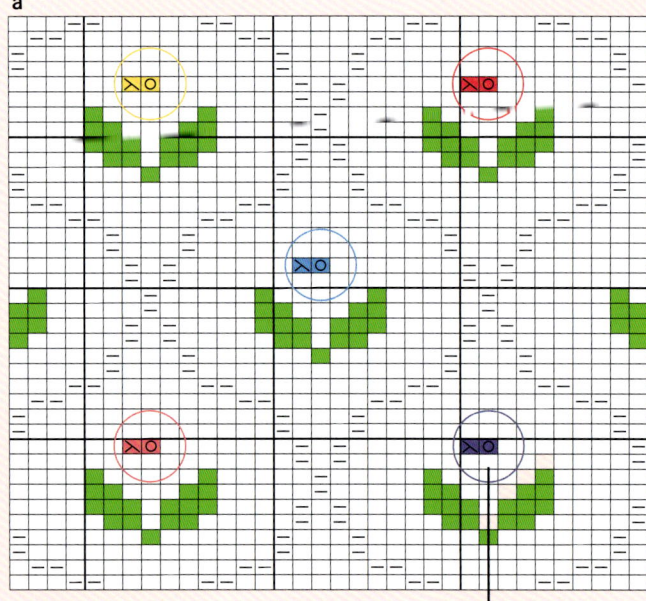

Lattice Pattern and Daisies

a
Yarn Used:
Jamieson's Spindrift
☐ #104 Natural White ■ #259 Leprechaun
Use the color of your choice for the flower.
Other Material: Camel yellow color felt (washed)

b
Yarn Used:
Puppy British Fine
☐ #021 Light Beige ☐ #031 Pink ■ #080 Yellow Green
Other Material: White color felt (washed)

Shared Materials:
Knitting Needles: Straight Needles Size 4 (3.25 mm, UK Size 10)
Panel: 34 stitches × 38 rows
Gauge (10 cm - 4" square): 28 stitches, 36 rows

Difficulty: ★☆☆

* Refer to page 27 for instructions on embroidering the daisies.
* Preparing the yarn for colorwork:
  Leaf (green): 55 cm - 21⅝" long pieces

Point
This is an easy-to-make, cute swatch that makes use of the eyelet stitch. Enjoy how the look of the swatch changes depending on your color choices and the way you embroider.

Flower embroidery position

1.5 cm - ⅝"
Layer felt on the back.

1.5 cm - ⅝"
Cut the felt at around 2.5 cm/1" in diameter, and after completing the embroidery, trim the excess.

a: Blanket stitch on the outside creates a sharp and clear finish.

b: Blanket stitch on the inside gives a soft and fluffy feel.

Lesson 2	# How to Embroider Daisies
	With a simple pattern, add embroidery to make a daisy.

1 The swatch has a hole where the daisy will be embroidered, and the colorwork for the leaves is complete. Prepare a piece of felt that is larger than the embroidery area, along with embroidery floss. Felt might shrink or bleed color, so be sure to wash it beforehand.

2 Place felt behind hole and pin in place with sewing pins.

3 Using a sewing needle and thread, do a running stitch 5 mm - ⅛" away from the edge of the hole. It's a good idea to pull the knot into the felt to hide it.

4 Thread the embroidery needle and pick up a small section of the felt with a single stitch. Do not knot the end of the embroidery floss and begin embroidering. Keep the floss length between 30 ~ 40 cm - 11⅞" ~ 15¾"; longer threads may break.

5 Thread the needle out near the edge of the hole and start a blanket stitch (buttonhole stitch).

6 Insert the needle next to the previous stitch and use the embroidery stitches as a guide to vertically pick up one stitch of the knitted fabric. Loop the thread around the needle and pull it through.

7 Insert the needle into fabric again, next to the previous stitch, and continue stitching in the same way. Stitch tightly to avoid gaps.

8 Stitch around the entire hole. At the end, bring the needle out to the felt side, but do not knot the floss. Instead, pass the needle through the felt and cut the floss.

9 Cut the excess felt into a circle to finish.

Various Styles of Daisy Embroidery

The blanket stitch is worked from the outside of the flower to the center. Since there is no border along the outside, it creates a softer impression.

The blanket stitch is worked outward, giving the flower a more defined shape.

Two layers of embroidery. The white stitches are densely embroidered, while the red stitches are spaced out, starting from the middle of the white stitches.

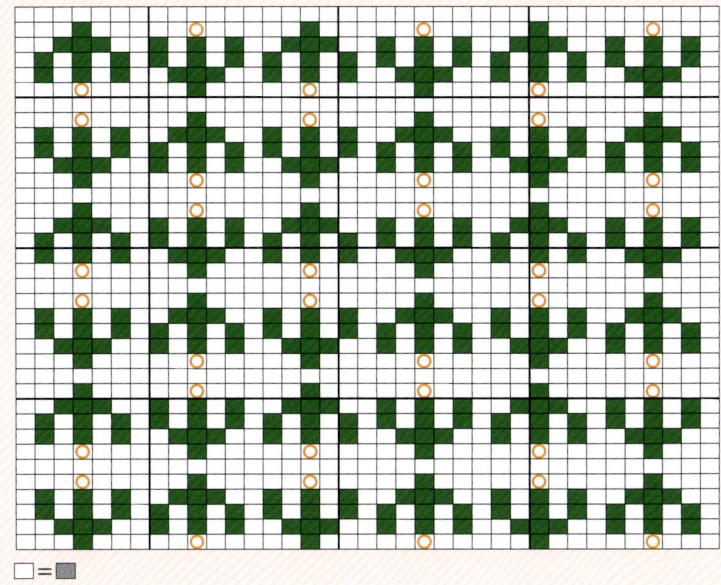

Up & Down Dandelions

Yarn Used:
Puppy British Fine
■ #009 Gray ■ #055 Green ☐ #066 Yellow
Knitting Needles: Straight Needles Size 5 (3.50 mm)
Crochet Hook Size 2/0 (2.00 mm, UK Size 14)
Panel: 47 stitches × 36 rows
Gauge (10 cm - 4" square): 30 stitches, 30 rows

Difficulty: ★☆☆

* Refer page 123 for bobble stitch crochet.

◯ = ⚘
2 Half Double Crochet Cluster Stitch
Crochet hook: Size 2/0 (2.00 mm)

Upward daisy: background color yarn
Downward daisy: bobble stitch yarn

Point
It's best to crochet the bobble stitch tightly, ensuring that the yarn carried across doesn't loosen.

☐ = ■

Primroses

Yarn Used:
Puppy British Fine
■ #003 Navy Blue ■ #080 Yellow Green ☐ #066 Yellow
Knitting Needles: Straight Needles Size 4 (3.25 mm, UK Size 10)
Crochet Hook Size 2/0 (2.00 mm, UK Size 14)
Panel: 33 stitches × 42 rows
Gauge (10 cm - 4" square): 28 stitches, 34 rows

Difficulty: ★☆☆

* Refer page 123 for bobble stitch crochet.

◯ = ⚘ Background color

2 Half Double Crochet Cluster Stitch
Crochet hook: Size 2/0 (2.00 mm)

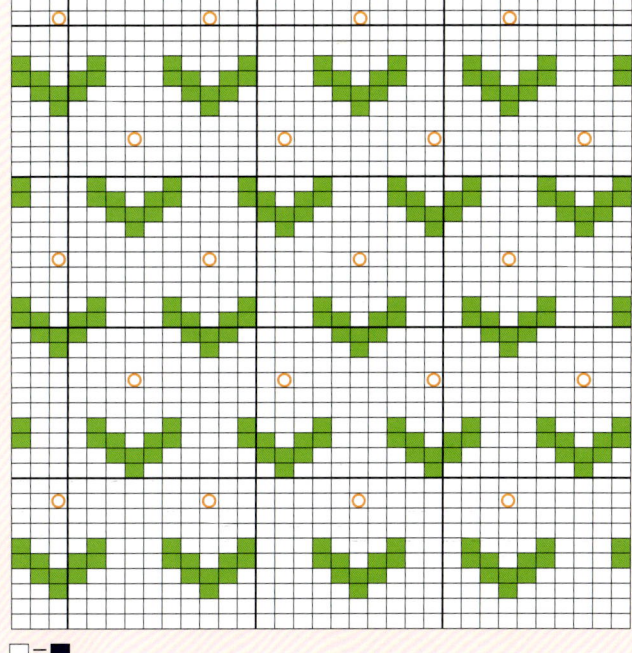

☐ = ■

a

b

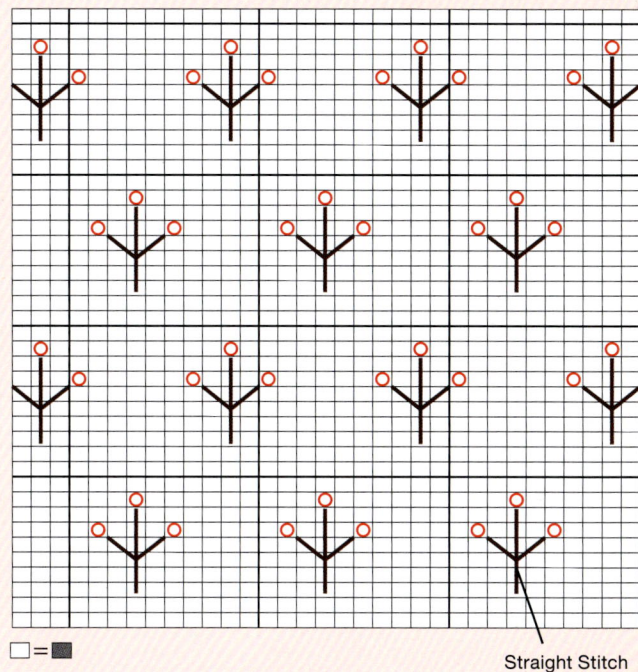

Straight Stitch

Red Berries – Rose Madder

Yarn Used:
Puppy British Fine
■ #009 Gray ■ #006 Red ■ #022 Burnt Brown
Knitting Needles: Straight Needles Size 4 (3.25 mm, UK Size 10)
Crochet Hook Size 2/0 (2.00 mm, UK Size 14)
Panel: 33 stitches × 41 rows
Gauge (10 cm - 4" square): 28 stitches, 38 rows

Difficulty: ★☆☆

* Refer page 123 for bobble stitch crochet.

◯ = Background color

2 Half Double Crochet Cluster Stitch
Crochet hook: Size 2/0 (2.00 mm)

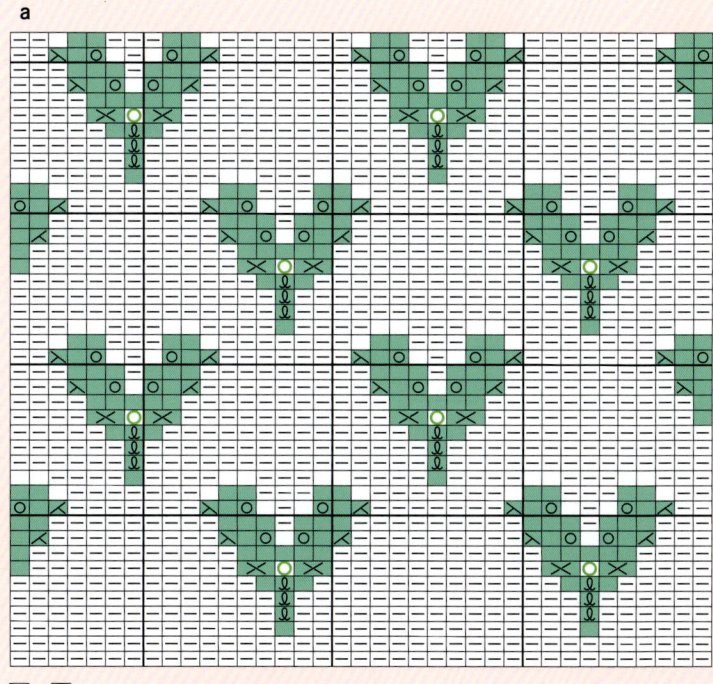

a

Purl the background color yarn
When changing yarn, knit both background and Mistletoe color yarns.

Pull through with crochet hook
Chain 1
Slip stitch into the increase
Slip, knit 2 together, pass slipped stitch over
◯ Knit the bobble stitch for 1 row
Increases

Mistletoe

a
Yarn Used:
Jamieson's Spindrift
■ #119 Mooskit/Sholmit ■ #769 Willow ■ #780 Lime
Knitting Needles: Straight Needles Size 4 (3.25 mm, UK Size 10)
Crochet Hook Size 3/0 (2.25 mm, UK Size 13)
Panel: 37 stitches × 42 rows
Gauge (10 cm - 4" square): 28 stitches, 34 rows

b
Yarn Used:
Puppy British Fine
□ #001 White ■ #091 Pistachio ■ #055 Green
Puppy Kid Mohair Fine
□ #2 White
Knitting Needles: Straight Needles Size 4 (3.25 mm, UK Size 10)
Crochet Hook Size 3/0 (2.25 mm, UK Size 13)
Panel: 37 stitches × 42 rows
Gauge (10 cm - 4" square): 26 stitches, 34 rows

* The background color is knitted with two strands: British Fine #001 and Kid Mohair Fine.

Difficulty: ★★☆

* For bobble stitch knitting, refer to page 122.
* Preparing the yarn for colorwork:
  Mistletoe: 100 cm - 39⅜" long pieces
  Bobble stitch: 45 cm - 17¾" long pieces

I created a cardigan using two variations of the Buttercup pattern from page 12. The front is made of two separate pieces (left and right), while the back and each sleeve are single rectangular pieces. Because the pattern is dense, the cardigan's shape remains simple, allowing room for creativity.

Instructions...page 130

Draping this shawl over your shoulders provides warmth, and its soft color evokes a sense of calm. Like the cardigan on page 32, this sleeveless shawl is constructed by joining rectangular pieces. However, using a different knitting pattern and omitting the sleeves creates a distinct look, even with a similar design.

Instructions... page 133

Structure of a Knitted Garment

In this book, various creative ideas are used to make knitting patterns more enjoyable. One of these ideas is the garment's structure. By avoiding techniques like increases and decreases in sweaters, you can knit in straight rows and join the pieces, allowing you to focus on the colorwork without worry. This helps you progress through your project smoothly and allows you to fully enjoy the charm of your colorwork patterns.

 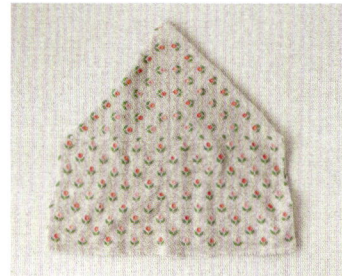 

Here we see a shawl and cardigan made by simply joining rectangular pieces. The shawl is made by joining three rectangles, while the cardigan is made by joining five rectangles. The front pieces are aligned at the center back, and the design also creates a collar.

This bolero is made by joining two rectangular pieces. The pieces are joined at the center back, and each sleeve seam is grafted. Finally, the collar and cuffs are knitted to complete the bolero.

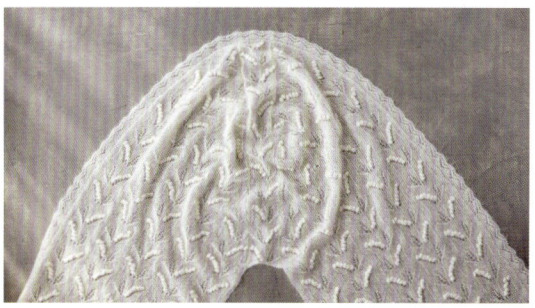 

This hooded Lily-of-the-Valley shawl is a large project, so it will take time, but this project is also made from rectangle knitted pieces. Knit two long rectangles for the sides and then join them together from the hood gusset section. The hood area includes decreases and increases, but the shape is simple, so you can knit it without confusion.

This project with its unique balloon-like shape, involves knitting rectangular pieces while dividing the neckline into left and right sections. Finally, pick up the stitches for one cuff and the collar to complete the garment.

This patchwork shawl was created from the idea of showcasing the cuteness of swatches in a complete piece. The swatches that make up the border require increases, but since they are small parts, they are easy to knit. This way, you can enjoy combining your favorite swatches.

The Mistletoe cowl is made slightly larger and fastened with a brooch to create a stylish look. It looks cute when worn loosely, and it's also lovely when worn like a collar, as shown in the photo. Feel free to enjoy and experiment with styling.

Instructions...page 136

Column 1	Tips for Simplifying

Many of the patterns in this book involve knitting with multiple colors, which might seem a bit challenging at first. However, there are plenty of techniques to make the knitting process easier. This section introduces some of these helpful tricks.

1. Add Colors with Embroidery

See the two swatches on page 52. The pansy has embroidery for the flower center, leaves, and thin stem. The leaves use the outline stitch to hide the V-shaped knit stitches around the leaf, and the thin stem uses the chain stitch to create a natural curve.

The daisy design includes a leaf motif colorwork and buttonhole-like opening (the knitting itself is surprisingly simple). A yellow felt piece is sewn behind the opening, and a blanket stitch is worked with two colors of embroidery floss (see page 27). While the knitting is very easy, the result is impressive - 'Wow, how did you achieve this?'

Adding embroidery not only increases the color options but also adds a handcrafted element, making the finished product look more intricate and detailed.

Outline stitch for the leaves, chain stitch for the stem, and straight stitch and French knot for the flower.

Blanket stitch for the petals.

2. About Carrying Yarn Across

When designing patterns, managing yarn floats is crucial. Decisions on whether vertical floats can be easily handled or how many stitches are acceptable for horizontal floats affect the tidying of yarn tails later on. Fewer yarn tails result in a thinner, more beautiful fabric, but long horizontal floats can cause the yarn to catch or the stitches to tighten.

For example, consider the Pansy and One Stitch pattern on page 52. If the number of rows between the single colorwork stitches is odd, you will need to cut the yarn each time to avoid issues. Therefore, it's best to have an even number of rows between floats in this case.

If you're carrying (floating) the yarn vertically, aim for an even number of rows between floats. For horizontal floats, keep the span to about 5 cm - 2" to avoid problems.

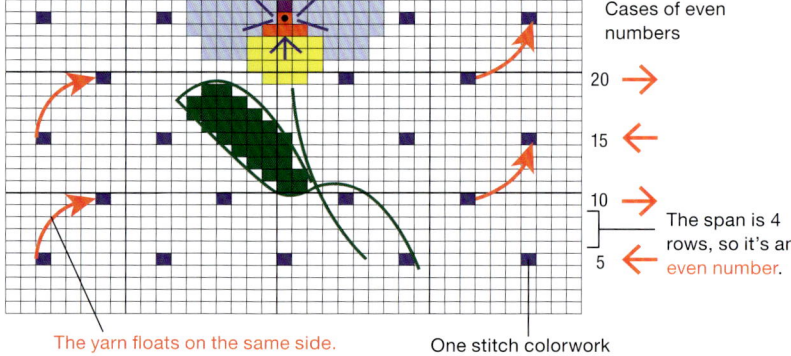

One Stitch Colorwork

Cases of even numbers

The yarn floats on the same side.

One stitch colorwork

The span is 4 rows, so it's an even number.

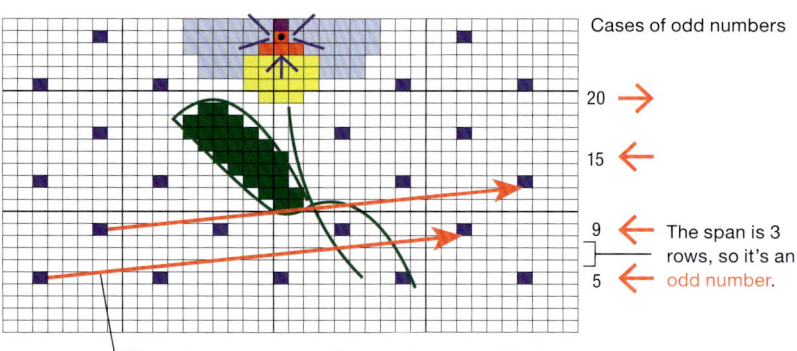

Cases of odd numbers

The span is 3 rows, so it's an odd number.

Since the yarn does not float on the same side, it will need to carry across diagonally over a long distance, which means you'll need to cut it once.

3. Simplifying Colorwork (Pre-cutting Yarn)

Although it's going to be more work for yarn management, the knitting can be made easier by avoiding horizontal floats and pre-cutting the yarn to the necessary lengths for the colorwork pattern.

For example, in the Rosebuds pattern on page 51, prepare yarn lengths of 45 cm - 17¾" for the bud color and 200 cm - 78¾" for the leaf and stem colors. While preparation may be a bit challenging, having the yarn pre-cut to the required lengths prevents tangling and makes knitting easier, avoiding issues with fabric pulling. This method is used for many patterns, such as the cherries on pages 66 and 68 and the grapes on page 76.

When viewed from the back, you will see that the yarn does not float to the next section. Since the flower area is worked in stockinette stitch and the surrounding area in garter stitch, this also prevents the yarn from creating unwanted thickness.

4. Using Stitch Markers

Stitch markers are essential for accurately knitting repeated patterns. By placing these small markers at the beginning of each pattern repeat, you can significantly simplify the process. This is especially effective for lace patterns. For example, the Holly and Leaf Lace pattern on page 104 and the Lily-of-the-Valley pattern on page 108 require stitch markers.

Additionally, stitch markers are very helpful for colorwork patterns such as the Thistle Bolero on page 62 and the Rosebuds pattern on page 50.

Place a stitch marker for each pattern repeat to keep track.

5. Starting with a Coaster

So, where should you begin? Even if you're an experienced knitter, it's recommended to knit a gauge swatch before starting on a garment. It's a small extra step, but it's important as it helps gauge the tension of your knitting.

For beginners, starting with a coaster is a great idea. Each chart indicates how many stitches and rows make up a 10 cm - 4" square. Refer to the coaster instructions (see page 156) and calculate the number of stitches and rows for the pattern you choose. It's okay if the pattern doesn't fit perfectly at first – just adjust by trimming or adding as needed. The key is to start knitting.

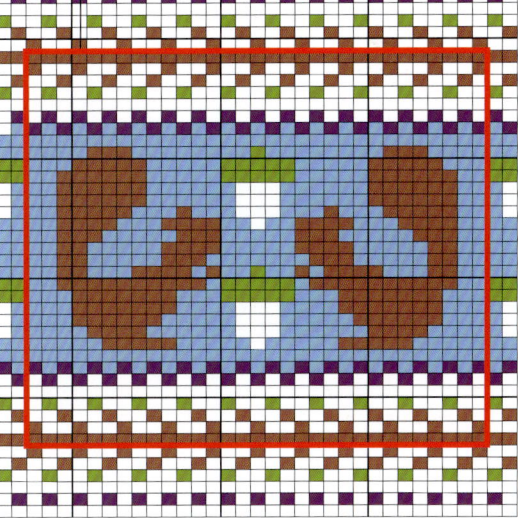

31 stitches on row 33

For example, the coaster on page 118 uses the squirrel and border motifs from the Squirrels and Acorns swatch on page 91. However, you can include two squirrels as shown in the swatch. In this case, center the design with an acorn and set the width to 31 stitches for even placement on both sides.

Large Flowers In this section, the designs feature a single, large, well-defined flower, rather than smaller ones. They create a strong impact and leave a lasting impression.

Large Rose

Yarn Used:
Jamieson's Spindrift
- #655 China Blue
- #550 Rose
- #788 Leaf
- #580 Cherry
- #570 Sorbet
- #772 Verdigris
- #585 Plum
- #390 Daffodil

Knitting Needles: Straight Needles Size 5 (3.50 mm)
Panel: 36 stitches × 38 rows
Gauge (10 cm - 4" square): 26 stitches, 32 rows

Difficulty: ★★☆

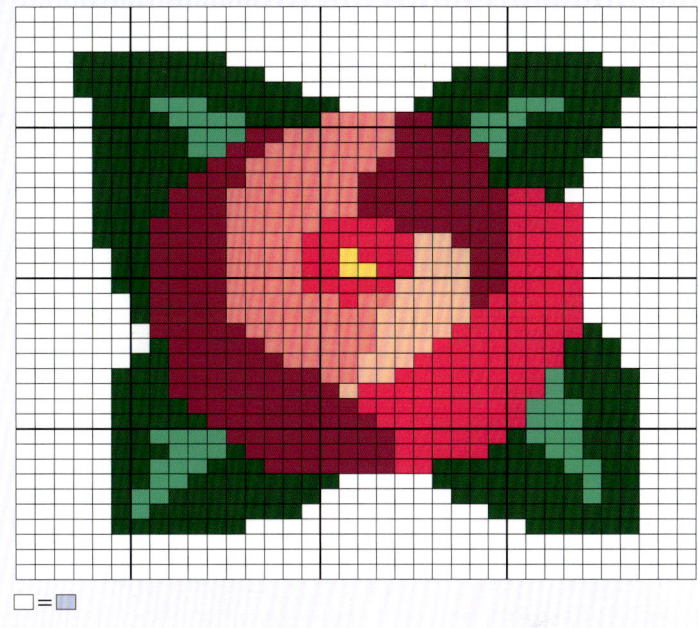

□ = □

a: #999, b: #599
French Knot (wrap twice)

a: #410, b: #780
Bullion Stitch (wrap 4 times)

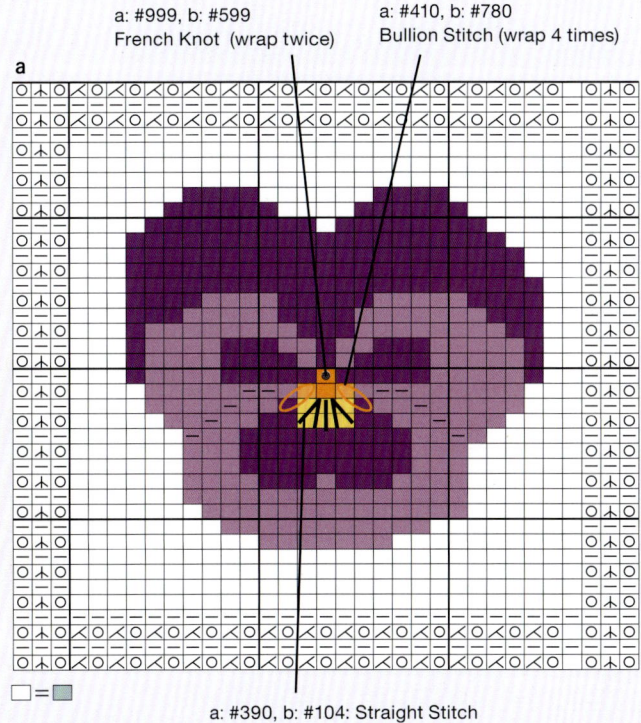

a: #390, b: #104: Straight Stitch

□ = □

Pansy & Openwork Border

Yarn Used:

a

Jamieson's Spindrift
- #720 Dewdrop
- #616 Anemone
- #599 Zodiac
- #390 Daffodil
- #410 Cornfield
- #999 Black

b

Jamieson's Spindrift
- #788 Leaf
- #616 Anemone
- #599 Zodiac
- #390 Daffodil
- #104 Natural White
- #780 Lime

Shared Materials:
Knitting Needles: Straight Needles Size 4 (3.25 mm, UK Size 10)
Panel: 33 stitches × 40 rows
Gauge (10 cm - 4" square): 26 stitches, 32 rows

Difficulty: ★★☆

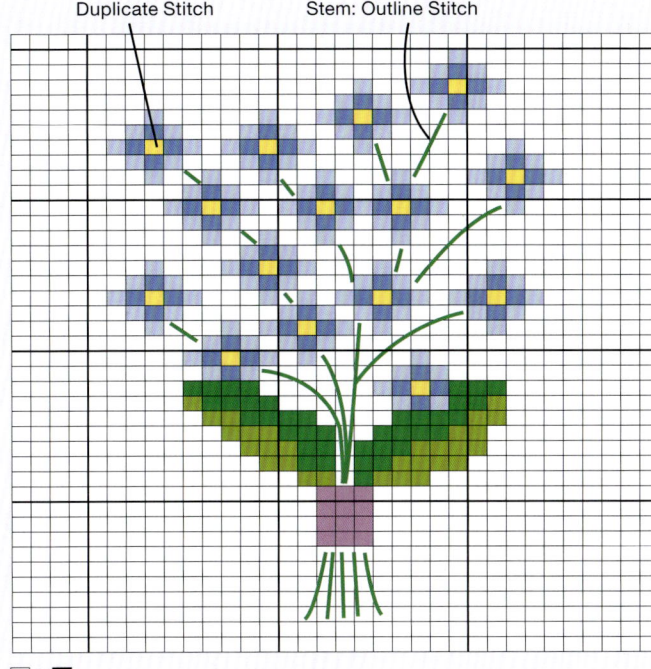

Forget-Me-Not Bouquet

Yarn Used:
Jamieson's Spindrift
■ #999 Black ☐ #655 China Blue ■ #815 Ivy
■ #665 Bluebell ■ #800 Tartan ■ #390 Daffodil
■ #616 Anemone
Knitting Needles: Straight Needles Size 5 (3.50 mm)
Panel: 34 stitches × 41 rows
Gauge (10 cm - 4" square): 28 stitches, 30 rows

Difficulty: ★★☆

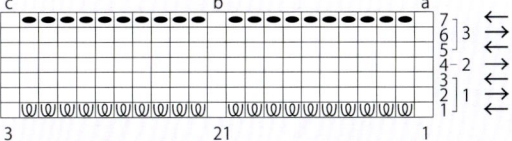

Ribbon row 1: knit 1, 10 backwards loop increases, knit 1, 10 backwards loop increases, knit 1
Ribbon rows 2-6: knit across row, pull the yarn tightly between points a, b, and c, folding it into a loop.
Ribbon row 7: Knit 1, bind off 10, knit 1, bind off 10, knit 1 (use background color yarn to knit, use ribbon color yarn to bind off)
See page 44 for the instructions.

Redcurrant

a
Yarn Used:
Puppy British Fine
■ #009 Gray ■ #066 Yellow ■ #007 Ultramarine
■ #006 Red
Knitting Needles: Straight Needles Size 5 (3.50 mm)
Panel: 32 stitches × 38 rows
Gauge (10 cm - 4" square): 28 stitches, 32 rows

b
Yarn Used:
Puppy Shetland
■ #31 Gray ■ #54 Yellow ■ #53 Ultramarine
■ #29 Red
Knitting Needles: Straight Needles Size 6
  (3.75 mm, UK Size 9)
Panel: 32 stitches × 38 rows
Gauge (10 cm - 4" square): 23 stitches, 27 rows

Difficulty: ★★☆

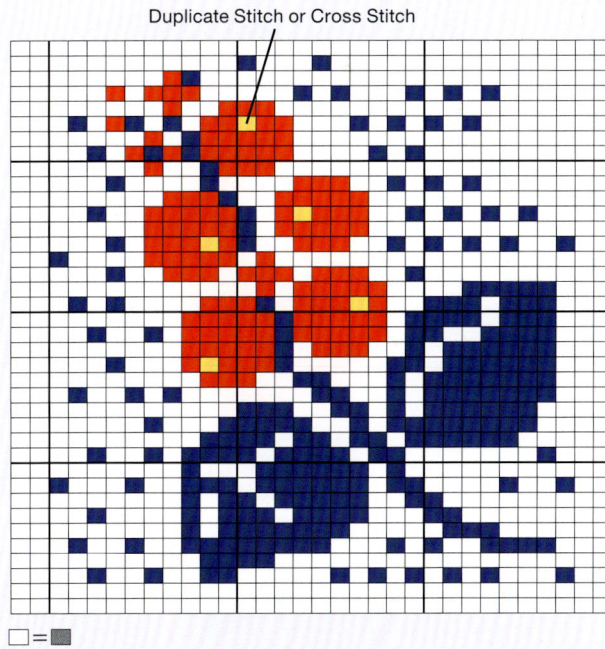

Lesson 3 — How to Knit a Ribbon

This is a method for knitting a ribbon three-dimensionally. Only three stitches for the three rows (labeled as a, b, c in the chart) are picked up from the base panel. The rest is the three-dimensional portion of the ribbon, so you won't knit the base panel itself. Note that you will be knitting three rows within a single row. Refer to the chart on page 43.

1 Knit the first stitch of the ribbon. This will be the first stitch (a) on the chart.

2 Make ten backwards loop increases.

3 You have made ten increases. There should be ten stitches on the right needle.

4 Knit the next stitch on the left needle. This will be the second stitch (b) on the chart.

5 Again, make ten backwards loop increases. Now, on either side of the second stitch (b), you have ten stitches on the right needle.

6 Knit the next stitch on the left needle. This will be the third stitch (c) on the chart.

7 Turn your work and purl the row. Just work the ribbon portion by turning your work.

8 You have purled back to the first stitch (a). You have now completed the two segments of the first row.

9 When starting the next row, make sure to cross the background color yarn with the ribbon color yarn. If you don't, a gap will form between the ribbon and the fabric.

10 Knit across the third segment of the first row in the background color. Since this is the last segment of the first row, knit until the end of the row. As you finish the ribbon portion, pull the yarn tightly. The background yarn (light blue) will carry across the back of the ribbon.

11 For the second row (which is the fourth row of the ribbon), purl across the row. This row does not require separate work on the ribbon.

12 Knit the first segment of the third row (the fifth row of the ribbon). Start from the beginning of the row and change the yarn color at the ribbon section. Knit the third stitch (c) as well.

13. Turn your work over and purl the ribbon portion only. This will be the second segment of the third row of the base panel (the sixth row of the ribbon).

14. You have purled up to the first stitch (a) of the ribbon. Don't forget to cross the background color yarn with the ribbon color yarn before starting the next row.

15. Turn your work. Knit the third segment of the third row (the seventh row of the ribbon). This will be the last row for the ribbon, so you will start binding off. First, knit the initial stitch with the background color yarn.

16. Pick up the ribbon color yarn and knit two stitches. Bind off by passing the first stitch over the second stitch.

17. Repeat this, binding off nine stitches in total, and leave the 10th stitch on the needle.

18. Next stitch is the stitch (b). Knit it with the background color yarn. Bind off the ribbon color yarn.

19. Pull the background color yarn tightly to fold the ribbon in half, forming the shape.

20. Continue binding off with the ribbon color yarn, and for the final stitch (c), knit it with the background color yarn and bind off the ribbon color yarn.

21. Again, pull the background color yarn tightly to fold the ribbon in half.

22. Continue knitting with the background color yarn to the end of the row. This completes the three-dimensional ribbon. The yarn carried on the wrong side will be hidden inside the folded ribbon.

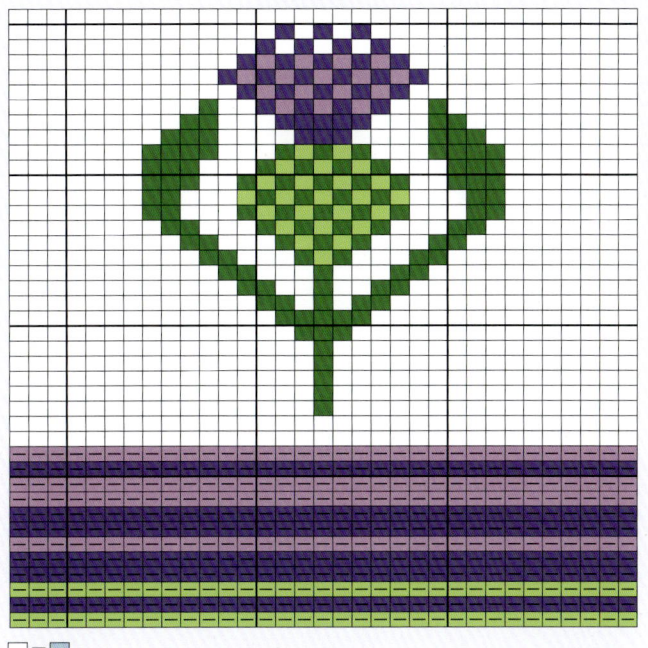

☐ = ☐

Thistle

Yarn Used:

Jamieson's Spindrift

☐ #929 Aqua ■ #1300 Aubretia ■ #616 Anemone,
■ #259 Leprechaun ■ #815 Ivy

Knitting Needles: Straight Needles Size 4 (3.25 mm, UK Size 10)
Panel: 33 stitches × 41 rows
Gauge (10 cm - 4" square): 25 stitches, 32 rows

Difficulty: ★★☆

* Preparing the yarn for colorwork:
  Flower (#1300): 90 cm - 39⅜" long pieces
  Flower (#616): 50 cm - 19¾" long pieces
  Involucre (#259): 60 cm - 23⅝" long pieces
  Leaf (#815): 240 cm - 94½" long pieces

☐ = ■

Dandelion

Yarn Used:

Puppy British Fine

■ #092 Turquoise ■ #055 Green ■ #037 Brown ☐ #066 Yellow

Knitting Needles: Straight Needles Size 4 (3.25 mm, UK Size 10)
Panel: 33 stitches × 41 rows
Gauge (10 cm - 4" square): 28 stitches, 32 rows

Difficulty: ★★☆

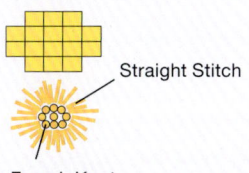

Straight Stitch

French Knot
(wrap once)

Embroider the flower part on top.

Snowdrops

Yarn Used:
Jamieson's Spindrift
■ #655 China Blue □ #304 White ■ #788 Leaf
■ #785 Apple

Other Materials:
Beads: MIYUKI Seed Beads Round 8/0 #1
Knitting Needles: Straight Needles Size 4 (3.25 mm, UK Size 10)
Panel: 34 stitches × 42 rows
Gauge (10 cm - 4" square): 25 stitches, 32 rows

Difficulty: ★★☆

Point
When knitting a narrow, single-stitch stem, after knitting the next stitch, pull the stem color yarn tight. This will help create a neat finish.

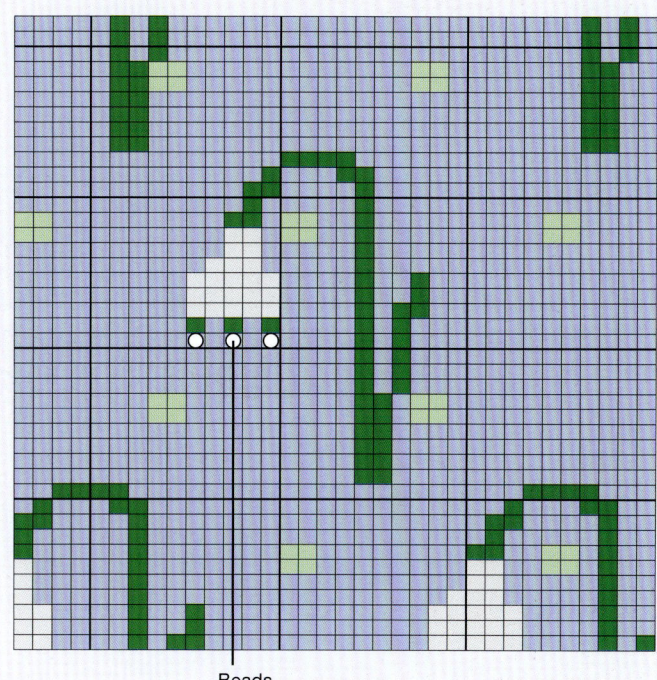

Beads

□ = ■

French Knot (wrap twice)
Embroider over #999

Poppies

Yarn Used:
Jamieson's Spindrift
■ #517 Mantilla ■ #540 Coral ■ #271 Flame
■ #259 Leprechaun ■ #599 Zodiac ■ #999 Black
■ #805 Spruce

Knitting Needles: Straight Needles Size 4 (3.25 mm, UK Size 10)
Panel: 34 stitches × 44 rows
Gauge (10 cm - 4" square): 28 stitches, 38 rows

Difficulty: ★★☆

* Prepare small skeins of yarn corresponding to the number of flowers that will fit within the project's width for the intarsia of large flowers.

a.
b.

Climbing Roses

Yarn Used:

Jamieson's Spindrift

■ #315 Heron   ■ #259 Leprechaun   □ #390 Daffodil
■ #585 Plum   ■ #188 Sherbet   ■ #580 Cherry

Knitting Needles: Straight Needles Size 4 (3.25 mm, UK Size 10)
Panel: 34 stitches × 42 rows
Gauge (10 cm - 4" square): 26 stitches, 30 rows

Difficulty: ★★☆

* Preparing the yarn for colorwork:
 Flower center (#390): 35 cm - 13¾" long pieces
 Petal (#585): 30 cm - 11⅞" long pieces
 Petal (#188): 45 cm - 17¾" long pieces
 Petal (#580): 25 cm - 9⅞" long pieces

Rosebuds

Yarn Used:

a
Puppy Chaska
□ #10 White
Puppy - ALBA
■ #5139 Red   ■ #1185 Green   ■ #1170 Pink

b
Jamieson's Spindrift
■ #580 Cherry,   ■ #259 Leprechaun,
■ #540 Coral,   □ #390 Daffodil

Shared Materials:
Knitting Needles: Straight Needles Size 4
 (3.25 mm, UK Size 10)
Panel: 40 stitches × 48 rows
Gauge (10 cm - 4" square): 26 stitches, 40 rows

Difficulty: ★★★

* Preparing the yarn for colorwork:
 Rosebud: 45 cm - 17¾" long pieces
 Leaves, Stems: 200 cm - 78¾" long pieces

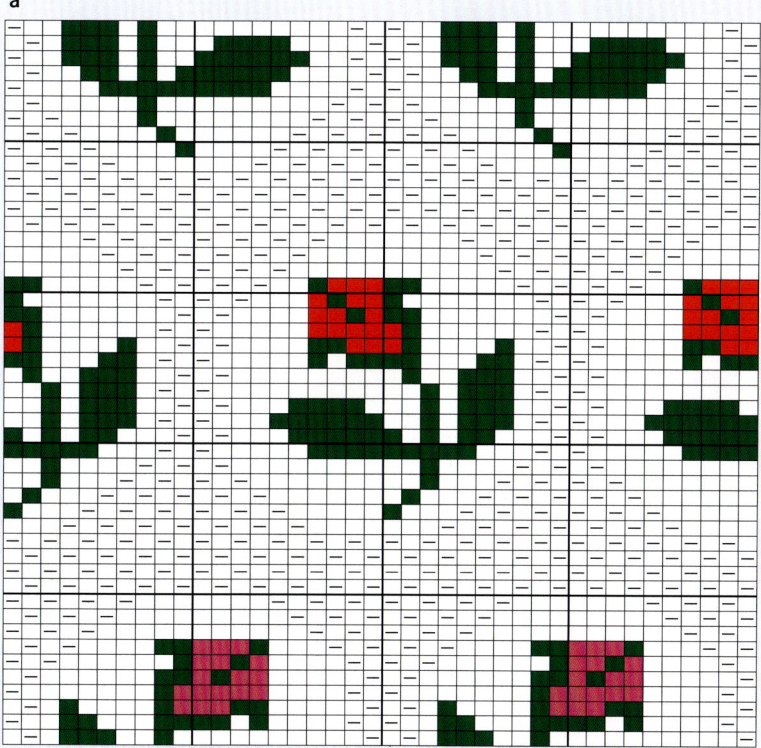

a

51

Pansy and One Stitch Patterns

Yarn Used:
Jamieson's Spindrift
- #105 Eesit ■ #629 Lupin ■ #788 Leaf
- #400 Mimosa ■ #470 Pumpkin
- #599 Zodiac ■ #655 China Blue
- ■ #999 Black

Knitting Needles: Straight Needles Size 4
(3.25 mm, UK Size 10)
Panel: 38 stitches × 40 rows
Gauge (10 cm - 4" square): 26 stitches, 32 rows

Difficulty: ★☆☆

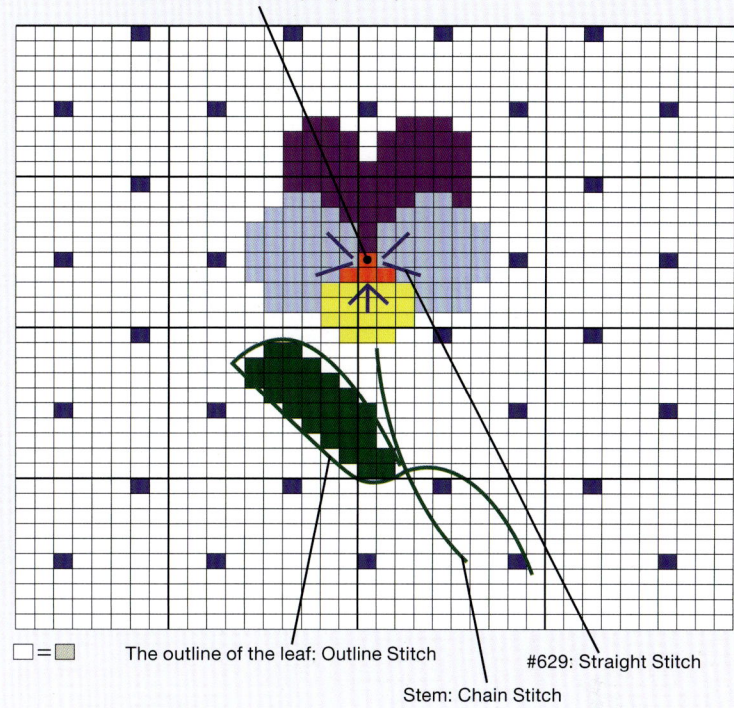

#999: French Knot (wrap twice)

□ = ▨   The outline of the leaf: Outline Stitch   #629: Straight Stitch
Stem: Chain Stitch

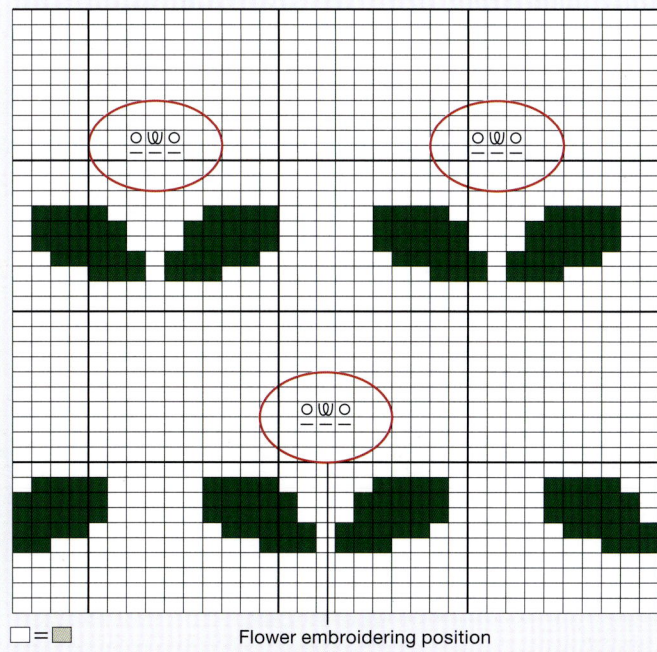

Large Daisies

Yarn Used:
Jamieson's Spindrift
- #105 Eesit ■ #525 Crimson ■ #788 Leaf
- □ #304 White

Other Materials: Camel yellow color felt (washed)
Knitting Needles: Straight Needles Size 4
(3.25 mm, UK Size 10)
Panel: 34 stitches × 40 rows
Gauge (10 cm - 4" square): 26 stitches, 32 rows

Difficulty: ★☆☆

*Refer to page 27 for embroidering the daisy.

□ = ▨   Flower embroidering position

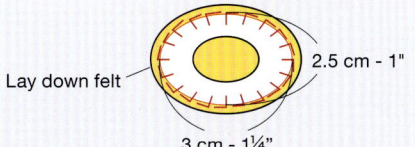

Lay down felt   2.5 cm - 1"
3 cm - 1¼"

First, use White (#304) to work blanket stitch along the outer edge. Then, use Crimson (#525) to work shorter blanket stitch with gaps in between on top.

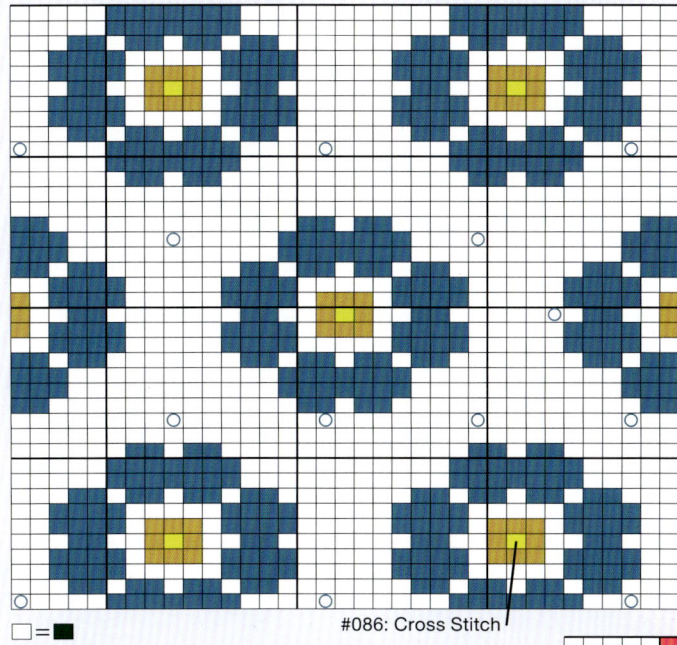

#086: Cross Stitch

□ = ■

Cornflowers

Yarn Used:
Puppy British Fine
■ #034 Deep Green ■ #092 Turquoise ■ #035 Mustard
□ #086 Neon Yellow
Knitting Needles: Straight Needles Size 5 (3.50 mm)
Crochet Hook Size 2/0 (2.00 mm, UK Size 14)
Panel: 35 stitches × 40 rows
Gauge (10 cm - 4" square): 28 stitches, 32 rows

Difficulty: ★★☆

* Refer page 123 for bobble stitch crochet.

◎ = 🧶

2 Half Double Crochet Cluster Stitch
Crochet hook: Size 2/0 (2.00 mm)

Pink Daisies

Yarn Used:
Jamieson's Spindrift
□ #122 Granite ■ #188 Sherbet ■ #815 Ivy
■ #271 Flame
Knitting Needles: Straight Needles Size 4
(3.25 mm, UK Size 10)
Panel: 35 stitches × 40 rows
Gauge (10 cm - 4" square): 28 stitches, 32 rows

Difficulty: ★☆☆
* Preparing the yarn for colorwork:
  Petals: 90 cm - 35½" long pieces
  Leaves, Stems: 70 cm - 27½" long pieces
  Flower center: 20 cm - 7⅞" long pieces

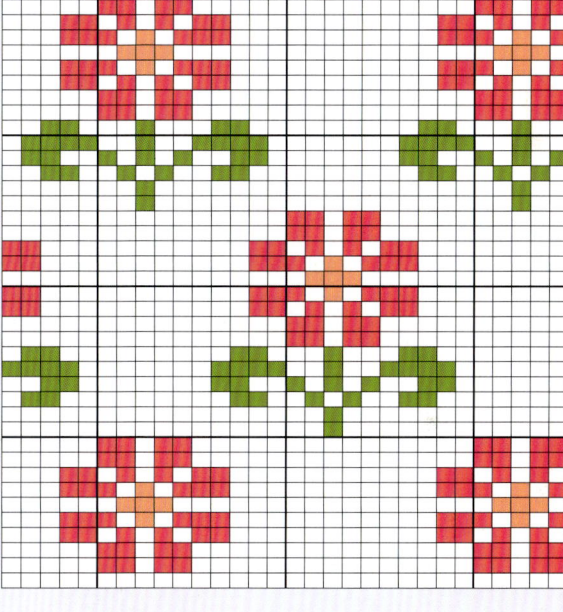

□ = □

Cross stitch with the two shades of yellow held together.

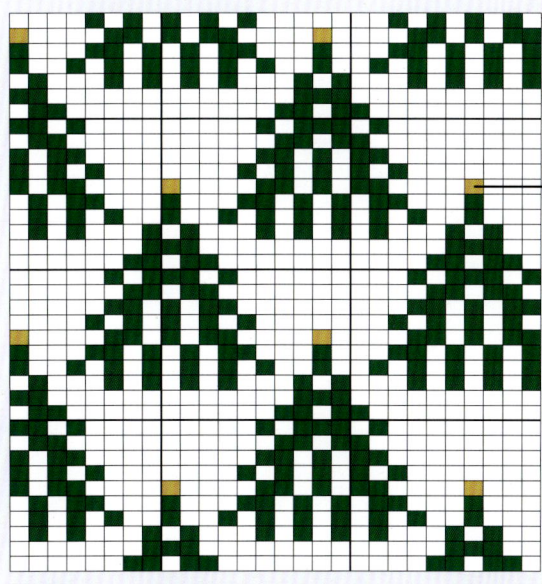

□ = ■

Fir Trees

Yarn Used:
Puppy Shetland
□ #9 Blue Gray ■ #14 Green
Puppy British Fine
□ #066 Yellow □ #086 Neon Yellow
Knitting Needles: Straight Needles Size 5 (3.50 mm)
Panel: 34 stitches × 40 rows
Gauge (10 cm - 4" square): 26 stitches, 28 rows

Difficulty: ★☆☆

55

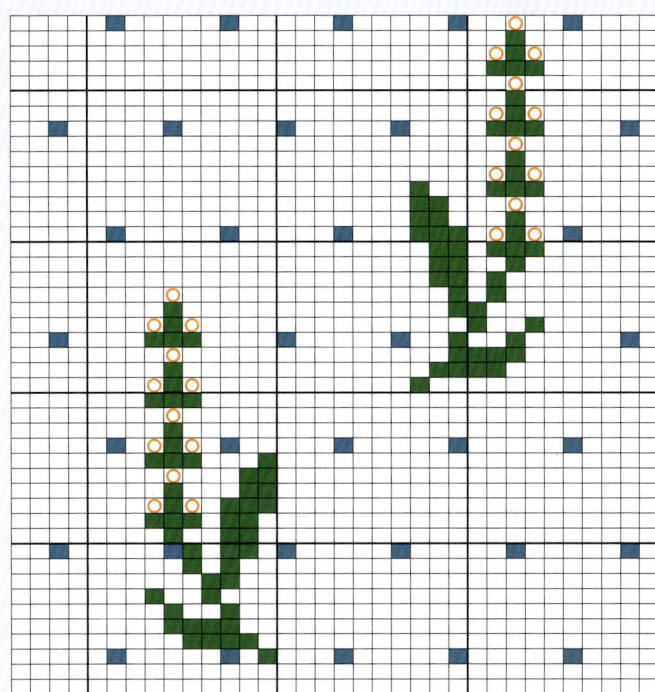

Mimosas

Yarn Used:
Puppy British Fine
☐ #001 White ■ #066 Yellow ■ #092 Turquoise ■ #055 Green
Knitting Needles: Straight Needles Size 4 (3.25 mm, UK Size 10)
Crochet Hook Size 2/0 (2.00 mm, UK Size 14)
Panel: 34 stitches × 45 rows
Gauge (10 cm - 4" square): 26 stitches, 34 rows

Difficulty: ★☆☆

◎ = 🌰

* Refer page 123 for bobble stitch crochet.
2 Half Double Crochet Cluster Stitch
Crochet hook: Size 2/0 (2.00 mm)

◎ = 🌰
2 Half Double Crochet Cluster Stitch
Crochet hook: Size 2/0 (2.00 mm)

Saphire Berries

Yarn Used:
Puppy British Fine
■ #040 Beige ■ #037 Brown ■ #007 Ultramarine
Knitting Needles: Straight Needles Size 4 (3.25 mm, UK Size 10)
Crochet Hook Size 2/0 (2.00 mm, UK Size 14)
Panel: 34 stitches × 43 rows
Gauge (10 cm - 4" square): 28 stitches, 36 rows

Difficulty: ★☆☆

* Refer page 123 for bobble stitch crochet.

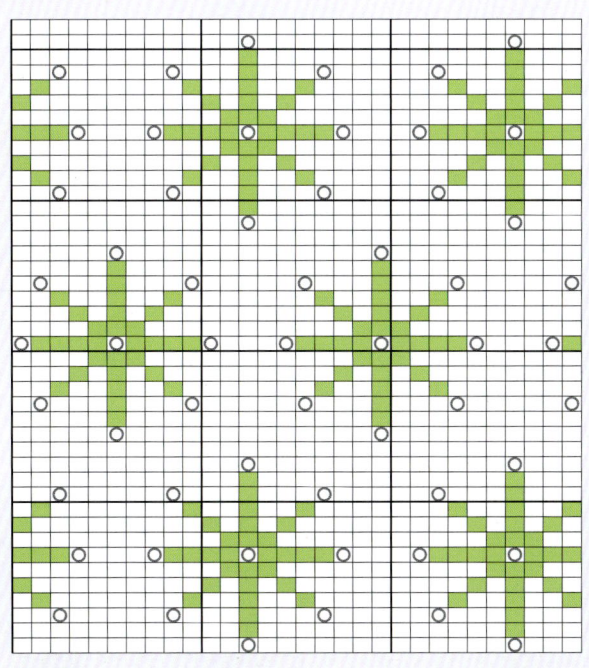

☐ = ■

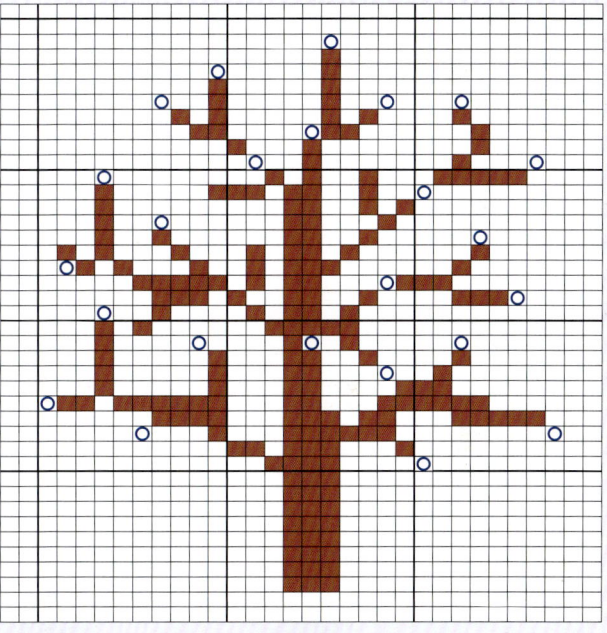

☐ = ☐

Fennel

Yarn Used:
Jamieson's Spindrift
■ #684 Cobalt ■ #780 Lime ☐ #304 White
Knitting Needles: Straight Needles Size 5 (3.50 mm)
Crochet Hook Size 2/0 (2.00 mm, UK Size 14)
Panel: 35 stitches × 42 rows
Gauge (10 cm - 4" square): 28 stitches, 32 rows

◎ = 🌰
2 Half Double Crochet Cluster Stitch
Crochet hook: Size 2/0 (2.00 mm)

Difficulty: ★★☆

* Refer page 123 for bobble stitch crochet.

a
b

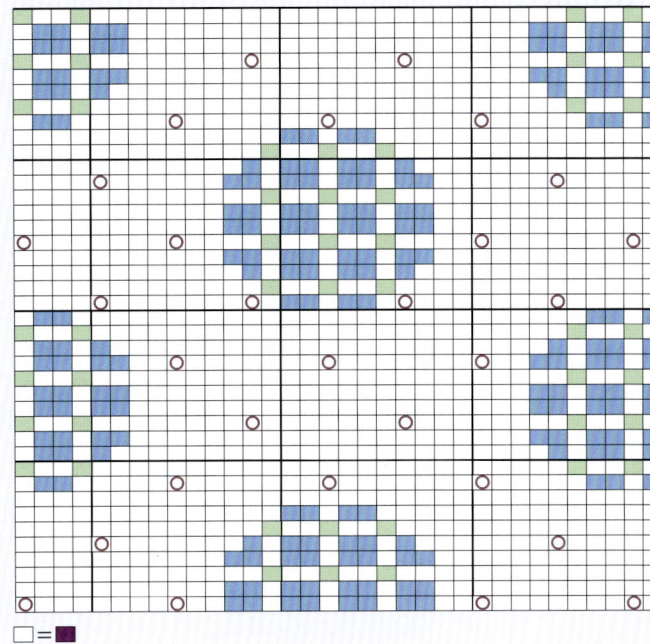

Hydrangeas

Yarn Used:
Jamieson's Spindrift
■ #599 Zodiac ■ #660 Lagoon ■ #785 Apple
■ #617 Lavender
Knitting Needles: Straight Needles Size 5 (3.50 mm)
　　　　　　　　　Crochet Hook Size 2/0 (2.00 mm, UK Size 14)
Panel: 34 stitches × 40 rows
Gauge (10 cm - 4" square): 24 stitches, 30 rows

Difficulty: ★★☆

* Refer page 123 for bobble stitch crochet.

2 Half Double Crochet Cluster Stitch
Crochet hook: Size 2/0 (2.00 mm)

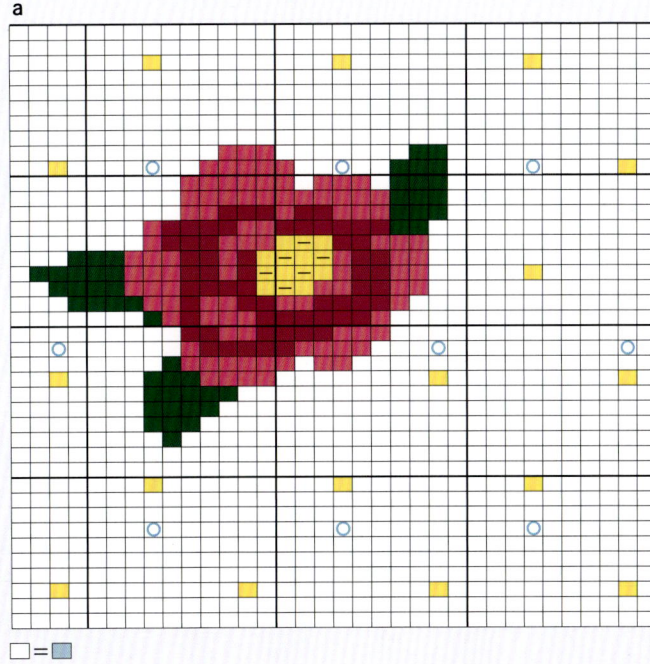

a

Bobble Stitches and Rose

Yarn Used:
a
Jamieson's Spindrift
■ #929 Aqua ■ #517 Mantilla ■ #575 Lipstick
■ #788 Leaf ■ #390 Daffodil
Knitting Needles: Straight Needles Size 4 (3.25 mm, UK Size 10)
　　　　　　　　　Crochet Hook Size 3/0 (2.25 mm, UK Size 13)
Panel: 34 stitches × 40 rows
Gauge (10 cm - 4" square): 26 stitches, 34 rows

b
Puppy British Fine
■ #008 Black ■ #066 Yellow ■ #006 Red ■ #013 Dark Red
■ #055 Green ■ #080 Yellow Green
Knitting Needles: Straight Needles Size 4 (3.25 mm, UK Size 10)
　　　　　　　　　Crochet Hook Size 3/0 (2.25 mm, UK Size 13)
Panel: 34 stitches × 40 rows
Gauge (10 cm - 4" square): 28 stitches, 38 rows

Difficulty: ★★☆

* Refer page 123 for bobble stitch crochet.

* Preparing the yarn for colorwork:
　Petals (#517): 110 cm - 43¼" long pieces
　Petals (#575): 180 cm - 70⅞" long pieces
　Leaves (#788): 100 cm - 39⅜" long pieces
　Flower center (#390): 45 cm - 17¾" long pieces

2 Half Double Crochet
Cluster Stitch

Crochet hook: Size 3/0
(2.25 mm)

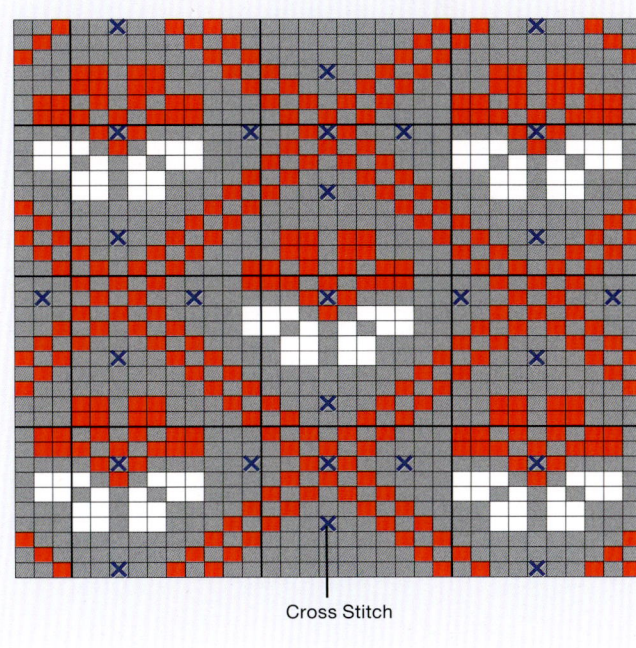

Cross Stitch

Latvian Flowers

Yarn Used:
Puppy British Fine
■ #009 Gray ■ #007 Ultramarine ■ #006 Red
□ #001 White
Knitting Needles: Straight Needles Size 5 (3.50 mm)
Panel: 33 stitches × 37 rows
Gauge (10 cm - 4" square): 28 stitches, 30 rows

Difficulty: ★★☆

Diagonal Flowers

Yarn Used:
ROWAN Felted Tweed
■ #195 Gray ■ #200 Pink
Knitting Needles: Straight Needles Size 5 (3.50 mm)
Panel: 35 stitches × 44 rows
Gauge (10 cm - 4" square): 25 stitches, 36 rows

Difficulty: ★★☆

Point
It's easier to knit symmetrical patterns, like the one on this page, in the round by focusing only on the right side.

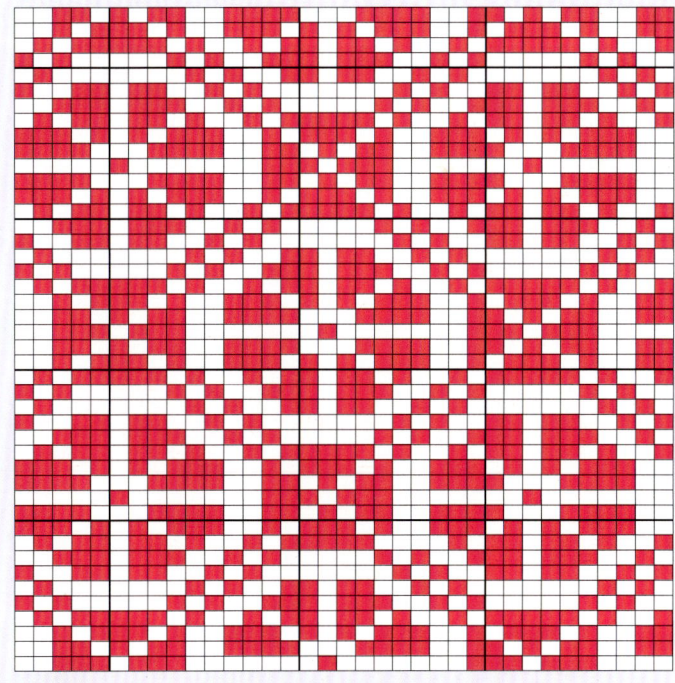

□ = ■

61

This is a thistle-patterned bolero that can be quickly thrown on. The design makes the most of the large thistle pattern, providing plenty of width to fully cover your back, while the front maintains a sleek look with only the sleeves and collar visible. Thanks to the generous width, the sleeves also have a cute, gathered look.

Instructions...page 138

Column 2 — Choosing Yarn and Creating an Image

Choosing yarn is both a great joy and one of the most challenging decisions. When selecting yarn to depict the natural flowers featured in this book, you might wonder: Should I use natural colors? Or should I create a palette from my own imagination? How many colors should I include? Is the color I envision even available as yarn?

Start by imagining the design in your mind. Then, try translating that image onto paper using colored pencils, and see how it could correspond to yarns available to you. While it might seem difficult to "imagine" the design, if you're inspired to knit a pattern from this book, take a walk and observe the colors in nature. If a breeze is blowing, you might think, "Ah, the fresh green leaves looked so beautiful with the gentle wind," and that memory could spark an idea to combine greens, blues, whites, and yellows. It all begins with what you feel!

For beginners, start by choosing a project with fewer colors and using a simple straight yarn that's easy to unravel if needed. Once you've gained some experience, try incorporating more colors, three-dimensional knitting techniques, and even experiment with mohair.

After you've chosen a pattern, transfer it onto graph paper and color it in. As you physically mark "two red stitches, three white stitches," you will start to memorize the pattern, making it easier to knit than expected. This is one of the key methods I hold dear – definitely give it a try!

1. How Colors and Yarn Can Transform a Design

Let's compare these five Lily-of-the-Valley swatches. The light blue version, knitted in a single color, emphasizes the three-dimensional effect of the design. The next three swatches – light yellow-green, green, and navy – all have the flowers knitted in white, but the change in background color creates a different mood. The green feels natural, the light yellow-green gives off a soft, gentle impression, and the navy adds a sharp, crisp look. There's also a gray version with black flowers, which creates a chic and sophisticated look. Try copying the pattern you want to knit and color it in with colored pencils. This exercise helps visualize the design much more clearly than just imagining it in your head.

The shawl on page 115 is knitted with white mohair. Changing the yarn texture can dramatically transform the overall impression of the finished project.

2. Swatches in Different Colors

Here is the Thistle pattern in various colors. The white background swatch has a vibrant and lively feel, while the gray background swatch gives a chic, mature look, and the navy background swatch has a youthful feel. Since the thistle is Scotland's national flower and Shetland, where this yarn is from, is part of the northern Scottish Islands, I focused on preserving the significance of the thistle's color while varying the background to change the overall impression. Knitting this pattern reminds me of Shetland's rugged landscape and the warm smiles of the friendly islanders.

The light blue version on page 62 is a color combination I personally want to wear. I enjoyed playing with different color combinations and knitting multiple swatches before deciding on the color for the actual garment. You can also sew your sample swatches together to create a bag – it's a wonderful way to use them!

I worked the stripes in a purl stitch to create a blending effect between the colors for the finished project. It's a simple, but highly effective technique.

3. Swatches with Different Yarns

These two swatches were knitted with the same stitch and row counts, but you'll notice the differences in size. The larger swatch was made with medium-weight yarn on size 6 (3.75 mm) needles, while the smaller one was knitted with fine yarn on size 4 (3.25 mm) needles. Naturally, the gauge (stitches and rows per 10 cm - 4 ") differs as well, which will affect the stitch and row count needed for larger projects like garments or blankets. The thickness and weight of the fabric also change, so choosing yarn based on what you want to create is essential. For items like bags, you might prefer a denser fabric, while garments can be adjusted to your desired softness. Always swatch first to understand the yarn's characteristics and ensure it's the right fit for your project.

Fruits

Employing three-dimensional stitches, like the bobble stitch, enhances the cuteness of the patterns presented in this section.

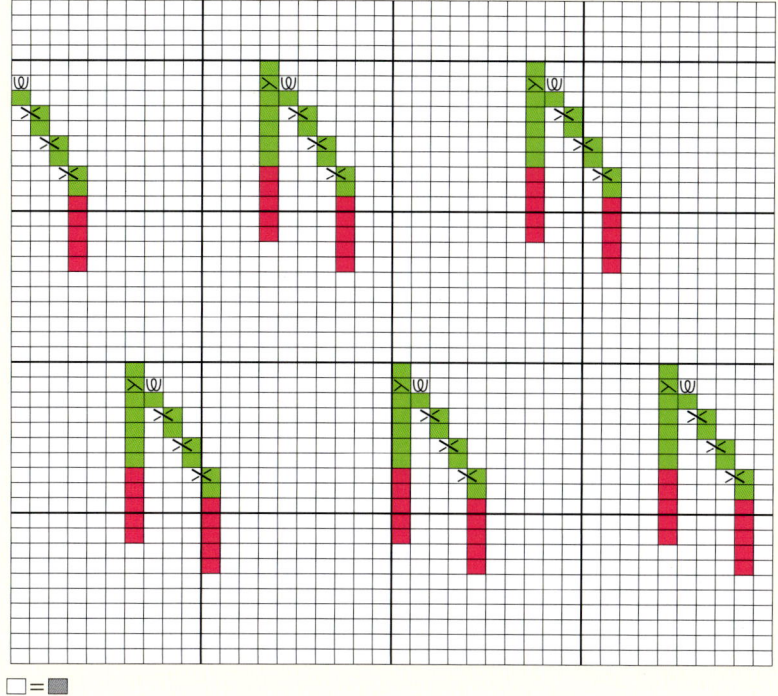

Two Cherries

Yarn Used:
Puppy British Fine
■ #009 Gray   ■ #085 Neon Pink
Puppy Shetland
■ #47 Yellow Green
Knitting Needles: Straight Needles Size 4
(3.25 mm, UK Size 10)
Crochet Hook Size 3/0
(2.25 mm, UK Size 13)
Panel: 36 stitches × 44 rows
Gauge (10 cm - 4" square): 28 stitches, 36 rows

Difficulty: ★☆☆

* Preparing the yarn for colorwork:
  Cherries: 90 cm - 35½" long pieces
  Stems: 45 cm - 17¾" long pieces
* See page 70 for instructions on knitting the cherry intarsia colorwork.

Bobble Stitch for 5 rows
Pull through with crochet hook

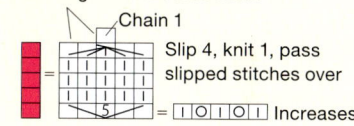

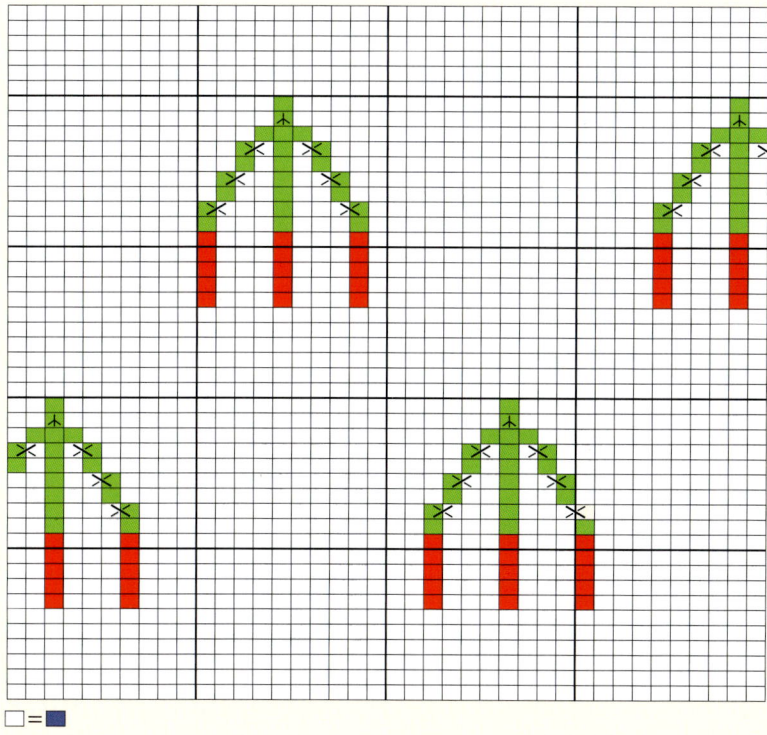

Three Cherries

Yarn Used:
Puppy Shetland
■ #17 Cobalt Blue   ■ #29 Red
■ #47 Yellow Green
Knitting Needles: Straight Needles Size 6
(3.75 mm, UK Size 9)
Crochet Hook Size 4/0
(2.50 mm, UK Size 12)
Panel: 27 stitches × 40 rows
Gauge (10 cm - 4" square): 22 stitches, 30 rows

Difficulty: ★☆☆

* Preparing the yarn for colorwork:
  Cherries: 150 cm - 59" long pieces
  Stems: 90 cm - 35½" long pieces
* See page 70 for instructions on knitting the cherry intarsia colorwork.

Bobble Stitch for 5 rows
Pull through with crochet hook

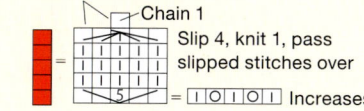

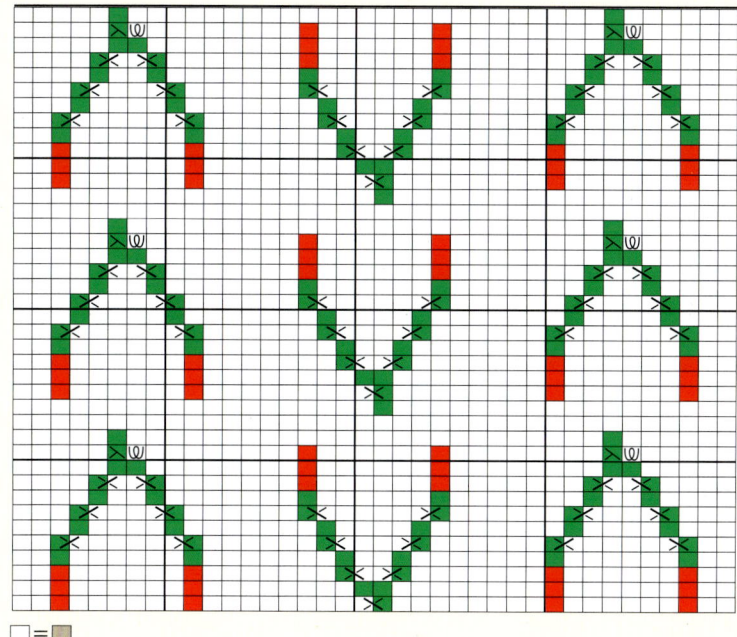

Up & Down Cherries

Yarn Used:
Puppy ALBA
☐ #1087 Beige ■ #5139 Red ■ #1185 Green
Knitting Needles: Straight Needles Size 5 (3.50 mm)
Crochet Hook Size 4/0
(2.50 mm, UK Size 12)
Panel: 38 stitches × 40 rows
Gauge (10 cm - 4" square): 28 stitches, 32 rows

Difficulty: ★★☆

* Preparing the yarn for colorwork:
  Cherries: 120 cm - 47¼" long pieces
  Stems: 55 cm - 21⅝" long pieces
* See page 71 for instructions on knitting the cherry intarsia colorwork.

Note: For the bobble stitches, the color of each piece of yarn – pulled through the backing with a crochet hook – will differ depending on the cherry's positioning (upward, downward).

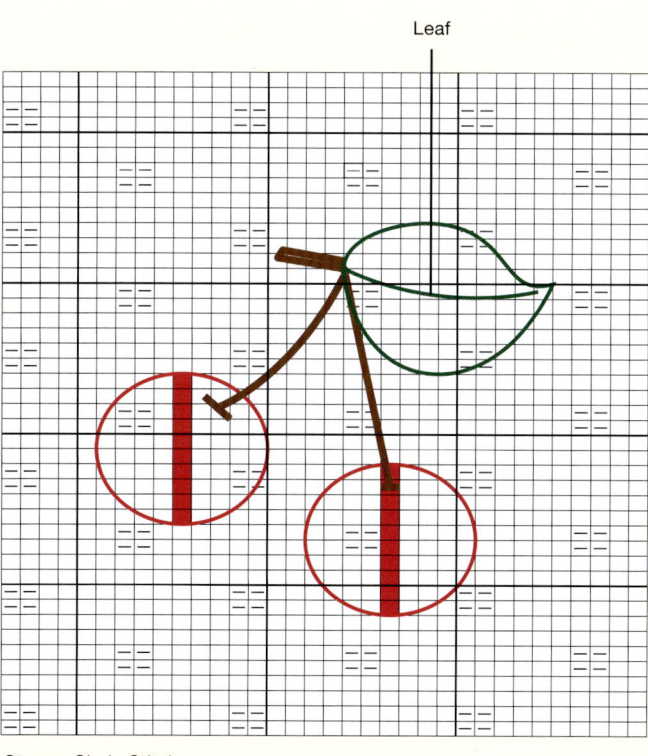

Leaf

Stems: Chain Stitch
Sew the leaf motif (knitted separately) along its centerline to attach it.

Large Cherry

Yarn Used:
Jamieson's Spindrift
☐ #655 China Blue ■ #525 Crimson ■ #788 Leaf
■ #879 Copper
Knitting Needles: Straight Needles Size 4
(3.25 mm, UK Size 10)
and for leaf, Size 2 (2.50 mm)
Crochet Hook Size 3/0
(2.25 mm, UK Size 13)
Panel: 34 stitches × 44 rows
Gauge (10 cm - 4" square): 26 stitches, 38 rows

Difficulty: ★☆☆

* Preparing the yarn for colorwork:
  Cherries: 90 cm - 35⅜" long pieces
* See page 70 for instructions on knitting the cherry intarsia colorwork.

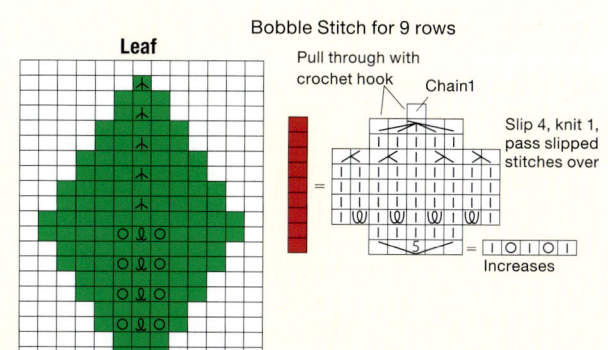

Lesson 4: How to Knit Cherries

Explained with the cherries on pages 66 and 68. Cut the yarn, for both the cherry and the stem, to required lengths. Refer to the diagrams on pages 67 and 69.

Instructions for Two and Three Cherry Patterns

1. One stitch before changing the yarn to knit the cherry, slide the red yarn between the working yarn and the project. Knit one stitch with the cherry colored yarn.

2. Pass the yarn over the right needle to make a second increase.

3. For the third increase, insert the needle into same stitch and knit.

4. Yarn over to create a fourth increase and knit into the same stitch for a fifth. Here, we can see that five increases were made. Continue knitting with the panel color (white) to the end of the row. The first row is complete.

5. Begin knitting the second row. Lay the cherry yarn over the background color yarn one stitch before where the knitting begins for the cherry. Knit once with the panel color (white).

6. Switch to the cherry color and purl across the five increases made in the previous steps.

7. After the fifth purl, switch to the background color (white) and purl to the end of the row.

8. Turn the working project over and begin knitting the third row. Cross the background colored yarn and cherry yarn one stitch before where the cherry knitting begins. Knit one stitch with the background color.

9. Switch to the cherry yarn and knit five stitches. Switch to the background color (white), then continue to knit to the row's end. For the fourth row, proceed like the previous row, but purl instead.

10. Use the panel color for the fifth row. Move five cherry color stitches onto the crochet hook.

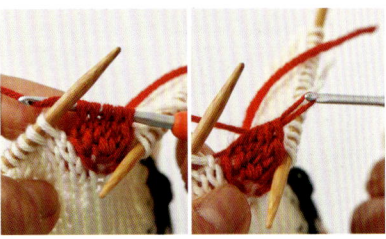

11. Pass the yarn over the crochet hook and pull through to decrease to a single stitch.

12. Pass the yarn over the crochet hook to make a single chain stitch. Place this stitch back onto the knitting needle to complete the cherry.

Up & Down Cherries

1 Similar to the cherry on page 70, make three increases from one stitch. Knit, yarn over, and knit. This forms the first row of the first cherry segment.

2 Turn the working project around and work the second row of the first segment of the cherry. Purl the first stitch of the cherry.

3 Backwards loop cast-on to make one increase.

4 Purl the second stitch, then make another backward loop cast-on to create another increase. Purl the third stitch. Two increases were made to make five stitches.

5 Turn the work around. Cross the background color and cherry yarn to knit the third row of the first cherry segment.

6 Knit five stitches. Now the first segment of the cherry is done. Proceed to knit with the background colored yarn to the row's end.

7 Begin working on the second row of the main panel. From the edge, proceed with background colored yarn. Change the yarn to cherry and knit five stiches. The second cherry segment has only one row. Change the yarn back to the background color and knit to the row's end.

8 Work the third cherry segment in a similar manner to the first segment. Begin the row with the background color, then switch to the cherry yarn for the third segment of the first row (fifth row of the cherry). Turn to knit the second row of the third segment (sixth row of the cherry).

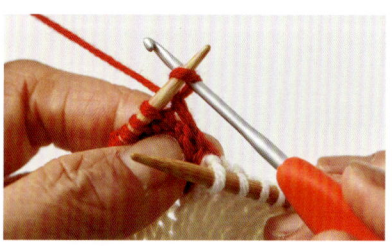

9 Pick up five stitches of the third row of the third cherry segment (seventh row of the cherry) with the crochet hook.

10 Yarn over the crochet hook and pull through to decrease to one stitch. Make one chain stitch with the crochet hook.

11 Place the stitch back onto the knitting needle to complete the cherry. This cherry has more volume than the one on page 70 as the work is turned on the first, third, fourth, and seventh rows of the cherry.

The yarn crosses at the back like so.

71

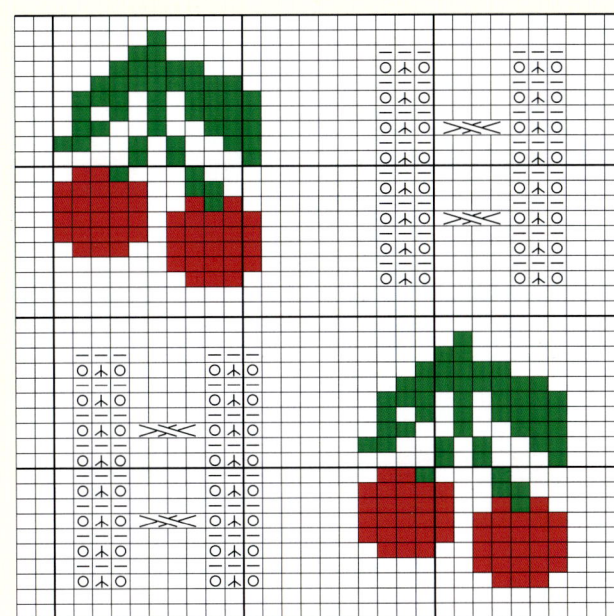

Openwork and Cherries

Yarn Used:
Jamieson's Spindrift
■ #710 Gentian ■ #525 Crimson ■ #790 Celtic
Knitting Needles: Straight Needles Size 4 (3.25 mm, UK Size 10), Cable Needle
Panel: 32 stitches × 40 rows
Gauge (10 cm - 4" square): 28 stitches, 36 rows

Difficulty: ★☆☆

* Preparing the yarn for colorwork:
  Leaves: 115 cm - 45¼" long pieces
  Cherries: 105 cm - 41⅜" long pieces

□ = ■

Cherry Intarsia

Yarn Used:
Puppy Shetland
■ #30 Light Gray ■ #23 Wine Red
■ #55 Opera ■ #47 Yellow Green ■ #14 Green
Knitting Needles: Straight Needles Size 6 (3.75 mm, UK Size 9)
Panel: 33 stitches × 40 rows
Gauge (10 cm - 4" square): 24 stitches, 31 rows

Difficulty: ★☆☆
* Preparing the yarn for colorwork:
  Cherry (each): 40 cm - 15¾" long pieces
  Leaves (yellow green): 85 cm - 33½" long pieces
  Leaves (green): 35 cm - 13¾" long pieces

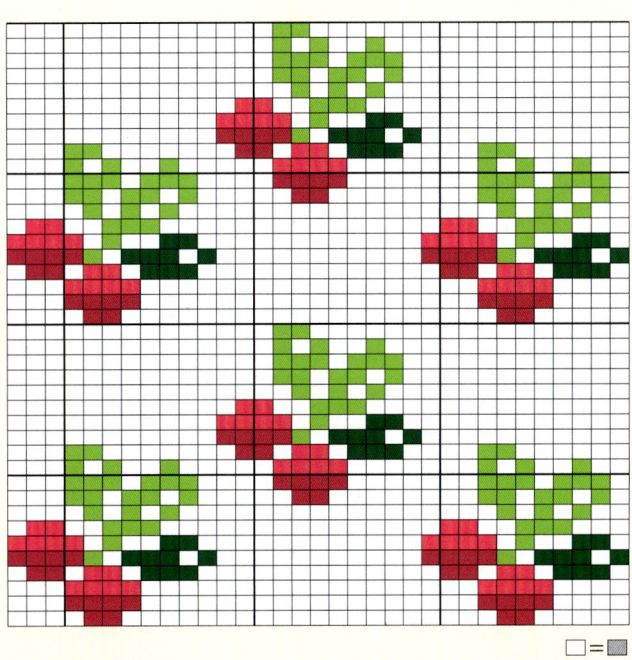

□ = ▨

Cross Stitch

Blueberries

Yarn Used:
Puppy ALBA
■ #1112 Dark Green
Puppy Shetland
■ #14 Green ■ #47 Yellow Green ■ #56 Purple ■ #17 Cobalt Blue
Puppy British Fine
■ #037 Brown
Knitting Needles: Straight Needles Size 6 (3.75 mm, UK Size 9)
Panel: 34 stitches × 38 rows
Gauge (10 cm - 4" square): 24 stitches, 32 rows

Difficulty: ★☆☆

□ = ■

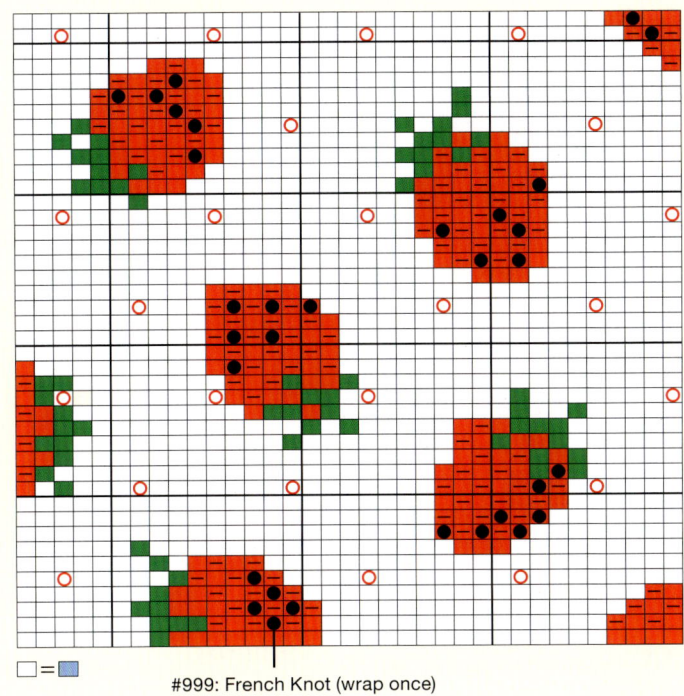

#999: French Knot (wrap once)

☐ = 🟦

* The strawberry intarsia on the swatch in the photo (page 74) is upside down.

Dancing Strawberries

Yarn Used:
Jamieson's Spindrift
🟦 #660 Lagoon 🟥 #500 Scarlet 🟩 #800 Tartan
⬛ #999 Black
Knitting Needles: Straight Needles Size 5 (3.50 mm)
Crochet Hook Size 2/0
(2.00 mm, UK Size 14)
Panel: 35 stitches × 42 rows
Gauge (10 cm - 4" square): 28 stitches, 34 rows

Difficulty: ★★☆

* Preparing the yarn for colorwork:
  Strawberries: carry yarn across
  Leaves: 40 cm - 15¾" long pieces

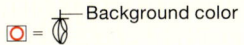
— Background color
⊙ =
2 Half Double Crochet Cluster Stitch
Crochet hook: Size 2/0 (2.00 mm)

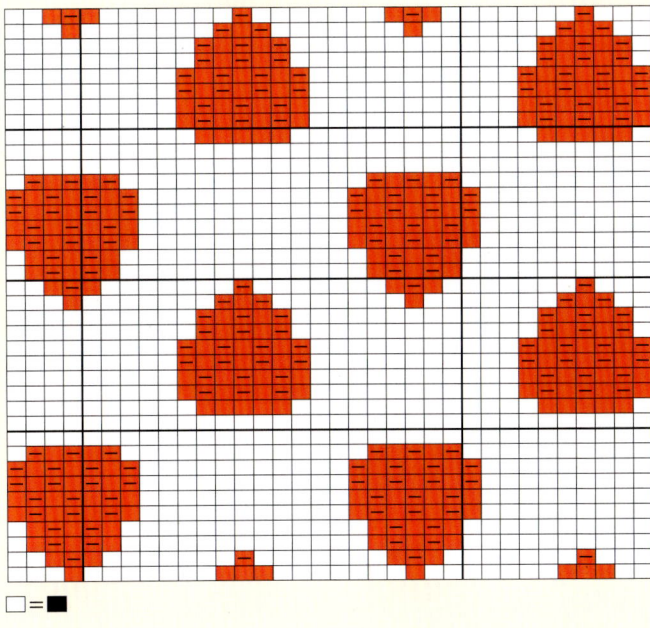

☐ = ⬛

Up & Down Strawberries

Yarn Used:
Puppy Shetland
⬛ #20 Navy Blue 🟥 #29 Red 🟩 #14 Green
Puppy British Fine
🟨 #066 Yellow
Knitting Needles: Straight Needles Size 6
(3.75 mm, UK Size 9)
Panel: 34 stitches × 42 rows
Gauge (10 cm - 4" square): 26 stitches, 30 rows
(after embroidered)

Difficulty: ★☆☆

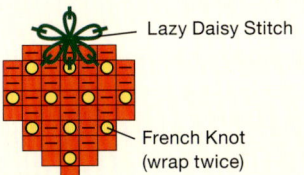
Lazy Daisy Stitch
French Knot (wrap twice)

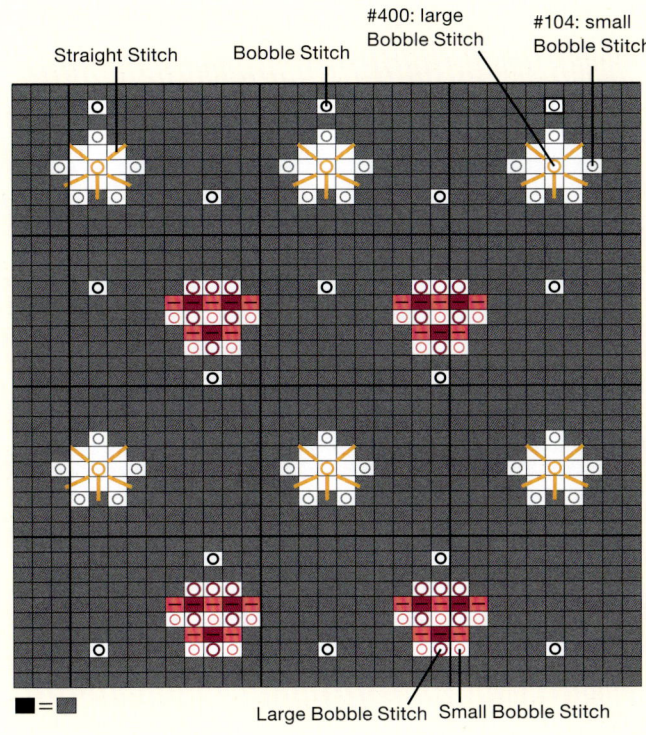

Raspberries

Yarn Used:

Jamieson's Spindrift

■ #999 Black ■ #188 Sherbet ■ #580 Cherry
□ #104 Natural White ■ #400 Mimosa
■ #800 Tartan

Knitting Needles: Straight Needles Size 5 (3.50 mm)
Crochet Hook Size 2/0
(2.00 mm, UK Size 14),
Size 3/0 (2.25 mm, UK Size 13)

Panel: 33 stitches × 40 rows

Gauge (10 cm - 4" square): 26 stitches, 34 rows

Difficulty: ★☆☆

* See page 122 for knitting bobble stitch, page 123 for bobble stitch crochet.

#800: Lazy Daisy Stitch
#188: small
#580: large

Large Bobble Stitch

3 Half Double Crochet Cluster Stitch
Crochet hook: Size 2/0 (2.00 mm)

Small Bobble Stitch
2 Half Double Crochet Cluster Stitch
Crochet hook: Size 2/0 (2.00 mm)

Bobble Stitch for 1 row
Pull through with crochet hook
Chain 1, Crochet hook: Size 3/0 (2.25 mm)
Slip stitch into the increase
Slip, knit 2 together pass slipped stitch over
= Increases

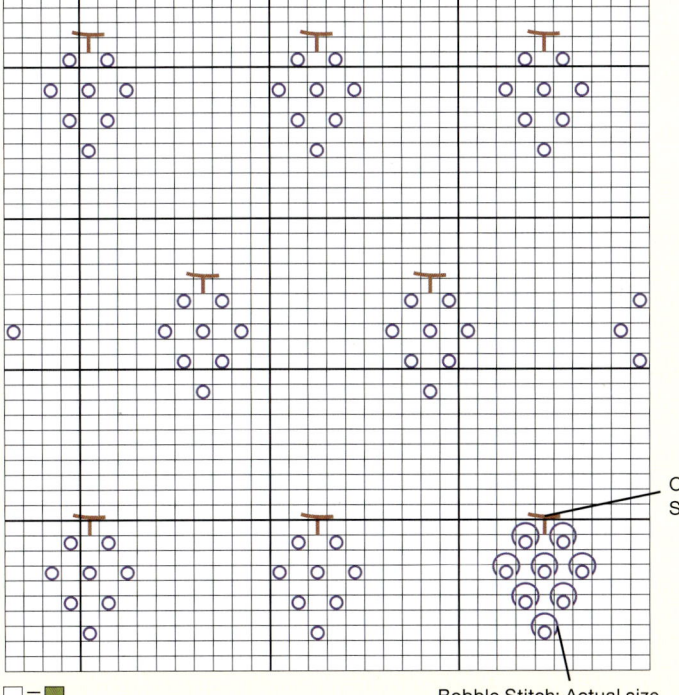

Grapes

Yarn Used:

Puppy British Fine

■ #028 Moss Green ■ #027 Purple ■ #037 Brown

Knitting Needles: Straight Needles Size 4 (3.25 mm, UK Size 10)
Crochet Hook Size 3/0 (2.25 mm, UK Size 13)

Panel: 34 stitches × 45 rows

Gauge (10 cm - 4" square): 26 stitches, 32 rows

Difficulty: ★☆☆

* Preparing the yarn for colorwork:
  Grapes: 250 cm - 98 3/8" long pieces
* For knitting the bobble stitch, refer to page 122.

Bobble Stitch for 1 row
Pull through with crochet hook
Chain 1
Slip stitch into the increase
Slip, knit 2 together pass slipped stitch over
= Increases

Point
Since the bobble stitch is knitted, there are rows with a lot of stitches. It's a fun pattern regardless with a firm, three-dimensional texture.

A bag knitted with the Up & Down Cherries pattern. The cherries are knitted throughout, making it incredibly cute. Since knitted bags tend to stretch, adding a separate lining will help maintain its shape. The leaves are knitted separately and looped through the handle.

Instructions...page 141

Column 3 — Adjusting to Your Own Size

Once you've chosen the pattern and project you'd like to knit, it's tempting to dive right in. However, it's essential to start with a swatch. Knit a sample that is 15 cm - 5⅞" square (following the pattern from the book), and then pin it flat with the wrong side facing up on an ironing board. Gently steam with an iron and let it cool. Knowing your gauge is crucial for adjusting the size of your project, which is explained below.

1. Understanding Your Guage

Measure your swatch with a ruler to see how many stitches and rows fit into 10 cm - 4" square. This is your "gauge." If your gauge matches the one listed on the pattern, you're good to go. If your stitches are looser (your gauge has more stitches per 10 cm - 4"), switch to a smaller needle size. If your stitches are tighter (fewer stitches per 10 cm - 4"), go up a needle size. A difference of about one stitch in a row is usually manageable, but if you're off by two stitches or more, you may need to adjust the needle size.

A good way to tell if your tension is right is by how the yarn moves on the needles while you're knitting. If the stitches glide smoothly, you're on track. If there's a big gap under each stitch, your tension is too loose. If the stitches feel tight and hard to move, your tension is too tight. That's why knitting needles are made in small increments – so you can match the right size to your tension. Find the needle size that works best for your knitting style. For garments, aim for a comfortable softness, while for small items or bags, a firmer fabric may be preferred. Taking the time to figure this out will ensure your project turns out just as you envision it.

2. Adjusting to Your Own Size

When knitting a garment or scarf, sizing is crucial. While most of the patterns in this book are designed to be "free-size," it's worth adjusting the size to suit your own preferences. There are three main ways to do this.

① **Change needle size without altering stitch or row count**
② **Use a thicker (or thinner) yarn**

By employing these methods, you can adjust the size of your fabric. These methods will affect the size and texture of your knitting.

For knitting needles, a change of one size alters the everything by about 5%. For example, switching from a 4 to a 5 will increase the project size by 5%, while going from a 4 to a 6 will increase everything by 10%. Similarly, reducing the needle size from a 4 to a 3 will decrease the size by the same percentage.

③ **Adjust stitch and row count without changing the needle or yarn**

If you want to keep the same needle size and yarn, you can adjust the overall stitch and row count to match your desired size. This allows you to modify the width or length without altering the texture or look of the pattern. For example, you might shorten the length while keeping the same width, or adjust the sleeve length by changing the number of ribbing or garter rows.

If you find it difficult to calculate your own stitch and row counts, a simple method is to use a piece of clothing you already own that fits well. Place the garment on a large piece of paper and trace the outline. Then, calculate how many stitches and rows your gauge requires to match that shape. Determine how many pattern repeats fit into the shape and distribute any extra stitches or rows evenly. Or adjust the pattern placement to match patterns along the seam. It's perfectly fine to calculate your adjustments using a reduced scale chart, but there's something particularly beneficial about working with a chart in its actual size. The process of developing a chart using the actual size of your project may help you to gain confidence for your next masterpiece.

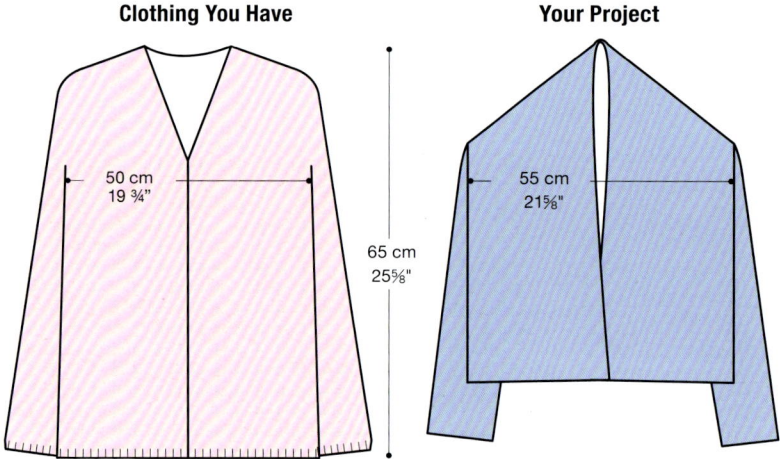

Since the design has a shorter length, if you want to make the width 5 cm - 2" smaller to match a sweater you usually wear, here's how you can adjust it. If the gauge of the knit you're making is 28 stitches and 30 rows, the width of 50 cm - 19¾" would equal 140 stitches. Next, consider how many pattern repeats fit into that width and distribute them evenly.
If the front and back don't need to match the pattern at the seam, it becomes easier. Distribute the pattern evenly from the center, leaving any extra stitches as they are to continue the pattern. Or, if it's close to a good stopping point for the pattern, you can add or subtract a few stitches.

3. Replacing with Another Pattern

If you want to knit the designs in this book using a different pattern, by all means, go for it!

Basically, the method is the same as adjusting the size to dimensions. First, figure out how many pattern repeats fit horizontally and vertically into the pattern, then distribute any extra space evenly. Thinking in actual size makes it easier to visualize, and it also helps when matching up the pattern along the seams, so I highly recommend it.

If you're replacing a pattern, consider changing the colors as well, not just the size. Knitting multiple test swatches might be a lot of work, so instead, try transferring the pattern onto graph paper and experiment with different color combinations, like a "blue version" or "pink version." This can turn into a fun, creative activity. As you color with pencils and engage your hands, you'll naturally discover your favorite color combinations.

Don't forget to occasionally check the width and length as you knit. You might find that your hands were tense and the stitches tighter when you knit the gauge, but as you got used to the pattern, your tension loosened up.

Also, keep in mind that knitting with circular needles tends to be looser than with straight needles. If you knitted your swatch with straight needles but plan to use circular needles for the project, be careful not to let your tension loosen too much. Since you're putting effort into the project, make sure to prepare throughly before knitting so you can enjoy the final result.

Enjoy! Let's start knitting! It's Fun!

Borders

These designs feature a horizontal pattern spanning two or more rows. The pattern combines geometric shapes and motifs, much like Fair Isle knitting.

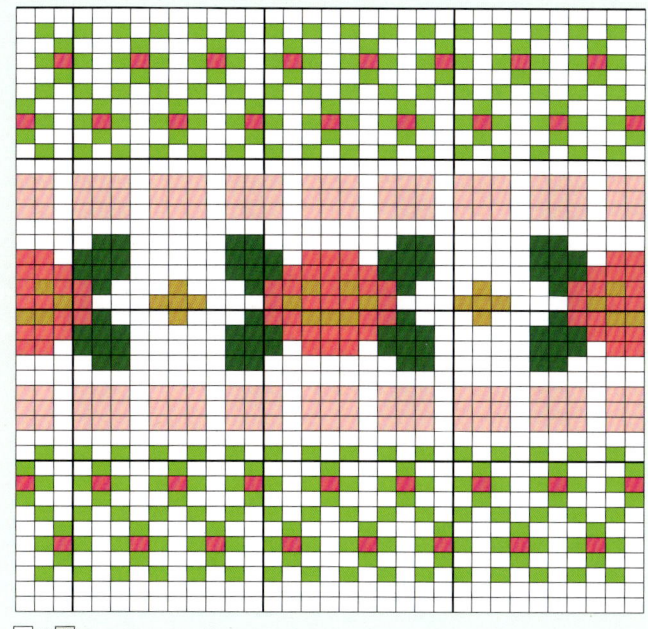

Border Pattern Roses

Yarn Used:
Puppy British Fine
☐ #021 Light Beige ■ #080 Yellow Green ■ #031 Pink
■ #055 Green ■ #035 Mustard ■ #068 Rose Pink
Knitting Needles: Straight Needles Size 4 (3.25 mm, UK Size 10)
Panel: 33 stitches × 40 rows
Gauge (10 cm - 4" square): 26 stitches, 32 rows

Difficulty: ★☆☆

Point
Carry the yarn horizontally to knit the border pattern. Make sure the background yarn and pattern color yarn run parallel on the wrong side as you knit.

Small Flower Ribbon

Yarn Used:
Jamieson's Spindrift
☐ #104 Natural White ■ #259 Leprechaun ■ #570 Sorbet
Knitting Needles: Straight Needles Size 4 (3.25 mm, UK Size 10)
Panel: 34 stitches × 40 rows
Gauge (10 cm - 4" square): 28 stitches, 32 rows

Difficulty: ★☆☆

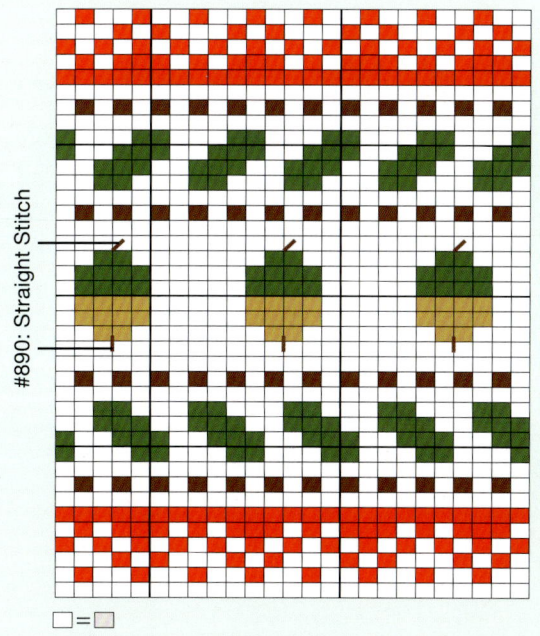

#890: Straight Stitch

Oak Tree

Yarn Used:
Jamieson's Spindrift
☐ #120 Eesit/White ■ #230 Yellow Ochre
■ #524 Poppy ■ #890 Mocha ■ #815 Ivy
Knitting Needles: Straight Needles Size 4 (3.25 mm, UK Size 10)
Panel: 34 stitches × 39 rows
Gauge (10 cm - 4" square): 26 stitches, 32 rows

Difficulty: ★☆☆

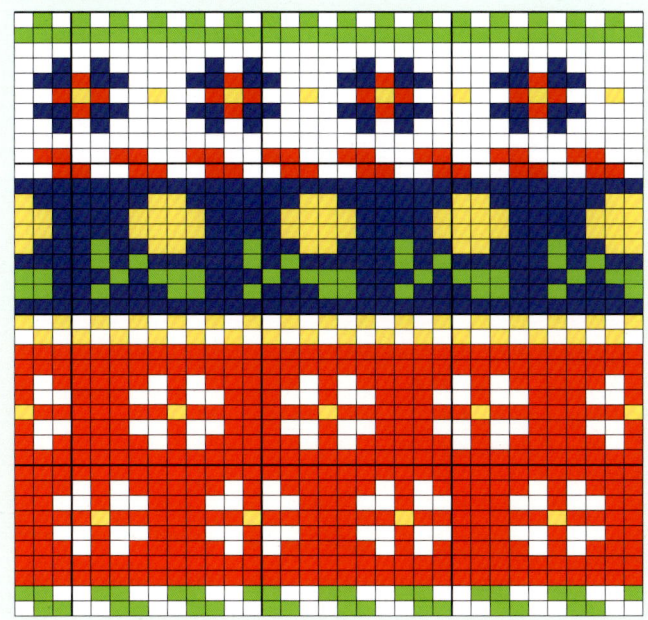

Flower Pattern Border

Yarn Used:
Puppy British Fine
■ #080 Yellow Green □ #001 White ■ #006 Red
■ #066 Yellow ■ #007 Ultramarine
Knitting Needles: Straight Needles Size 5 (3.50 mm)
Panel: 33 stitches × 40 rows
Gauge (10 cm - 4" square): 26 stitches, 32 rows

Difficulty: ★☆☆

Poin
The look of the border pattern changes depending on the color combination. Before knitting, make a sample with colored pencils to find your favorite color combination.

Fair Isle

Yarn Used:
Puppy British Fine
□ #021 Light Beige ■ #068 Rose Pink
■ #092 Turquoise ■ #062 Cobalt Blue
■ #053 Dark Purple ■ #080 Yellow Green
■ #091 Pistachio
Knitting Needles: Straight Needles Size 4
(3.25 mm, UK Size 10)
Panel: 35 stitches × 39 rows
Gauge (10 cm - 4" square): 28 stitches, 34 rows

Difficulty: ★☆☆

Violets

Yarn Used:

Jamieson's Spindrift

- #105 Eesit ■ #788 Leaf ■ #616 Anemone
- #410 Cornfield ■ #600 Violet ■ #136 Teviot
- #259 Leprechaun

Puppy Kid Mohair Fine ☐ #54 Light Beige

Knitting Needles: Straight Needles Size 4 (3.25 mm, UK Size 10)

Panel: 33 stitches × 42 rows

Gauge (10 cm - 4" square): 26 stitches, 32 rows

Difficulty: ★☆☆

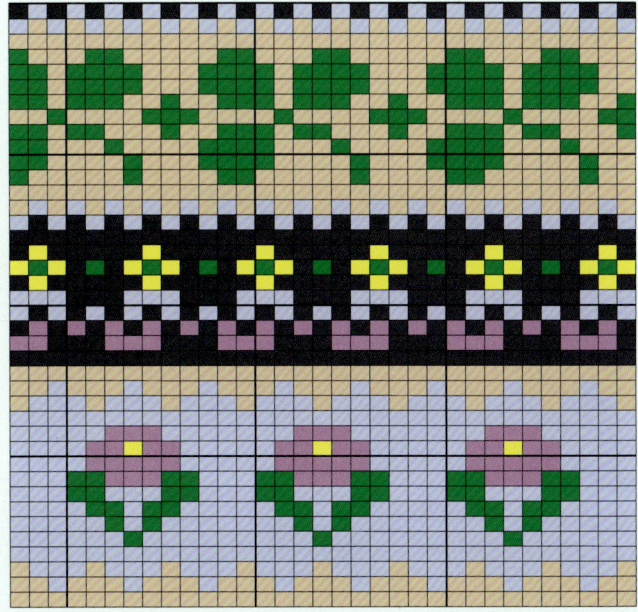

Daisies and Clovers

Yarn Used:

Jamieson's Spindrift

- ■ #123 Oxford ■ #342 Cashew ■ #616 Anemone
- ■ #400 Mimosa ■ #790 Celtic ■ #655 China Blue

Knitting Needles: Straight Needles Size 4 (3.25 mm, UK Size 10)

Panel: 33 stitches × 40 rows

Gauge (10 cm - 4" square): 26 stitches, 32 rows

Difficulty: ★☆☆

Roses and Rosebuds

Yarn Used:

a

Jamieson's Spindrift

- #580 Cherry #188 Sherbet
- #259 Leprechaun #390 Daffodil
- #470 Pumpkin

b

Jamieson's Spindrift

- #999 Black #525 Crimson #790 Celtic
- #390 Daffodil #104 Natural White

Shared Materials:
Knitting Needles: Straight Needles Size 5 (3.50 mm)
Panel: 34 stitches × 40 rows
Gauge (10 cm - 4" square): 26 stitches, 30 rows

Difficulty: ★☆☆

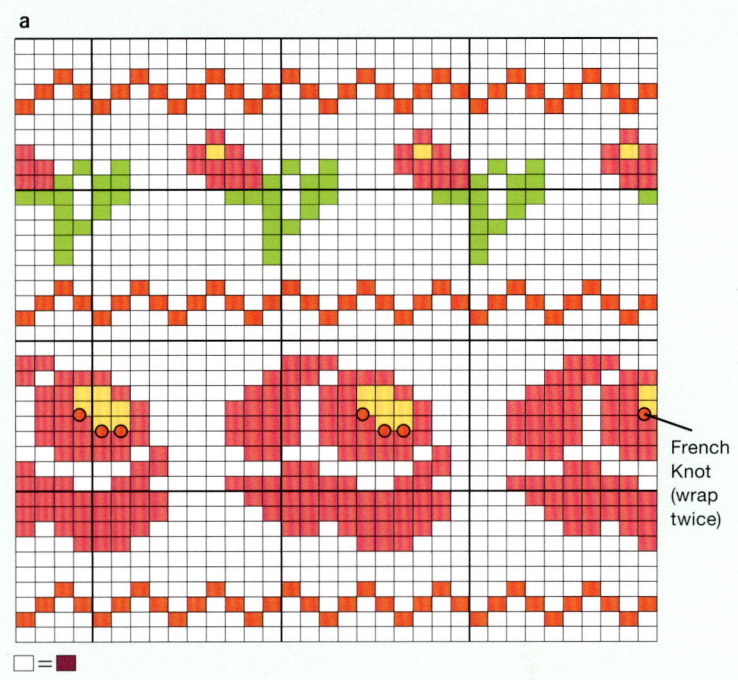

French Knot (wrap twice)

□ = ■

Ladybugs and Clovers

Yarn Used:

Jamieson's Spindrift

- #655 China Blue #999 Black #800 Tartan
- #500 Scarlet #104 Natural White

Knitting Needles: Straight Needles Size 5 (3.50 mm)
Panel: 34 stitches × 38 rows
Gauge (10 cm - 4" square): 26 stitches, 30 rows

Difficulty: ★☆☆

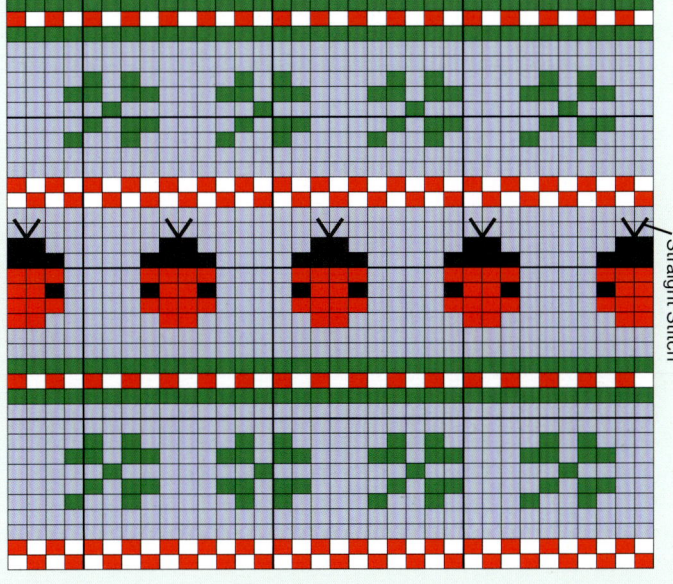

Straight Stitch

Point

One of the clovers has been turned into a four-leaf clover. This kind of playful variation can also be fun!

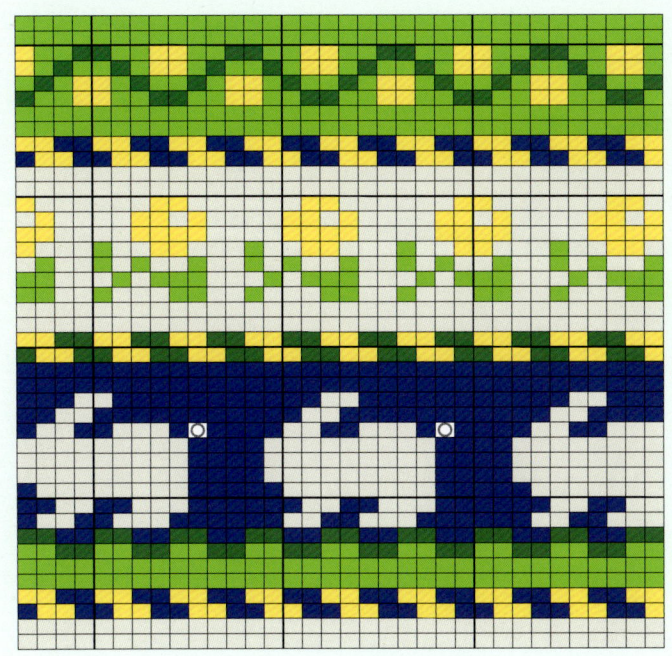

Dandelions and Rabbits

Yarn Used:

Puppy British Fine

☐ #021 Light Beige ■ #007 Ultramarine ☐ #066 Yellow

■ #055 Green ■ #080 Yellow Green

Puppy Kid Mohair Fine

☐ #54 Light Beige

Knitting Needles: Straight Needles Size 5 (3.50 mm)

Crochet Hook Size 3/0
(2.25 mm, UK Size 13)

Panel: 34 stitches × 42 rows

Gauge (10 cm - 4" square): 26 stitches, 30 rows

Difficulty: ★☆☆

* Knit the rabbit pattern using two strands: British Fine #021 and Kid Mohair Fine #54.

* Refer page 123 for bobble stitch crochet.

⊙ =

2 Double Crochet Cluster Stitch
Crochet hook: Size 3/0 (2.25 mm)

Squirrels and Acorns

Yarn Used:

Jamieson's Spindrift

☐ #342 Cashew ■ #1190 Burnt Umber ■ #815 Ivy

■ #599 Zodiac ☐ #660 Lagoon

Knitting Needles: Straight Needles Size 5 (3.50 mm)

Panel: 35 stitches × 44 rows

Gauge (10 cm - 4" square): 26 stitches, 30 rows

Difficulty: ★☆☆

☐ = ☐

Blueberries and Wild Roses

Yarn Used:
Jamieson's Spindrift
☐ #104 Natural White ■ #788 Leaf ■ #684 Cobalt
■ #585 Plum ■ #999 Black ■ #525 Crimson
Knitting Needles: Straight Needles Size 5 (3.50 mm)
Panel: 36 stitches × 39 rows
Gauge (10 cm - 4" square): 28 stitches, 28 rows

Difficulty: ★★☆

> *Point*
> You can create cute, chunky garments with medium-weight summer yarn or knit coasters with fine winter yarn! Let your imagination run wild.

Roses and Crowns

Yarn Used:
Puppy ALBA
☐ #0130 White ■ #5145 Navy Blue
■ #5139 Red ☐ #1109 Yellow
Knitting Needles: Straight Needles Size 5 (3.50 mm, UK Size 9)
Panel: 41 stitches × 42 rows
Gauge (10 cm - 4" square): 28 stitches, 30 rows

Difficulty: ★★☆

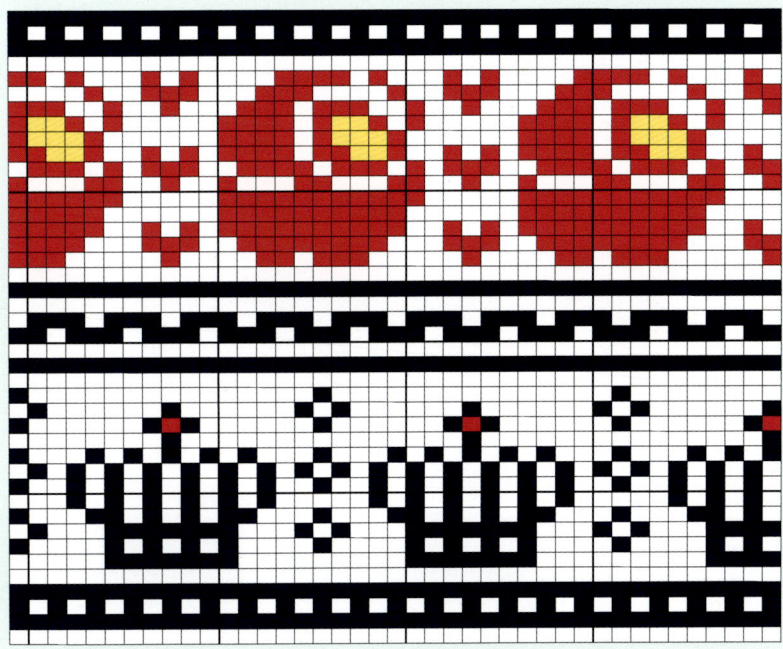

93

Berries

Yarn Used:

Jamieson's Spindrift

☐ #122 Granite ■ #788 Leaf ■ #585 Plum

Knitting Needles: Straight Needles Size 4
(3.25 mm, UK Size 10)

Panel: 34 stitches × 42 rows

Gauge (10 cm - 4" square): 28 stitches, 32 rows

Difficulty: ★☆☆

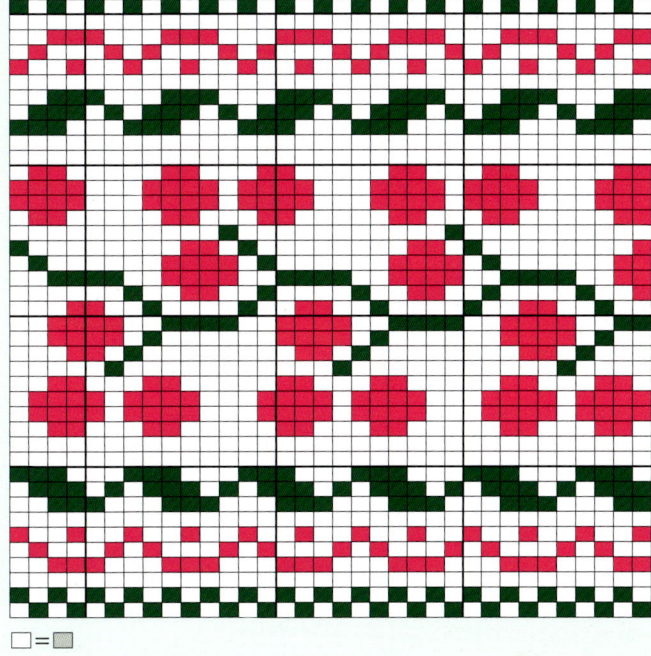

☐ = ☐

Dianthuses at Night

Yarn Used:

Puppy British Fine

■ #009 Gray ■ #085 Neon Pink ☐ #066 Yellow

Puppy Kid Mohair Fine

■ #51 Gray ■ #44 Opera

Knitting Needles: Straight Needles Size 5 (3.50 mm)

Panel: 34 stitches × 40 rows

Gauge (10 cm - 4" square): 26 stitches, 28 rows

Difficulty: ★☆☆

* Knit using two strands: British Fine and Kid Mohair Fine.

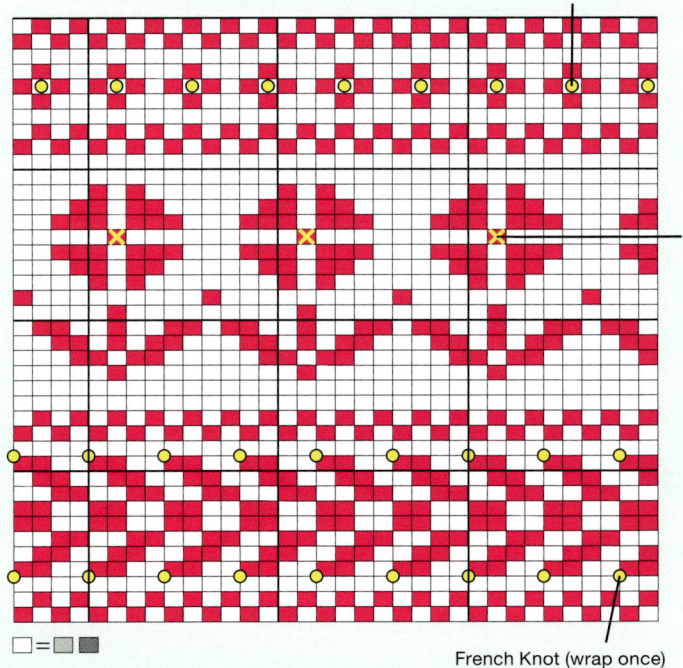

Knit with the background color yarn and then embroider afterward.

Cross Stitch

French Knot (wrap once)

☐ = ☐ ☐

Point

This pattern features embroidery as an accent. Use your preferred colors, whether you use embroidery floss or yarn.

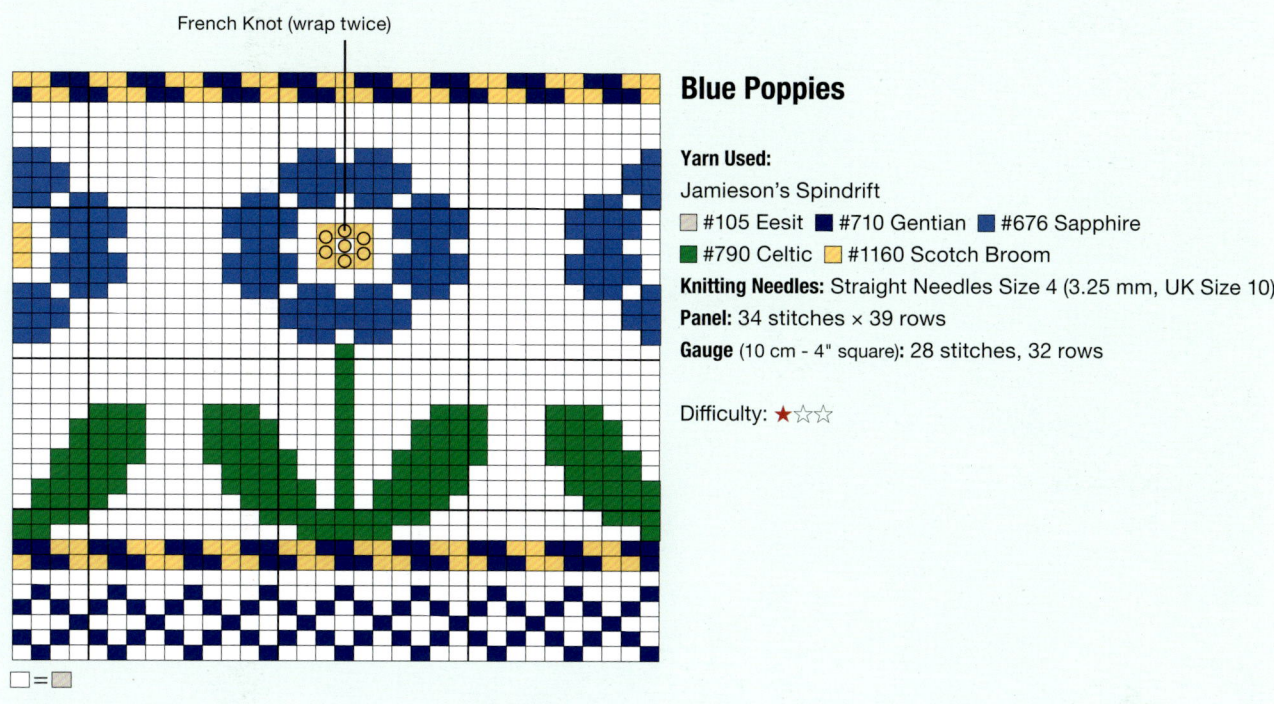

Blue Poppies

Yarn Used:
Jamieson's Spindrift
☐ #105 Eesit   ■ #710 Gentian   ■ #676 Sapphire
■ #790 Celtic   ☐ #1160 Scotch Broom
Knitting Needles: Straight Needles Size 4 (3.25 mm, UK Size 10)
Panel: 34 stitches × 39 rows
Gauge (10 cm - 4" square): 28 stitches, 32 rows

Difficulty: ★☆☆

Yellow Roses

Yarn Used:
Jamieson's Spindrift
☐ #104 Natural White   ☐ #660 Lagoon
■ #800 Tartan   ■ #684 Cobalt   ☐ #400 Mimosa
Knitting Needles: Straight Needles Size 5 (3.50 mm)
Panel: 33 stitches × 40 rows
Gauge (10 cm - 4" square): 26 stitches, 30 rows

Difficulty: ★☆☆

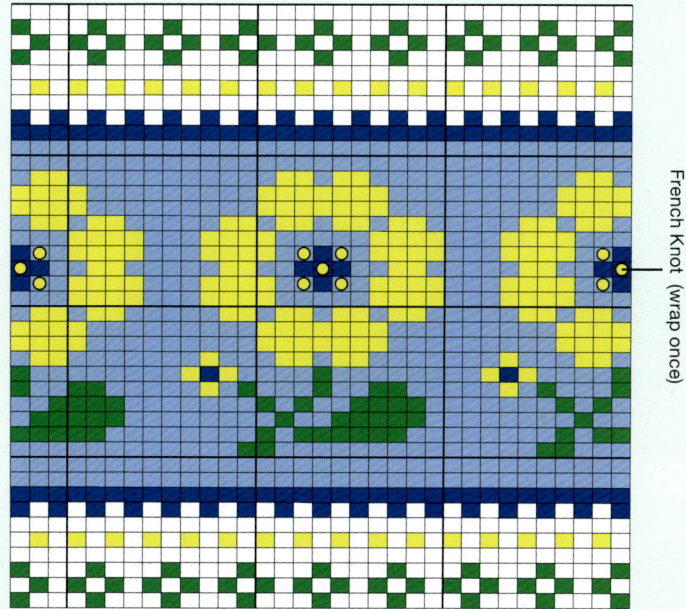

These items combine the traditional British teapot, Brown Betty, with the Rabbits pattern from page 90. The tea cozy and coaster help maintain the temperature of the tea, making them essential items for teatime enthusiasts. Be sure to knit them to fit the size of your own teapot.

Instructions...page 148

Short wrist warmers are appealing because they can be made quickly. With striped or small sequential patterns, they look cute around your wrist and accentuate your style. These examples use the Violets pattern from page 86 and the Mushrooms pattern from page 16.

Instructions...page 151

Solid Color Patterns

These are three-dimensional patterns knitted in a single color, like Aran or openwork. Although it may look complicated, they are essentially a repetition of the same stitches.

a

b

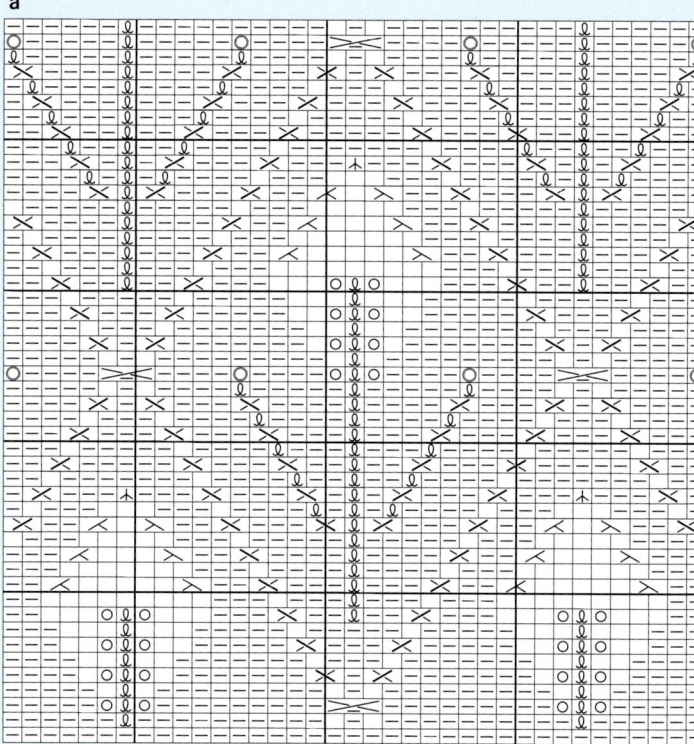

Leaves and Berries

a

Yarn Used:

Puppy Monarca

☐ #901 White

Knitting Needles: Straight Needles Size 7 (4.00 mm, UK Size 8)

Crochet Hook Size 6/0 (3.50 mm, UK Size 9)

Panel: 37 stitches × 48 rows

Gauge (10 cm - 4" square): 30 stitches, 22 rows

b

Yarn Used:

Puppy Shetland

■ #16 Blue

Puppy Kid Mohair Fine

■ #48 Blue Green

Knitting Needles: Straight Needles Size 6 (3.75 mm, UK Size 9), Cable Needle

Crochet Hook Size 5/0 (3.00 mm, UK Size 11)

Panel: 37 stitches × 48 rows

Gauge (10 cm - 4" square): 20 stitches, 30 rows

* Knit using two strands: British Fine #021 and Kid Mohair Fine #54.

Difficulty: ★☆☆

* For knitting the bobble stitch, refer to page 122.

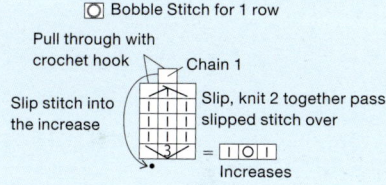

Crabapple Tree

Yarn Used:

Puppy Chaska

■ #50 Beige

Knitting Needles: Straight Needles Size 4 (3.25 mm, UK Size 10)

Crochet Hook Size 3/0 (2.25 mm, UK Size 13)

Panel: 25 stitches × 62 rows

Gauge (10 cm - 4" square): 24 stitches, 32 rows

Difficulty: ★★☆

* For knitting the bobble stitch, refer to page 122.

Point

As you knit, imagine the natural appearance of trees. For added fun, try changing the colors of the bobble stitches or swapping them out for beads!

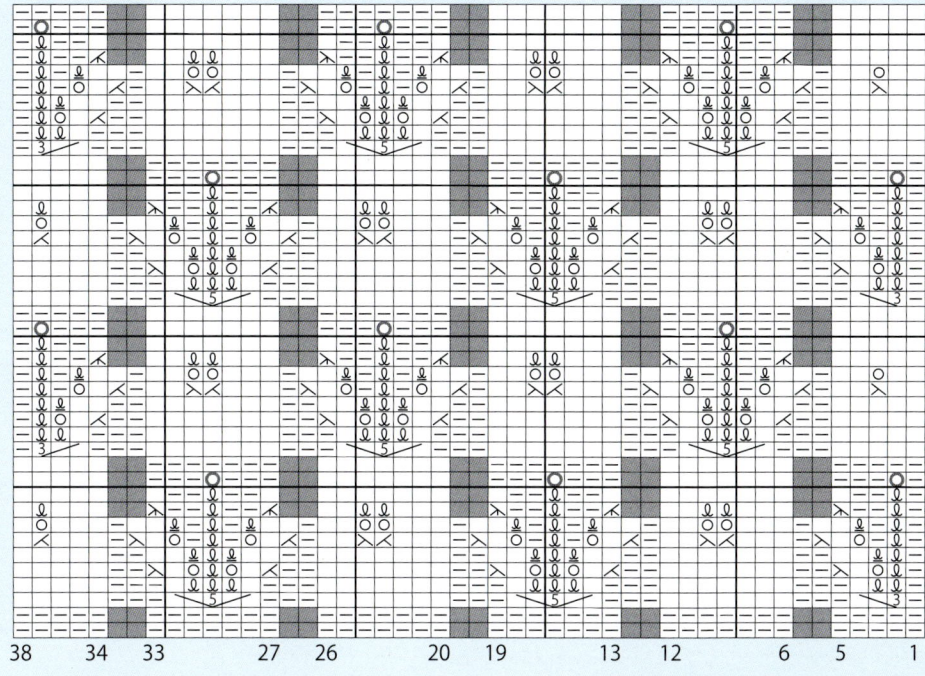

Tulips

Yarn Used:
Puppy ALBA
☐ #0130 White
Knitting Needles: Straight Needles Size 5 (3.50 mm)
Crochet Hook Size 4/0
(2.50 mm, UK Size 12)
Panel: 38 stitches × 42 rows
Gauge (10 cm - 4" square): 28 stitches, 36 rows

Difficulty: ★★★

* For knitting the bobble stitch, refer to page 122.

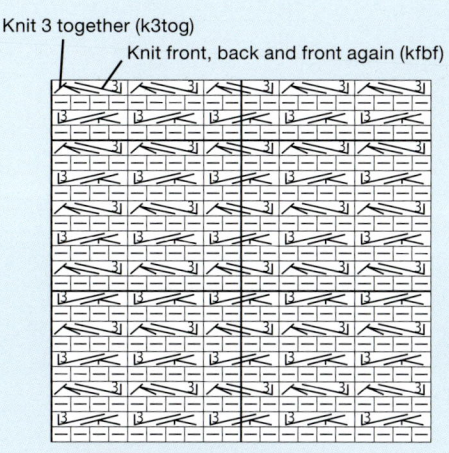

Trinity Stitch Berries

Yarn Used:
Puppy ALBA
■ #1170 Pink
Puppy Kid Mohair Fine
■ #44 Opera
Knitting Needles: Straight Needles Size 7 (4.00 mm, UK Size 8)
Panel: 26 stitches × 36 rows
Gauge (10 cm - 4" square): 20 stitches, 24 rows

Difficulty: ★★☆

* Knit using two strands: ALBA #1170 and Kid Mohair Fine #44.
* Refer to page 125 for trinity stitch.

a
b

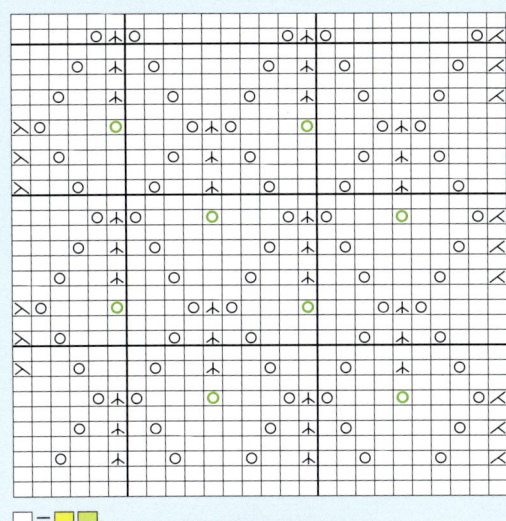

Leaf Lace Pattern

Yarn Used:
Puppy New2PLY
■ #260 Yellow
Puppy Kid Mohair Fine
■ #51 Lemon Yellow
Knitting Needles: Straight Needles Size 5 (3.50 mm)
Crochet Hook Size 4/0 (2.50 mm, UK Size 12)
Panel: 26 stitches × 32 rows
Gauge (10 cm - 4" square): 20 stitches, 29 rows

Difficulty: ★★☆

* Knit using two strands: New2PLY #260 and Kid Mohair Fine #51.

Point
Both patterns suit materials ranging from cotton to cashmere mohair. Take your time and knit carefully.

Hollies

a
Yarn Used:
Puppy British Fine
■ #091 Pistachio
Puppy Kid Mohair Fine
■ #51 Lemon Yellow
Knitting Needles: Straight Needles Size 6 (3.75 mm, UK Size 9)
Crochet Hook Size 5/0 (3.00 mm, UK Size 11)
Panel: 33 stitches × 41 rows
Gauge (10 cm - 4" square): 24 stitches, 30 rows

b
Yarn Used:
Puppy ALBA
■ #1185 Green ■ #5139 Red
Knitting Needles: Straight Needles Size 6 (3.75 mm, UK Size 9)
Crochet Hook Size 5/0 (3.00 mm, UK Size 11)
Panel: 33 stitches × 41 rows
Gauge (10 cm - 4" square): 24 stitches, 32 rows
Difficulty: ★★☆

* Knit using two strands: British Fine #091 and Kid Mohair Fine #51.

2 Half Double Crochet Cluster Stitch
Crochet hook: Size 5/0 (3.00 mm)

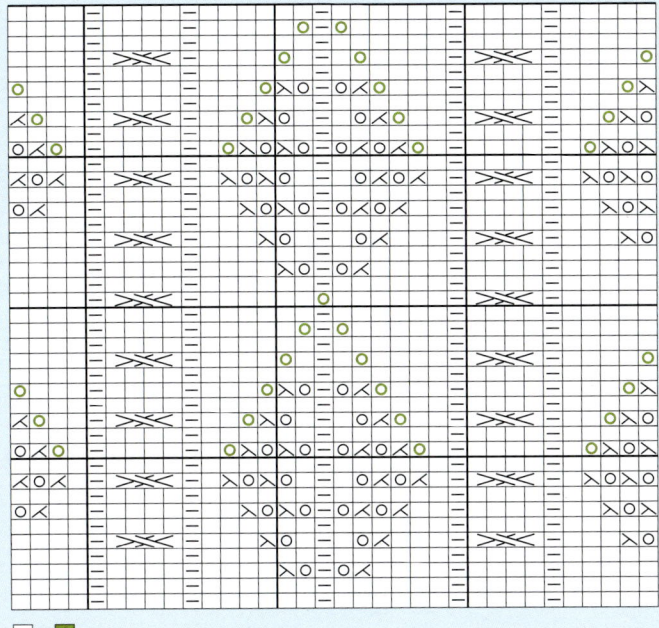

A Tree with Fruit

Yarn Used:
ROWAN Felted Tweed
■ #213 Yellow Green
Knitting Needles: Straight Needles Size 5 (3.50 mm)
　　　　　　　　Crochet Hook: Size 4/0 (2.50 mm, UK Size 12)
Panel: 34 stitches × 40 rows
Gauge (10 cm - 4" square): 26 stitches, 32 rows

Difficulty: ★★☆

* Refer page 123 for bobble stitch crochet.

◉ = 🧶

2 Half Double Crochet Cluster Stitch
Crochet hook: Size 4/0 (2.50 mm)

Point

Let's take a look at knitting 2 together in the lace section. The pattern is created by combining left-slanting and right-slanting decreases. In this case, they represent branches extending from a tree.

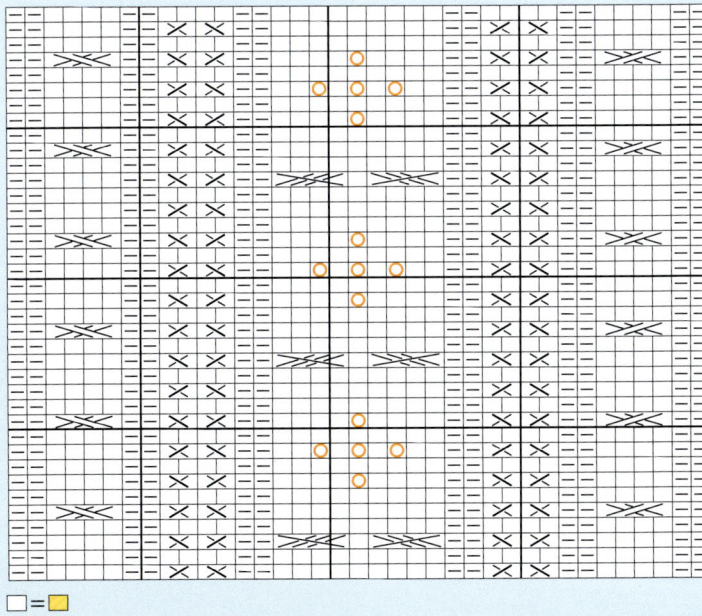

Cable Patterns and Bobble Stitch Flowers

Yarn Used:
Puppy ALBA
□ #1109 Yellow
Knitting Needles: Straight Needles Size 5 (3.50 mm)
　　　　　　　　Crochet Hook Size 4/0 (2.50 mm, UK Size 12)
Panel: 37 stitches × 38 rows
Gauge (10 cm - 4" square): 26 stitches, 32 rows

Difficulty: ★★☆

* For knitting the bobble stitch, refer to page 122.

◯ Bobble Stitch for 1 row

Pull through with crochet hook
Chain 1
Slip, knit 2 together pass slipped stitch over
Slip stitch into the increase
Increases

a

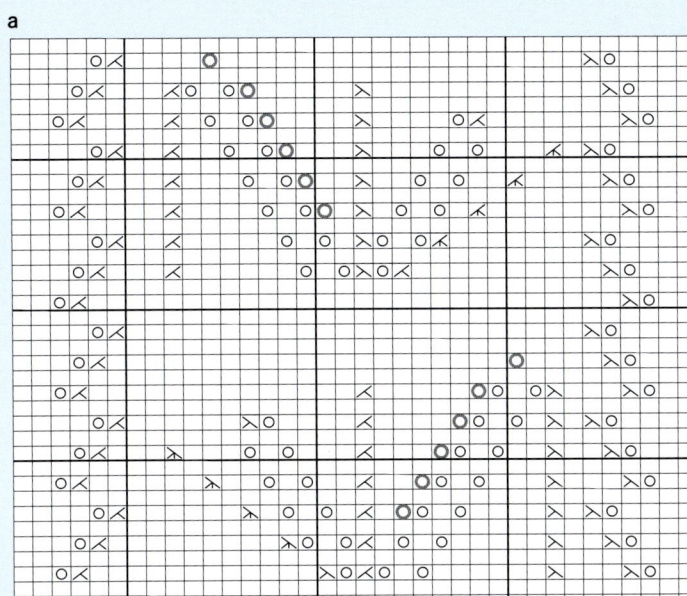

Lily-of-the-Valley-b has four stitches of lacework here.

Lily-of-the-Valley-b has four stitches of lacework here.

◉ Bobble Stitch for 1 row

Pull through with crochet hook
Chain 1
Slip, knit 2 together pass slipped stitch over
Slip stitch into the increase
= Increases

Lily-of-the-Valley

Yarn Used:

a

Puppy Chaska
☐ #10 White

Knitting Needles: Straight Needles Size 5 (3.50 mm)
Crochet Hook Size 4/0
(2.50 mm, UK Size 12)

Panel: 27 stitches × 38 rows

Gauge (10 cm - 4" square): 26 stitches, 32 rows

b

Puppy ALBA
■ #1185 Green ☐ #0130 White

Knitting Needles: Straight Needles Size 5 (3.50 mm)
Crochet Hook Size 4/0 (2.50 mm, UK Size 12)

Panel: 36 stitches × 38 rows

Gauge (10 cm - 4" square): 24 stitches, 32 rows

Difficulty: ★★☆

* For knitting the bobble stitch, refer to page 122.

Aran Pattern Bouquet

Yarn Used:

Puppy Shetland
☐ #50 White

Knitting Needles: Straight Needles Size 5 (3.50 mm)
Crochet Hook Size 4/0
(2.50 mm, UK Size 12)

Panel: 31 stitches × 40 rows

Gauge (10 cm - 4" square): 24 stitches, 36 rows

Difficulty: ★★☆

* For bobble stitch crochet, refer to page 123, and for smocking stitch instructions, refer to page 126.

◉ =
2 Half Double Crochet Cluster Stitch
Crochet hook: Size 4/0 (2.50 mm)

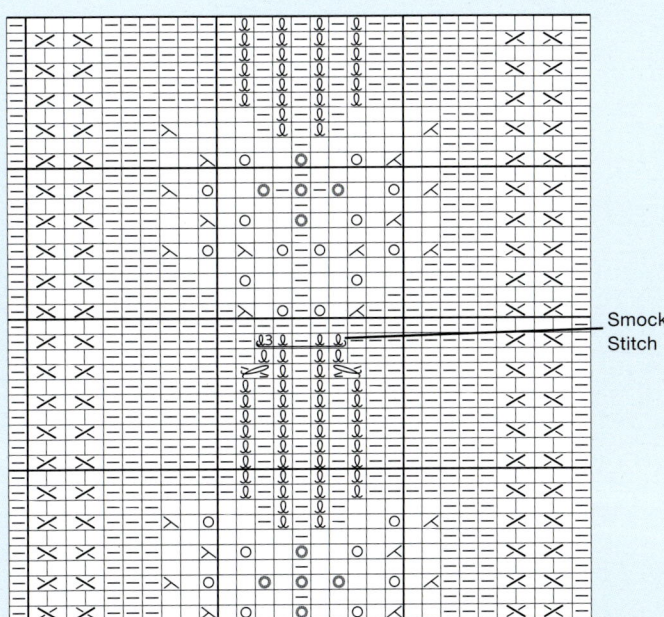

Smocking Stitch

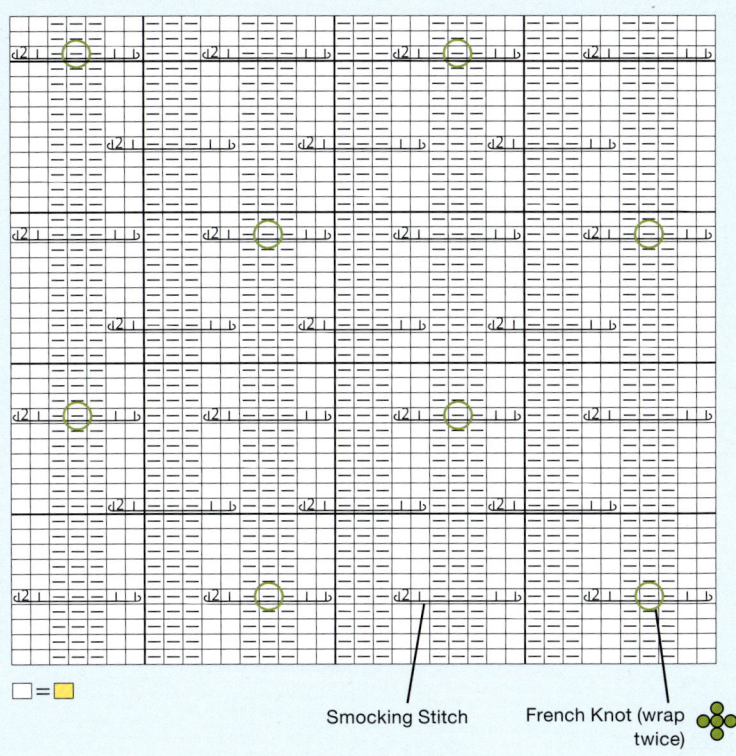

□ = □ (yellow)

Smocking Stitch

French Knot (wrap twice)

Smocking Flowers

Yarn Used:
Puppy ALBA
■ #1109 Yellow
Puppy British Fine
■ #091 Pistachio
Knitting Needles: Straight Needles Size 5 (3.50 mm), Cable Needle
Panel: 37 stitches × 44 rows
Gauge (10 cm - 4" square): 24 stitches, 34 rows

Difficulty: ★☆☆

* Refer to page 126 for smocking stitch instructions.

Point
Both are easier to knit than they look. They would also be suitable for making cute cushions or baby blankets.

Tyrolean

Yarn Used:
Puppy ALBA
■ #5145 Navy Blue ■ #5139 Red ■ #1185 Green
Knitting Needles: Straight Needles Size 5 (3.50 mm)
Crochet Hook Size 4/0
(2.50 mm, UK Size 12)
Panel: 34 stitches × 41 rows
Gauge (10 cm - 4" square): 26 stitches, 34 rows

Difficulty: ★☆☆

* For knitting bobble stitch, refer to page 122.

[◯] [◯] Bobble Stitch for 1 row
Pull through with crochet hook
Chain 1
Slip stitch into the increase
Slip, knit 2 together pass slipped stitch over
= Increases

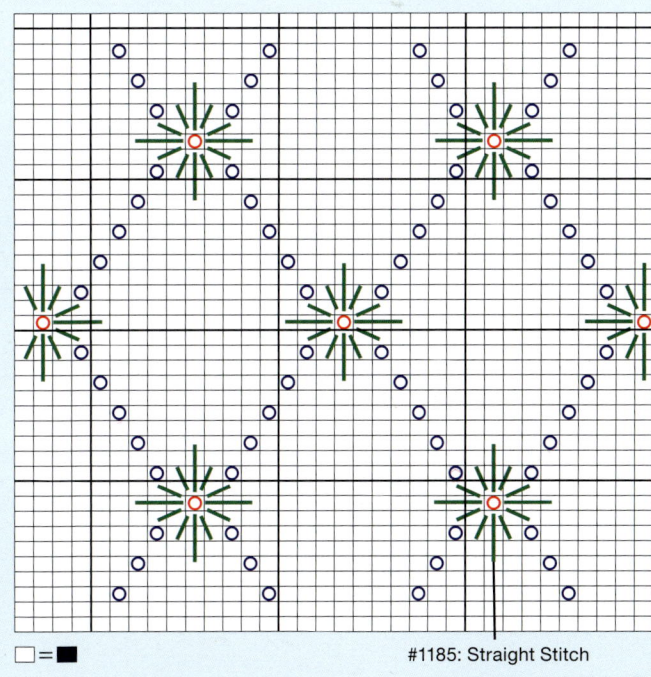

□ = ■

#1185: Straight Stitch

Aran Pattern Garden

Yarn Used:
Puppy Shetland
☐ #50 White
Puppy British Fine (for embroidering)
🟨 #066 Yellow 🟩 #080 Yellow Green 🟪 #031 Pink
🟦 #074 Light Blue 🟥 #006 Red 🟥 #068 Rose Pink
Knitting Needles: Straight Needles Size 5 (3.50 mm)
Panel: 34 stitches × 40 rows
Gauge (10 cm - 4" square): 38 stitches, 34 rows

Difficulty: ★☆☆

* When knitting garments, use needles one size larger for a slightly looser tension.

Point

Use your leftover fine yarn for embroidery. This way, you can use up your scraps while having fun. Using glossy cotton yarn will also change the overall look.

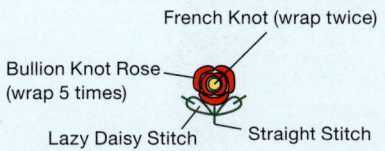

Flower embroidering position

French Knot (wrap twice)
Bullion Knot Rose (wrap 5 times)
Lazy Daisy Stitch — Straight Stitch

Cable & Smocking Stitch

Yarn Used:
Puppy ALBA
🟥 #5139 Red
Puppy British Fine (for embroidering)
☐ #001 White 🟨 #066 Yellow 🟩 #055 Green
Knitting Needles: Straight Needles Size 6 (3.75 mm, UK Size 9), Cable Needle
Panel: 34 stitches × 39 rows
Gauge (10 cm - 4" square): 30 stitches, 36 rows

Difficulty: ★☆☆

* Refer to page 126 for smocking stitch instructions.

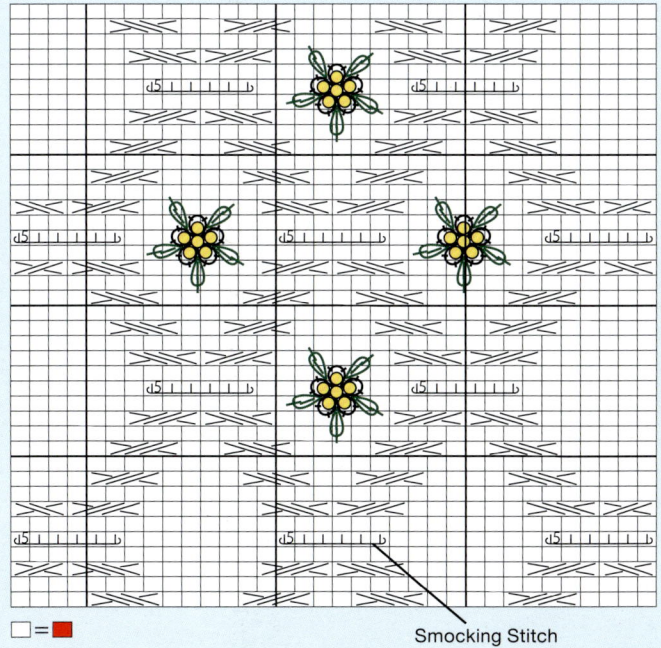

☐ = 🟥

Smocking Stitch

French Knot (wrap once) — Lazy Daisy Stitch Arrangement
Straight Stitch inside Lazy Daisy Stitch

113

These vibrant pink mohair hand warmers are quite striking. The vertically elongated design of the Crabapple Tree pattern is perfect for long hand warmers. Mohair yarn has a light, fluffy texture that can sometimes be tricky to knit, so this is a great place to start.
Instructions...page 152

The pure image of lily-of-the-valley, combined with the translucency and elegance of white mohair, makes this a perfect project. It's a long, hooded shawl, yet it's surprisingly light and soft. This is a coveted piece you'll want to devote your time to knitting with care.

Instructions…page 160

This garment features a unique lace pattern. Despite its loose and voluminous design, the lace's sheer quality gives it a light, airy feel. The collar and sleeves have smocking stitch design, with embroidery in a matching color adding a subtle accent.

Instructions ... page 145

Things You Can Make with Swatches

Using just one swatch, you can easily create charming patchwork items. Choose your favorite swatch to craft something truly special.

A brooch made only from the flower part of a swatch. Wrap a button and shape it into a circle or oval. Perfect as an accent for clothing or bags.

Instructions ... page 154

Here is the squirrel motif on page 90 made into a coaster. The eyes and the fluffy tail were embroidered afterward. Add a piece of felt to the back to give the coaster a sturdy finish.

Instructions ... page 156

The Small Red Roses pattern from page 10 and the Rosebuds pattern from page 50 are used to create pincushions. The soft texture makes for a pleasant pincushion. When making it, be sure to adjust the size to fit the base container you are using.

Instructions ... page 157

This is a small size item that frames a single flower. It looks charming on its own and stylish when displayed in a group. Enjoy adding embroidery to the swatch or experimenting with different arrangements.

Instructions ... page 158

This patchwork bag is made by joining your favorite swatches. Sew together twelve squares of the same size and one rectangular swatch for the bottom. It's charming even if the repeating patterns are cut off partway through. This approach allows you to make good use of test swatches without waste.

Instructions ... page 168

A patchwork shawl made by joining motifs lets you enjoy a variety of patterns. You can highlight narrow sections with stripes, add a large single flower, and have fun deciding where to place each swatch. Finish by knitting the lacy edges to give it a retro, charming look.

Instructions ... page 176

Lesson 5: How to Knit Bobble Stitches

There are two types: one for knitting with straight needles and one for crocheting. Straight needles are used for creating large bobbles, while crochet hooks are ideal for making small bobbles.

Weaving One Row Bobble Stitch (Bobble: three stitches, five rows)

* For crochet, use a crochet hook that is one size smaller than the knitting needles.

1. Knit the Lily of the Valley pattern on page 108. Without dropping the loop off the left needle, you will make increases. First, knit one stitch.

2. Next, yarn over the right needle. Do not drop the loop off the left needle.

3. For the third stitch, insert the needle into the same stitch and knit, then drop the stitches off the left needle. This will create an additional two stitches from the original one stitch.

4. Turn your work. Purl the three increases. The photo shows after purling three times.

5. Turn your work. Knit the three stitches. Then, turn your work and purl three stitches. Next, turn your work and transfer the three stitches to a crochet hook.

6. Wrap the yarn around the crochet hook, pull three stitches through. The stitches were decreased to one stitch.

7. Insert the crochet hook into the stitches you just worked, yarn over, and pull through.

8. Make one chain stitch.

9. Transfer the stitch back onto the right needle to complete the bobble stitch.

10. A nice, plump bobble stitch was made.

Crochet 2 Half Double Crochet Cluster Stitch

1. Change the yarn for the bobble stitch section. When working the first stitch, instead of using the knitting needle, use a crochet hook to yarn over and pull the yarn through. Do not drop the loop off the left needle.

2. Make two chain stitches.

3. Insert the crochet hook into the same stitch and work two half double crochet stitches, but only complete them halfway. Make sure the stitches match the length of the initial chain stitches. At this point, drop the loop off the left needle.

4. Yarn over and pull through three loops (you should have 5 loops on the hook). Hold the base of the loops with your finger to make this easier.

5. Make one chain stitch. Transfer this onto the right needle to complete the bobble stitch.

6. Whether you work the final chain stitch with the bobble yarn (left) or with the main color yarn (right) will determine if the bobble color carries over to the next row, slightly changing the appearance.

The bobble stitches in the tulip pattern on page 102 are made by working three stitches over five rows on a single row of the panel.

The Up & Down Dandelions on page 28 features bobbles stitch made with 2 half double crochet cluster stitches.

Lesson 6: How to Knit A Latvian Braid

Since this pattern features alternating colors, prepare two colors of yarn. This explanation uses a double Latvian braid.

1. On the row before the Latvian braid, knit in alternating colors.

2. Bring the yarn to the front and purl the next stitch.

3. Do the same with the next color, bringing the yarn to the front and purl.

4. For the third stitch (white), bring the white yarn under the red yarn and to the left.

5. Purl the third stitch with the white yarn. Be careful not to knit too tightly.

6. For the fourth stitch (red), bring the red yarn under the white yarn and to the left, and purl.

7. As you knit, the two yarns will twist, so untwist them as you go.

8. Continue alternating the two colors, bringing the yarn under and purl until you reach the end of the row. If you're only doing a single row Latvian braid, it's now complete.

9. For the next row, turn your work and knit. Just like the previous row, bring each yarn under the other and to the left as you knit.

10. Continue alternating the two colors on this row. When knitting in the round, only the front side is visible, so bring the yarn over and purl.

11. After finishing the row, the double Latvian braid is complete. One row will create a slanted pattern, while two rows will form horizontal V-shapes.

Lesson 7: How to Knit A Trinity Stitch

This is the stitch used for the bumpy texture on page 102.

1 First, purl one row.

2 For the second row, turn your work and purl the first stitch. Then, on the second stitch, make three increases. Knit one and bring the yarn to the front without dropping the loop off the left needle then purl into the same stitch.

3 For the third increase, bring the yarn to the back and knit into the same stitch. You have made three increases by working – knit one, purl one, knit one – into the same stitch.

4 On the next stitch, purl three stitches together (left-leaning decrease). Insert the right needle through all three stitches and purl them together.

5 Continue alternating between three stitch increases and purling three together across the row.

6 Turn your work and work the garter stitch across this row.

7 Now, three rows are complete.

8 For the fourth row, the order is reversed. Start with purling three together, then follow with three stitch increases.

9 Next, make three stitch increases. Work knit, purl, knit into same stitch. At the end of the fourth row, purl the last stitch, then purl three together. Insert the right needle through all three stitches and purl them together.

10 This completes one set of four rows. Continue this 4-row repeat to create the bumpy, three-dimensional trinity stitch pattern.

The result will be a bumpy, raised pattern.

Lesson 8: How to Knit A Smocking Stitch and Knot Stitch

These stitches create a horizontal pattern by wrapping or covering the yarn.

Seven-Stitch, Two-Wrap Smocking Stitch

1 Begin by knitting the smocking flower pattern on page 110. After the smocking stitch, purl three stitches.

2 Start the smocking stitch. Knit two, purl three, knit two.

3 Transfer the seven stitches on the right needle onto a cable needle.

4 Wrap the yarn counterclockwise around the seven stitches on the cable needle twice.

5 This is what it looks like after wrapping the yarn twice. Adjust the tension, making sure not to pull the yarn too tightly.

6 Transfer the seven stitches from the cable needle back to the right needle.

7 Pull the working yarn to prevent it from unwrapping.

8 Continue to work the next stitches. The smocking stitch is now complete.

Six-Stitch, Five-Wrap Knot Stitch and Embroidery: When combined with cable knitting, it adds more dimension and texture.

Three-Stitch Left-Slip Knot Stitch

1. These are the instructions for the knot stitch on page 24. Begin with yarning over on the right needle.
2. Insert the right needle into the third stitch on the left needle. Slip it over the first two stitches on the left needle and drop it off from the right needle.
3. Now, yarn over the right needle, while the left needle has a loop over two stitches.

4. Knit once inside each stitch of the loop.
5. This will create a small hole where the yarn over was.
6. Repeat this process to complete the row.

Lesson 9
How to Make A Duplicate Stitch (Embroidery)

Embroidery can add colors and patterns like intarsia after knitting is complete.

1. Embroider pistils and stamens at the center of the flower. Thread the needle with embroidery floss and pass it through the yarns carried on the back to prevent the floss from coming loose.
2. Bring the needle out through the center of the stitch you want to embroider. Pick up the stitches evenly on left and right where you intend to embroider.
3. Insert the needle back where the floss initially came out and bring the needle through to the back.

4. One stitch is complete.
5. For additional stitches, continue in the same manner: bring the needle out slightly below where you intend to embroider and bring the needle under the stitches to embroider.
6. The flower's center has been embroidered. For small sections, embroidering duplicate stitches can be more convenient than intarsia. Secure the floss on the back by threading it through the stitches, splitting the yarn.

Lesson 10: Joining Swatches

This method is how to join swatches when connecting pieces for items like shawls or bags.

1. Prepare two swatches

2. Align the two swatches with the right sides facing each other and pin them in place. Secure them at both ends, the center, and middle, adjusting the length as needed.

3. Use a crochet hook that is one size smaller than the knitting needles you used. Insert the hook into the first stitch of the first row.

4. Yarn over and pull through, then yarn over again and pull through the same loop.

5. Insert the crochet hook into the next stitch. Yarn over and pull the yarn through, then pull through the previous stitch as well. For garter stitch, pass the crochet hook through one of the gaps every two rows.

6. Continue joining in this manner. The right side will have a chain stitch appearance, while the wrong side will resemble backstitch.

7. Once joined, press with an iron to flatten the seam.

Instructions

Before You Begin

- Unit of measurement is primarily cm. Though this book provides measurements in inches, it should be noted that they are approximate conversions only.
- Completed work dimensions may differ from measurements given on diagrams.
- The yarn is listed in the following order: manufacturer, product name, color number, color name, and required amount.
- The gauge indicates the number of stitches and rows within a 10 cm/4" square.
- When knitting in the round, you can use either circular needles or double-pointed needles.
- The material quantities listed are sufficient for the project; however, it is recommended to have a little extra. For items such as hand warmers, the amount provided is enough for one pair.
- Please refer to the color pages for charts.
- For detailed instructions, refer to the instruction pages.

About Charts and Pattern Drafts

- Instructions include both charts and pattern drafts.

[Chart]

The chart uses stitch symbols, with each square representing one stitch and one row. The symbols reflect the stitches as seen from the right side of the work. When knitting in the round, you always work while looking at the right side, so follow the symbols exactly as shown.
In flat knitting, where the work is turned, the direction changes between rows. Odd-numbered rows are worked from the right side, and even-numbered rows from the wrong side. For right-side rows, follow the symbols as they appear. For wrong-side rows, work the opposite of the symbol (for example, if the symbol is for a knit stitch, you should purl).
Repeated symbols may be shortened using dashed lines. If the pattern continues onto another page, guide marks will indicate where to pick up the chart.

[Pattern Draft]

1 The number of foundation stitches, size, whether to knit in the round or flat, and whether stitches need to be picked up are indicated at the start.
2 The type of yarn and the needles to use are specified.
3 The starting position and the direction in which to knit.
4 The number of rows and dimensions (cm and inch) are provided. (4 shows where the stitch pattern or yarn changes.)
5 The total number of rows throughout the project.
6 Dashed lines indicate when knitting in the round.
7 Stitch increases and decreases are represented, showing repeated decreases or increases from bottom to top. For example, "Decrease 1 stitch 8 times each row" is shown from left to right.
8 The finishing method, including how to bind off stitches, is indicated. Binding off can be done with either knitting needles or a crochet hook.

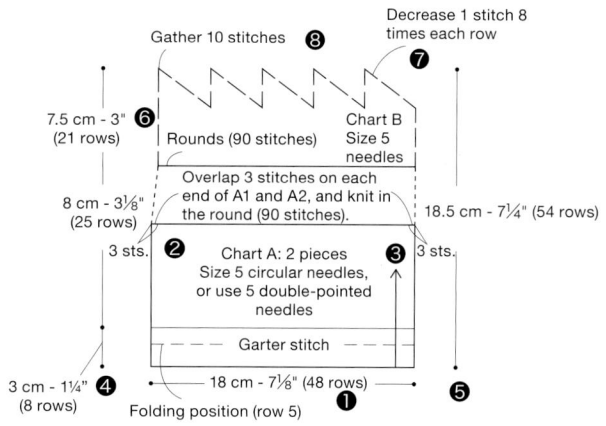

Page 32 Buttercup Cardigan

Finished Measurements: Width 55 cm - 21⅜" × Length 39 cm - 15⅜"

▶ Tools and Materials

Yarn
Puppy British Fine
#003 Navy Blue 250g / 8.8oz.
#066 Yellow 45g / 1.6oz.
#080 Yellow Green 45g / 1.6oz.

Other Material
A pair of belt parts if desired

Needles
Straight Needles:
Size 5 (3.50 mm, UK Size 9) – front panel,
Size 4 (3.25 mm, UK Size 10) – back panel, sleeve, hem
Crochet Hook:
Size 2/0 (2.00 mm, UK Size 14)

▶ Gauge

Front panel: 26 stitches, 30 rows
Back panel, Sleeve: 30 stitches, 32 rows

▶ Knitting and Assembly Instructions

① Cast on required number of stitches and knit according to the charts. Weave in the yarn ends and steam block.
② With the right sides together, join the front panels using a crochet hook.
③ Align the front and back panels with the right sides together, and join them using a crochet hook. Attach the sleeves, and seam the sides together using a crochet hook.
④ Steam block to shape.
⑤ Optionally, add belt, buttons, or other embellishments to your preference.

* Refer to page 13 for the Buttercups, Buttercup Border charts.

[Pattern A Chart: Front Panel Hem & Cuff]

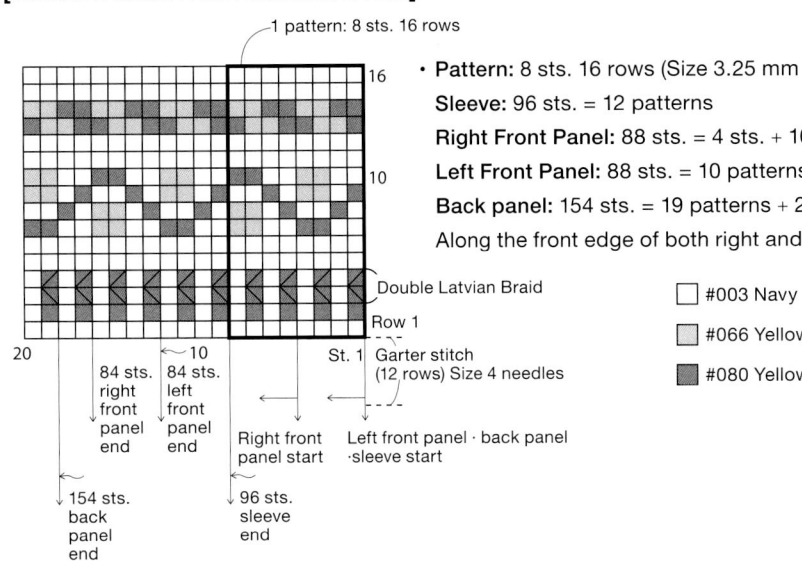

- **Pattern:** 8 sts. 16 rows (Size 3.25 mm needles)
  Sleeve: 96 sts. = 12 patterns
  Right Front Panel: 88 sts. = 4 sts. + 10 patterns + front edge (garter st.) 4 sts.
  Left Front Panel: 88 sts. = 10 patterns + 4 sts. + front edge (garter st.) 4 sts.
  Back panel: 154 sts. = 19 patterns + 2 sts.
  Along the front edge of both right and left front panels, add 4 sts.

□ #003 Navy Blue   □ Knit
□ #066 Yellow   ⊟ Purl
■ #080 Yellow Green   ⧄ Latvian Braid

[Pattern B Chart: Front Panel]

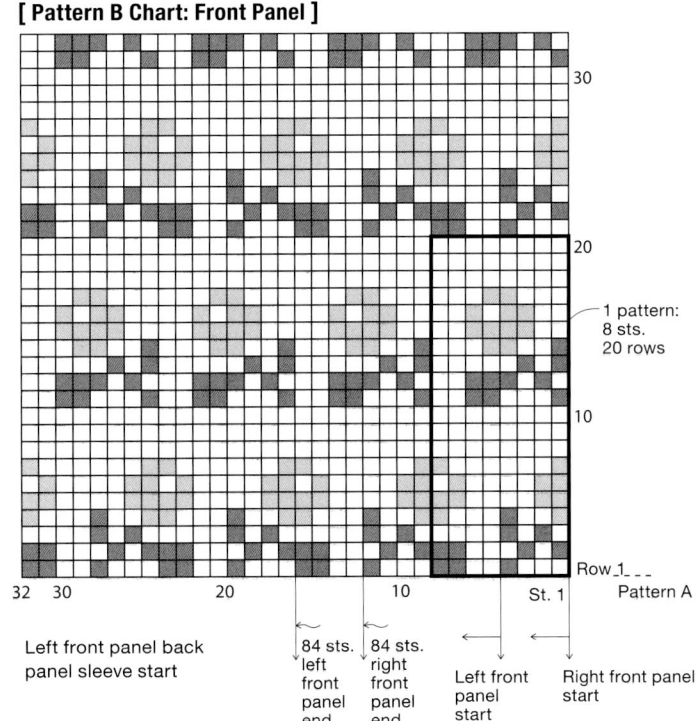

- **Pattern:** 8 sts. 20 rows (Size 5, 3.50 mm needles)

Right Front Panel:
88 sts. = 10 patterns + 4 sts. + front edge (garter st.) 4 sts.
178 rows = 8 patterns + 18 rows

Left Front Panel:
88 sts. = 4 sts. + 10 patterns + front edge (garter st.) 4 sts.
178 rows = 8 patterns + 18 rows

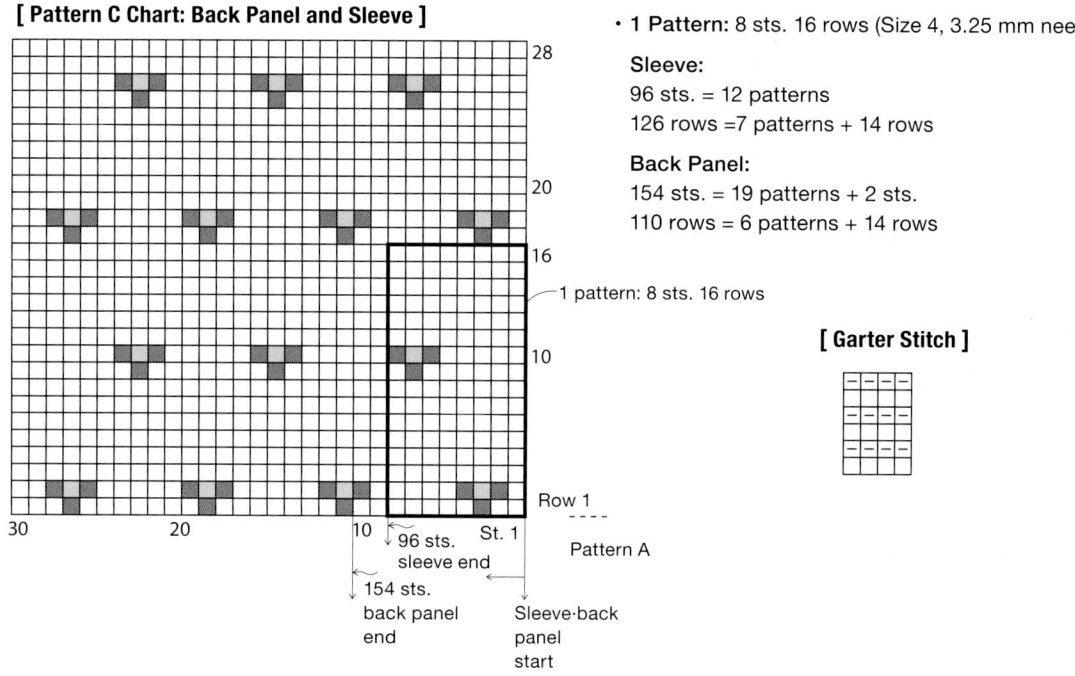

[Pattern C Chart: Back Panel and Sleeve]

- **1 Pattern:** 8 sts. 16 rows (Size 4, 3.25 mm needles)

Sleeve:
96 sts. = 12 patterns
126 rows = 7 patterns + 14 rows

Back Panel:
154 sts. = 19 patterns + 2 sts.
110 rows = 6 patterns + 14 rows

[Garter Stitch]

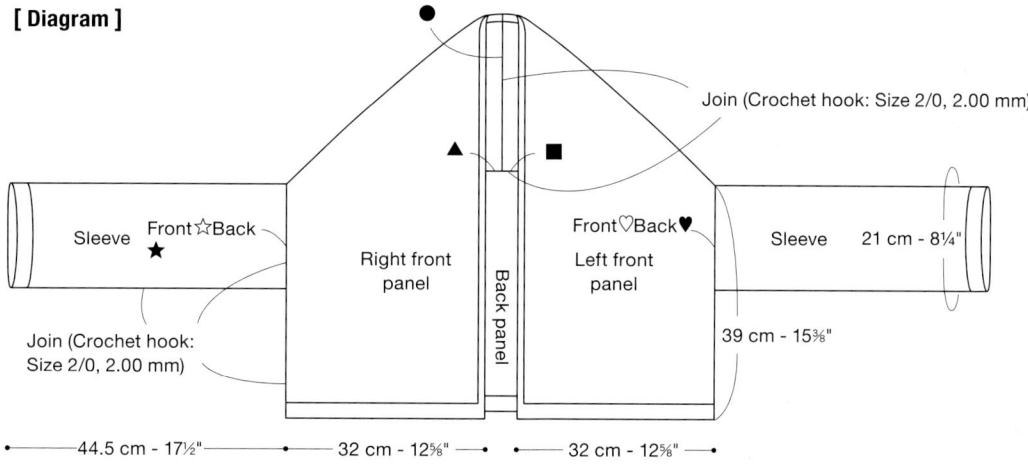

[Diagram]

Join (Crochet hook: Size 2/0, 2.00 mm)

Sleeve — Front☆Back★ — Right front panel — Back panel — Front♡Back♥ — Left front panel — Sleeve — 21 cm - 8¼"

Join (Crochet hook: Size 2/0, 2.00 mm)

39 cm - 15⅜"

44.5 cm - 17½" — 32 cm - 12⅝" — 32 cm - 12⅝"

Double Latvian Braid (flat knitting)

∗ As you knit the Latvian braid, the two colors of yarn will become twisted. Be sure to untwist as you knit.

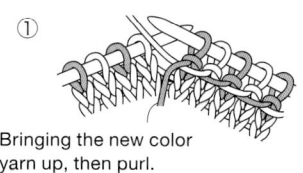

① Bringing the new color yarn up, then purl.

Bring the working yarn from below, then knit.

When viewed from the right side, the pattern will appear as shown above.

Knit pattern A up to the second row. For the third row, as shown in the chart, use yellow green (#080) and the background color yarn (#003), placing the background color yarn in front. Pick up the yellow green color yarn underneath the background color yarn, then purl.

For the fourth row (wrong side), keep both yarns on the right side of your work. Pick up the working yarn from below, then knit.

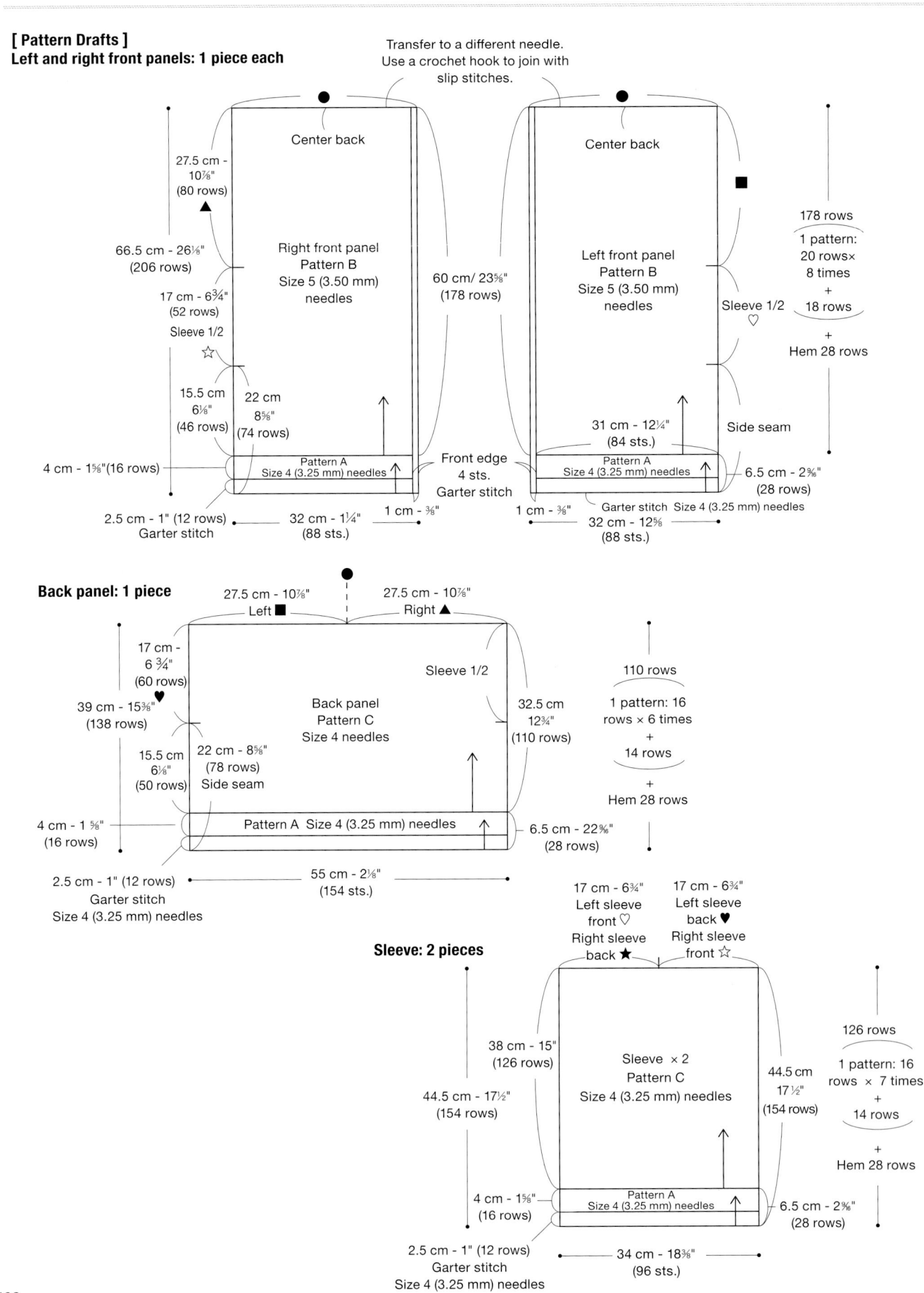

Page 34 Daisy Shawl

Finished Dimensions: Width 64 cm - 25¼" × Length 39 cm - 15⅜"

▶ Tools and Materials

Yarn
Jamieson's Spindrift
#105 Eesit 230g / 8.1 oz.
#259 Leprechaun 40g / 1.4 oz.
  55 cm - 21⅝" cut 292 pcs
#188 Sherbet 12g / 0.4 oz.
#570 Sorbet 12g / 0.4 oz.
  #188, #570: for embroidering daisies

* Refer to page 26 for the chart, page 27 for embroidering the daisy.

Other Material
2 pieces each of 20 × 20 cm - 7⅞" × 7⅞" square felt in yellow shades

Needles
Straight Needles: Size 4 (3.25 mm, UK Size 10)
Crochet Hook: Size 3/0 (2.25 mm, UK Size 13)

▶ Gauge
28 stitches, 32 rows

▶ Knitting and Assembly Instructions

① Begin by casting on required number of stitches. Knit according to the charts. Bind off only the back panel. Weave in the yarn ends and steam block.
② Embroider the flowers.
③ With the right sides facing, join the two front panels using the slip stitch with a crochet hook.
④ With the right sides facing, join the front and back panels using the slip stitch with a crochet hook.
⑤ Leaving the armhole openings, seam the sides using a crochet hook.
⑥ Wet block the piece and let it dry.

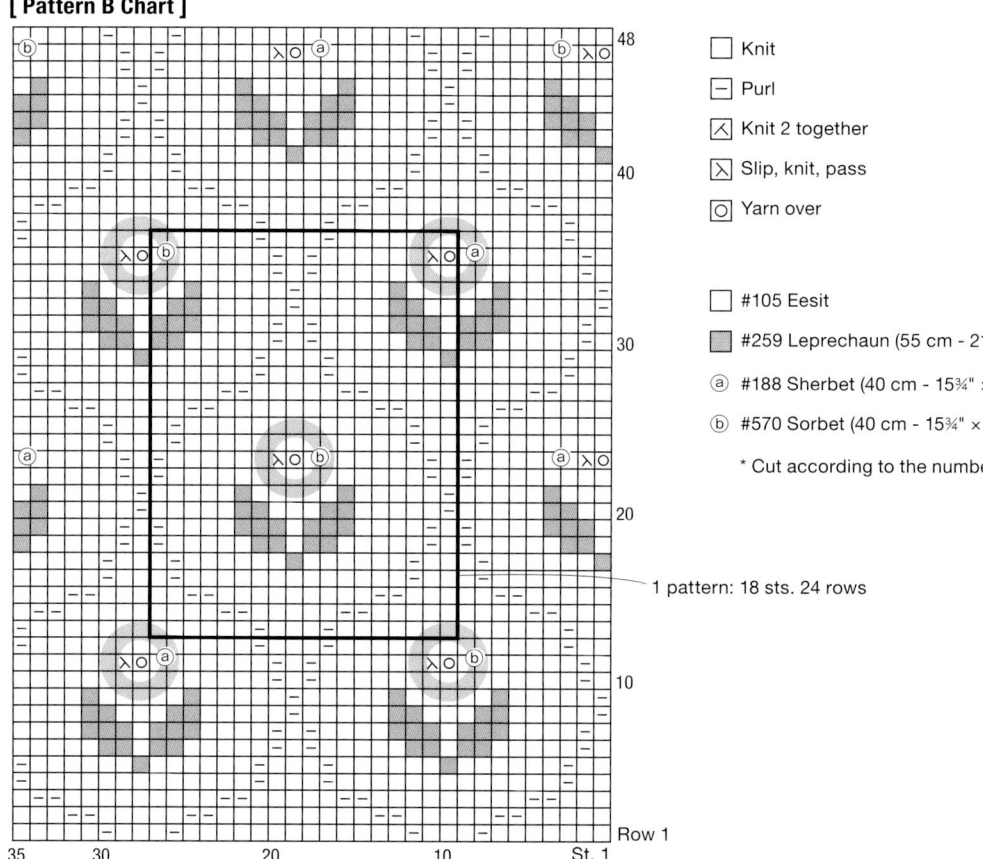

□ Knit
— Purl
⋋ Knit 2 together
⋌ Slip, knit, pass
○ Yarn over

□ #105 Eesit
■ #259 Leprechaun (55 cm - 21⅝" × 292 pcs)
ⓐ #188 Sherbet (40 cm - 15¾" × 133 pcs)
ⓑ #570 Sorbet (40 cm - 15¾" × 135 pcs)

* Cut according to the number of patterns.

[Daisy Embroidery]

① Sew a 2 ~ 2.5 cm - ¾" ~ 1" square felt piece to the center of the flower on the wrong side, aligning it with the hole.
② While looking at the right side, work blanket stitches.
③ Trim the excess felt into a circular shape.

* Felt may shrink or fade, so pre-cut 2 ~ 2.5 cm - ¾ ~ 1" squares and wash them in lukewarm water, then dry before use.

* For convenience, cut yarn prior into the necessary length for each flower, approximately 40 cm - 15¾".

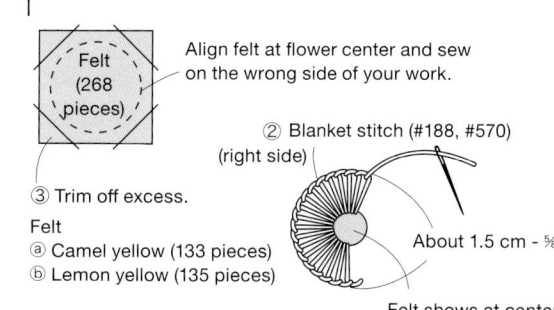

Align felt at flower center and sew on the wrong side of your work.
② Blanket stitch (#188, #570) (right side)
About 1.5 cm - ⅝"
③ Trim off excess.
Felt
ⓐ Camel yellow (133 pieces)
ⓑ Lemon yellow (135 pieces)
Felt shows at center

[Chart]

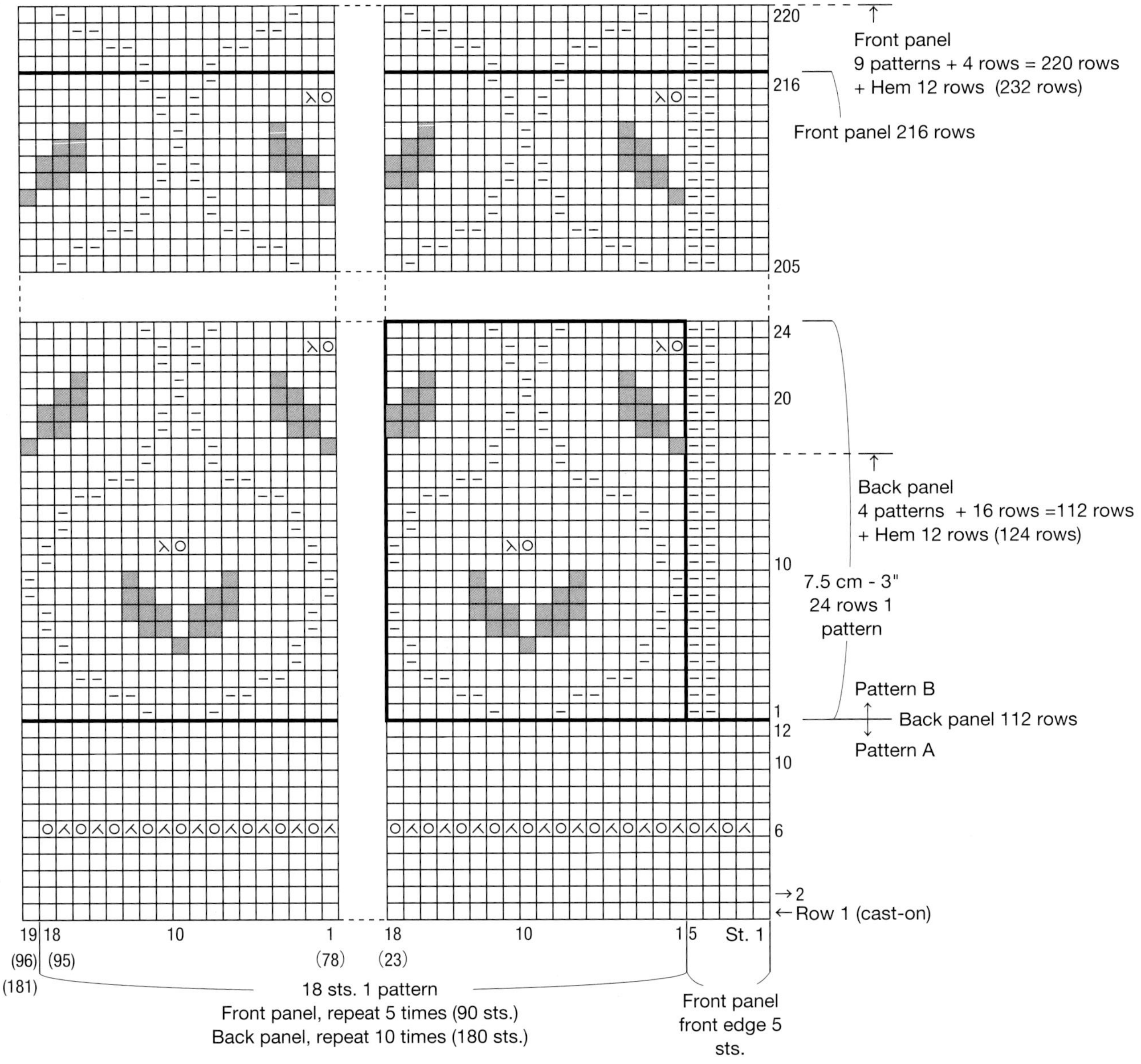

220
Front panel
9 patterns + 4 rows = 220 rows
+ Hem 12 rows (232 rows)
216
Front panel 216 rows
205
24
20
Back panel
4 patterns + 16 rows =112 rows
+ Hem 12 rows (124 rows)
10
7.5 cm - 3"
24 rows 1
pattern
Pattern B
1
Back panel 112 rows
12
Pattern A
10
6
→2
←Row 1 (cast-on)
19
18
10
1
18
10
1
5
St. 1
(96)
(95)
(78)
(23)
(181)
18 sts. 1 pattern
Front panel, repeat 5 times (90 sts.)
Back panel, repeat 10 times (180 sts.)
Front panel
front edge 5
sts.

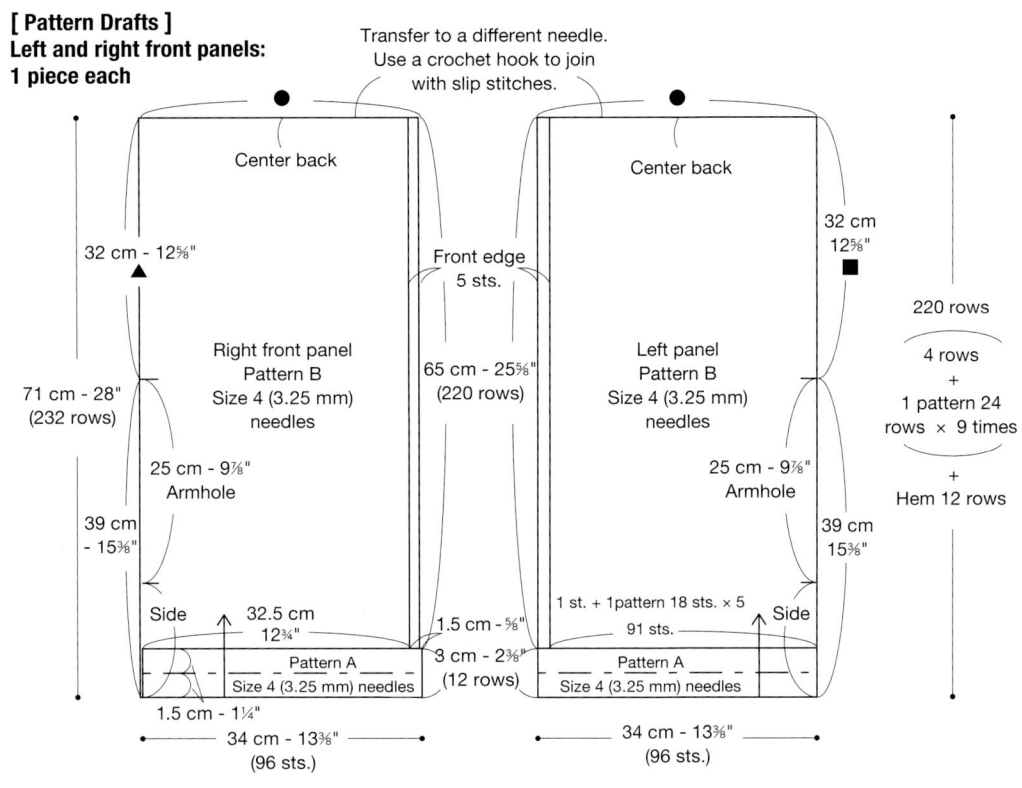
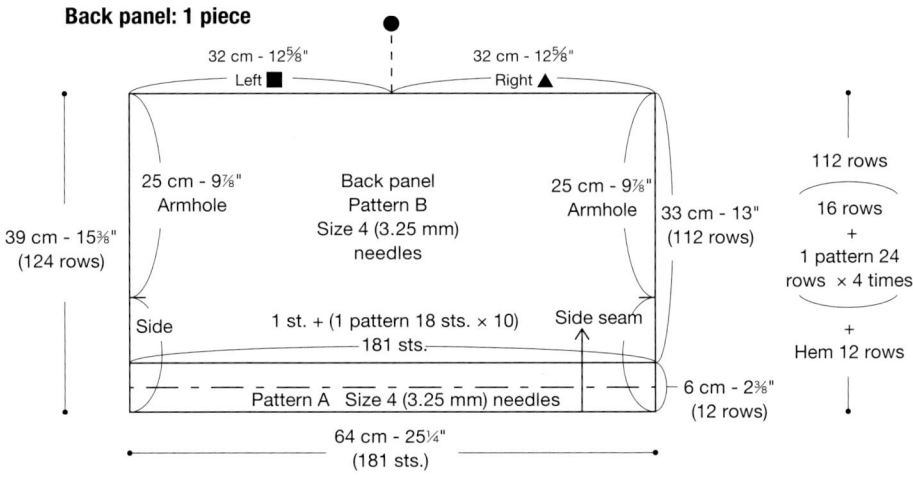
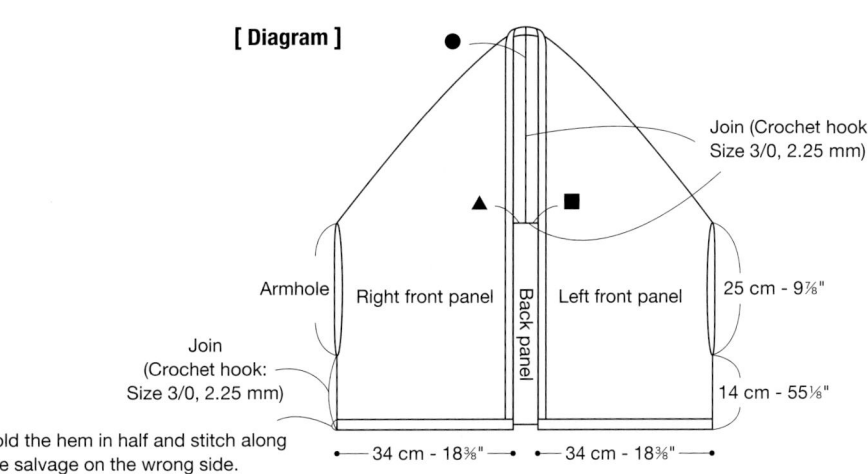

Page 36 Mistletoe Cowl

Finished Dimensions: Circumference of cowl 76 cm - 30" × Length 26 cm - 10¼"

▶ Tools and Materials

Yarn

Puppy British Fine

#024 Charcoal Gray 60g / 2.1 oz.

#080 Yellow Green 12g / 0.4 oz.
　100 cm - 39⅜" cut 50 pcs

#091 Pistachio 6g / 0.2 oz.
　45 cm - 17¾" cut 50 pcs

Puppy Kid Mohair Fine

#15 Gray 30g / 1 oz.

* Knit with two strands: #024 and #15
* For the chart, refer to page 31.

Other Material

One 5 cm - 2" in diameter fabric-covered button

5 × 5 cm - 2" × 2" square thick felt

5 × 5 cm - 2" × 2" square quilt batting

4.5 × 4.5 cm - 1¾" × 1¾" thick paper (cardstock)

One 3.5 cm - 1⅜" long brooch pin

Needles

Straight Needles: Size 5 (3.50 mm)

Crochet Hook: Size 4/0 (2.50 mm, UK Size 12)

Cable needle

▶ Gauge

24 sts. 28 rows

▶ Knitting and Assembly Instructions

① Cast on the required number of stitches and knit according to the charts. Bind off, weave in the yarn tails, and steam block.

② With the right sides facing each other, use the ladder stitch to join the piece into a circle.

③ Fold six rows along the top and bottom edges inward, and sew them down on the wrong side.

④ Steam block to shape the piece.

⑤ Make the brooch by knitting according to the chart. Bind off, weave in the yarn ends, and steam block to shape.

⑥ Cover the button with quilt batting and glue it in place.

⑦ Stitch around the edges of the knit fabric, cover the button with it, and pull the stitches tight to adjust the design's position.

⑧ Glue a piece of thick paper to the back of the button.

⑨ Insert the brooch pin into the felt and glue the felt onto the thick paper.

[Pattern Draft]

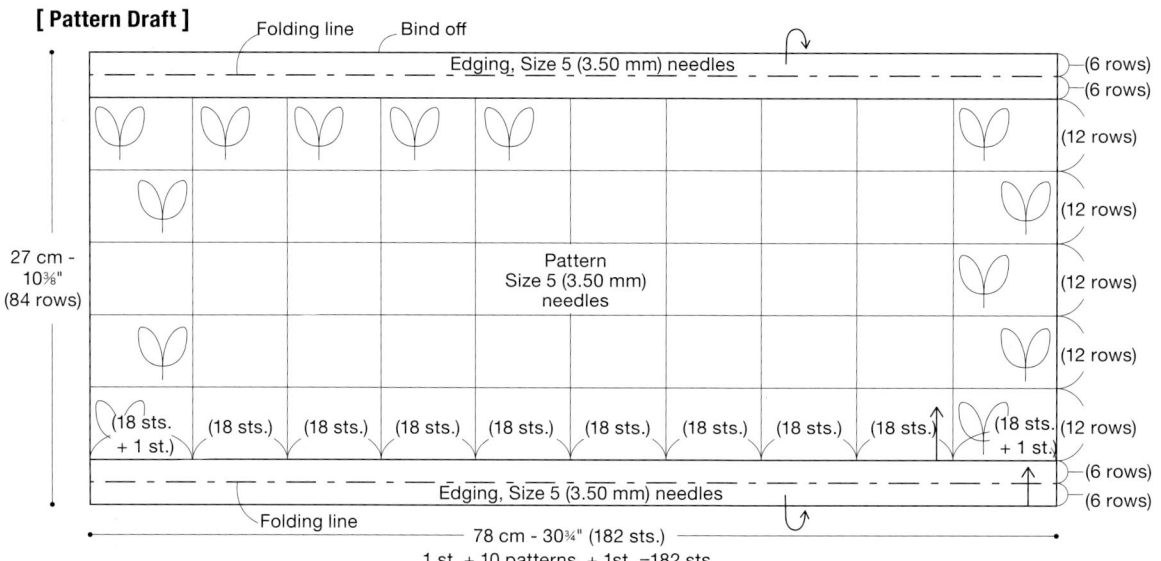

[Assembly]

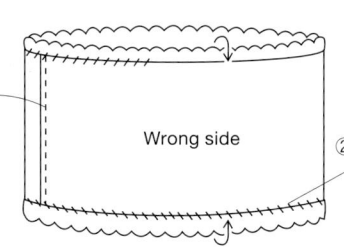

① With the right side facing, use ladder stitch to join both ends and form a circular shape.

② Fold the top and bottom edges to the wrong side and sew them in place.

[How to Make Brooch]

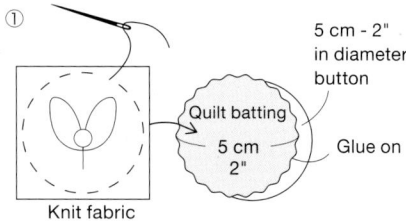

Stitch around the edges of the knit fabric and place it over the button covered with quilt batting.

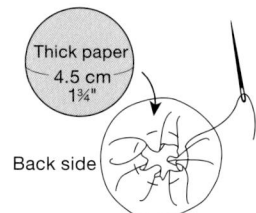

Pull the thread to adjust the fit around the button and ensure the pattern is correctly positioned on the outside. Glue a piece of thick paper to the back of the button.

③ Make small cuts in the felt, insert the brooch pin, and sew the center in place.

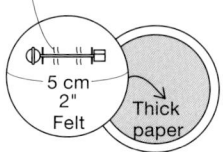

Check the front side and the orientation of the pin, then glue the felt onto the thick paper.

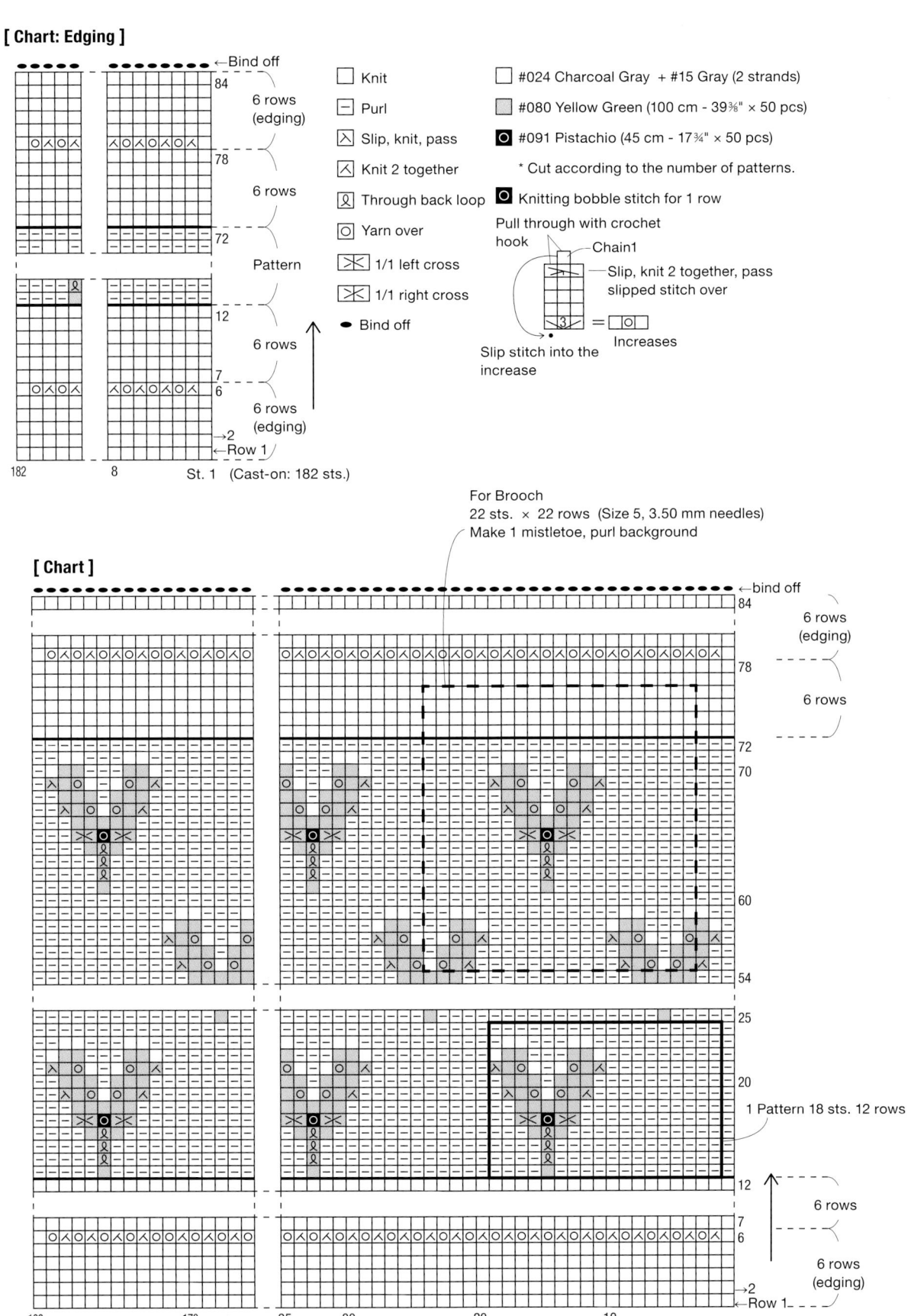

Page 62 Thistle Bolero

Finished Dimensions: Length 50 cm - 19¾", From center back to cuff: 74 cm - 29⅛"

▶ **Tools and Materials**

Yarn

Jamieson's Spindrift

#665 China Blue 225g / 7.9 oz.
#616 Anemone 8g / 0.2 oz.
#599 Zodiac 16g / 0.5 oz.
#769 Willow 10g / 0.3 oz.
#772 Verdigris 45g / 1.5 oz.

Except for China Blue, cut the yarn to the required length and number of pieces.

Yarn for provisional chain stitch as needed.

Needles

80 cm - 31½" circular needle, Size 5 (3.50 mm)

Straight Needles: Size 4 (3.25 mm, UK Size 10) (cuff)

Crochet Hook:
Size 4/0 (2.50 mm, UK Size 12),
6/0 (3.50 mm, UK Size 9)
(for provisional chain stitch)

▶ **Gauge**

26 sts. 31 rows

Pattern on Cuff: 28 sts. 52 rows

* For the chart, refer to page 47.

▶ **Knitting and Assembly Instructions**

① Start by casting on from a provisional chain, then knit two panels according to the chart. Weave in the yarn ends and steam block.

② Knit the cuffs. As you undo the provisional chain, place the stitches on the needle and knit according to the chart, then bind off. Weave in the yarn ends and steam block.

③ With the right sides facing each other, join the two panels using slip stitches with a crochet hook.

④ Fold the sleeves in half lengthwise with the right sides facing each other, and join the seams using a crochet hook up to the marked point (see page 128).

⑤ Knit the collar.

⑥ Wet block and let dry.

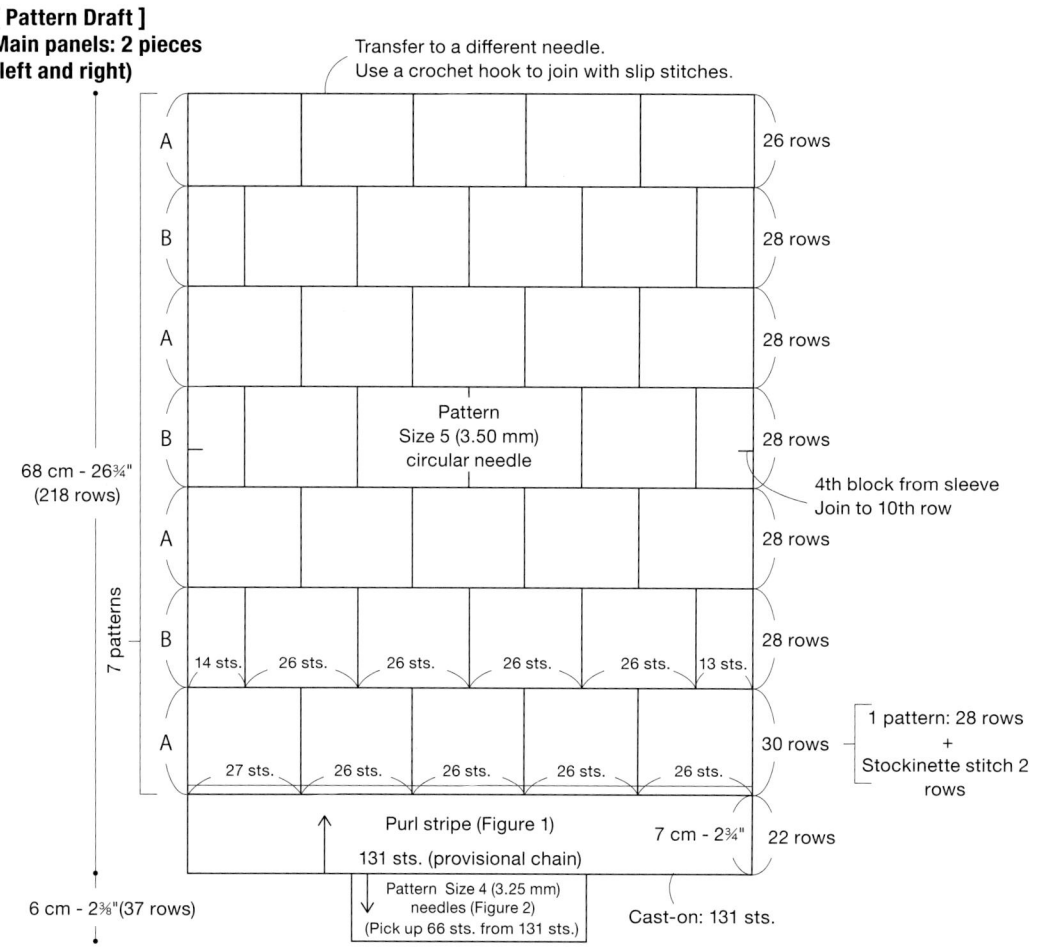

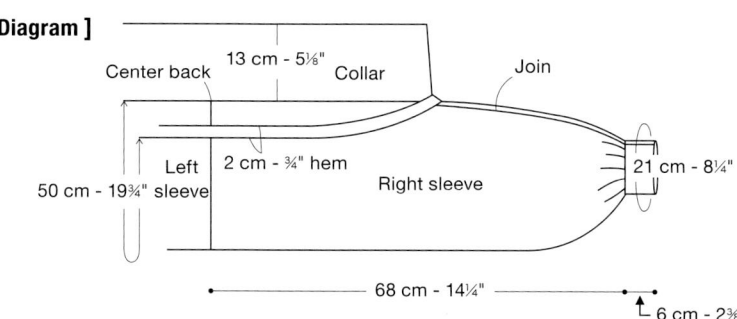

[How to Knit Collar]

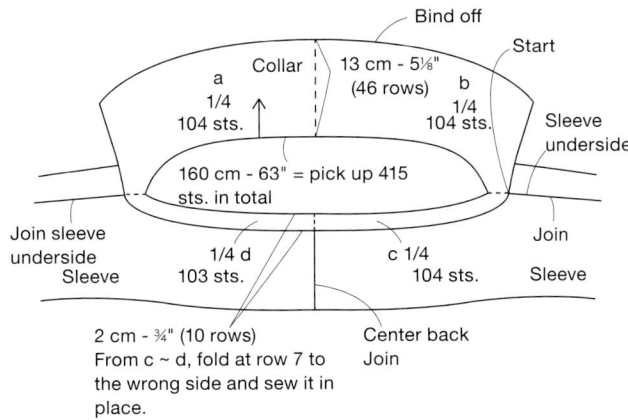

① While looking at the right side, pick up 415 stitches across 160 cm - 63".
Work 6 rounds of 1x1 ribbing using circular needles.
② On the 7th round, work (k2tog, yo) for 207 stitches of the hem (sections c and d), which is (k2tog, yarn over) × 103 times + 1 stitch.
Work 1x1 ribbing for sections a and b.
For the 8th and 9th rounds, work 1x1 ribbing for all sections (a, b, c, and d). On the 10th round, bind off 206 stitches of sections c and d (this becomes the hem, so bind off neither too tightly nor too loosely, ensuring even tension).
Add the remaining 1 stitch to sections a and b.
③ From here, switch to flat knitting (while still using circular needles) and continue. From the 11th round, follow the [Chart: Collar], decreasing stitches at the inside edges of the collar's left and right sides, and knit until the 46th row. On the 47th row, bind off all stitches (pay attention to maintain even tension).
* Use a crochet hook for the bind off and carefully check the collar as you work. If it doesn't come out well the first time, gently undo it and try again; this is an important part of the finishing process.
④ Steam block to shape the piece.

□ Knit	□ #665 China Blue
— Purl	■ #599 Zodiac (90 cm - 39⅜" × 32 pcs, 50 cm - 19¾" × 6 pcs)
⧹ Slip, knit, pass	■ #772 Verdigris (2.4 m - 94½" × 32 pcs, 1.3 m - 51⅛" × 6 pcs)
⧸ Knit 2 together	▨ #616 Anemone (50 cm - 19¾" × 32 pcs, 35 cm - 13¾" × 6 pcs)
○ Yarn over	▨ #769 Willow (60 cm - 23⅝" × 32 pcs, 40 cm - 15¾" × 6 pcs)
• Bind off	* Cut according to the number of patterns.
∨ Slip stitch (without knitting, transfer a stitch to the right needle)	

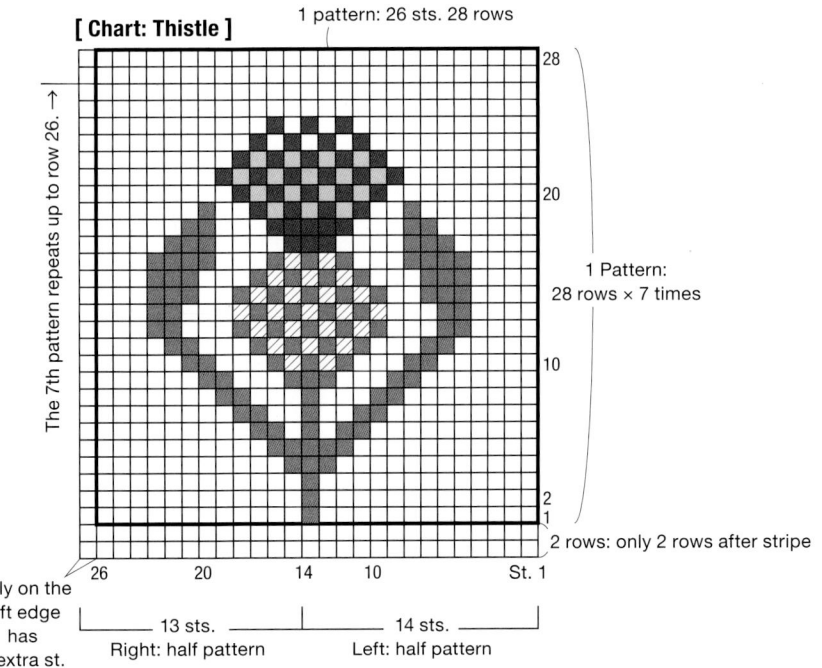

[Chart: Stripes on Sleeve Figure 1]

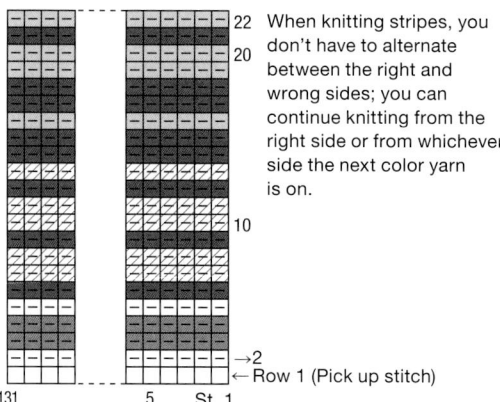

When knitting stripes, you don't have to alternate between the right and wrong sides; you can continue knitting from the right side or from whichever side the next color yarn is on.

[Chart: Cuff Pattern Figure 2]

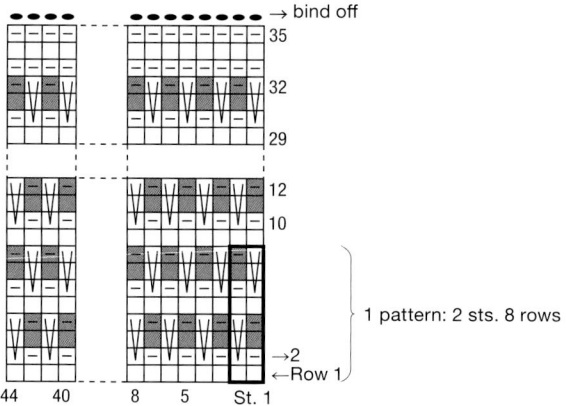

1 pattern: 2 sts. 8 rows

[How to Knit a Sleeve]

① Undo the provisional chain while placing the stitches onto the needle.
② Work k2tog in the background yarn for 131 stitches, then knit 1 on the remaining stitch to have a total of 66 stitches.
③ On the next row, work ssp on every other stitch on the wrong side to reduce to 44 stitches.
④ Following the chart (Figure 2), work 32 rows (8 rows per pattern, repeated 4 times). Then, work garter stitch for the next 3 rows. On the following row, bind off while working on the wrong side. Weave in the yarn ends and steam block.

How to Knit

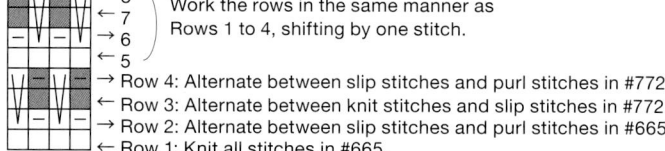

Work the rows in the same manner as Rows 1 to 4, shifting by one stitch.

→ Row 4: Alternate between slip stitches and purl stitches in #772.
← Row 3: Alternate between knit stitches and slip stitches in #772.
→ Row 2: Alternate between slip stitches and purl stitches in #665.
← Row 1: Knit all stitches in #665.

[Chart: Collar]

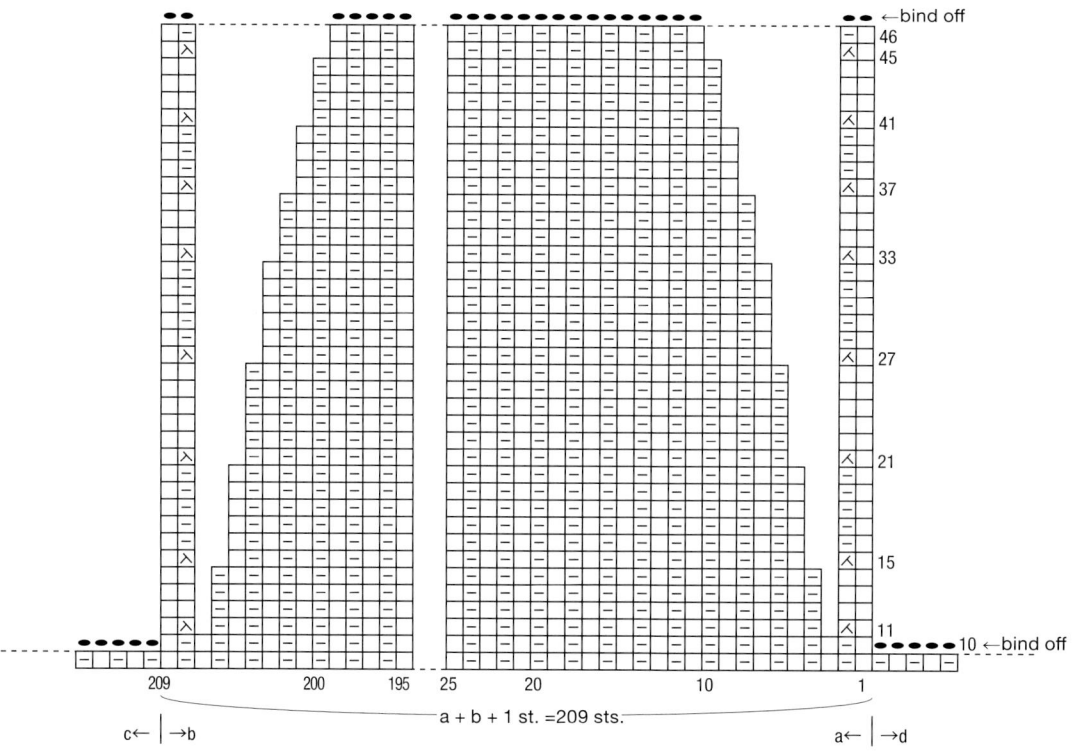

Page 78 Cherry Bag

Finished Dimensions: Width: 43 cm - 17" × Height: 27 cm - 10⅝" × Depth: 9 cm - 3½"

▶ **Tools and Materials**

Yarn
Puppy ALBA
#1082 Light Beige 120g / 4.2 oz.
#5139 Red 50g / 1.7 oz.
  120 cm - 47¼" × cut 92 pieces
#1185 Green 35g / 1.2 oz.
  55 cm - 21⅝" × cut 92 pieces
* For the chart, refer to page 69; for the knitting instructions, page 71.

Other Material
60 × 45 cm - 23⅝" × 17¾" fusible quilt batting
90 × 45 cm - 35½" × 17¾" fabric for the lining (including inner pocket)
120 cm - 47¼" long, 1 cm - ⅜" wide red grosgrain ribbon
One bamboo button, 3 cm - 1¼" in length
A pair of bamboo handle, inner width 16.5 cm - 65"

Needles
Straight Needles: Size 5 (3.50 mm)
Crochet Hook:
Size 3/0 (2.25 mm, UK Size 13),
5/0 (3.00 mm, UK Size 11)

▶ **Gauge**
28 sts. 32 rows

▶ **Knitting and Assembly Instructions**

① Cast on the required number of stitches and knit according to the charts. Bind off, weave in the yarn tails, and steam block.

② Align the knitted fabric with the right sides facing each other and use a crochet hook to slip stitch the sides and bottom gusset from the opening down to 8 cm - 3⅛".

③ Create an inside pocket and sew it to the lining, then attach fusible quilt batting to the back. Sew the sides and bottom gusset of the lining, folding over and sewing the sides and opening.

④ Insert the lining into the knitted bag and sew from the opening to the beginning of the seaming. Gather the lining's opening with running stitch and attach it to the first row of the knitted ribbing.

⑤ Wrap quilt batting around the handles and secure with stitches. Wrap the handles in the handle slot and sew them to the first round of the ribbing, then sew the sides closed.

⑥ Knit a double chain and sew it to the inside, then attach the bamboo button to the opposite side. Sew the grosgrain ribbon so that it covers the gathers on the inside.

⑦ Knit and attach decorative leaves.

[Pattern Draft]
Main body: 1 piece

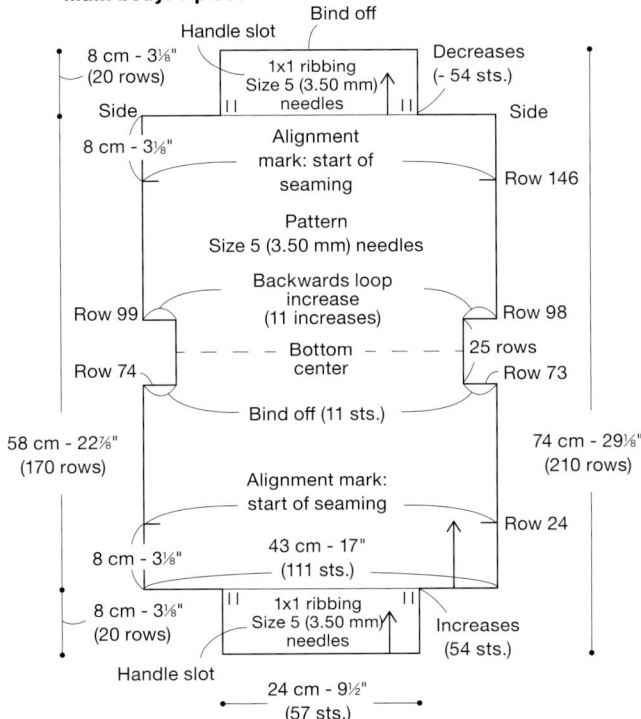

Lining: 1 piece
Fusible quilt cotton batting: 1 piece

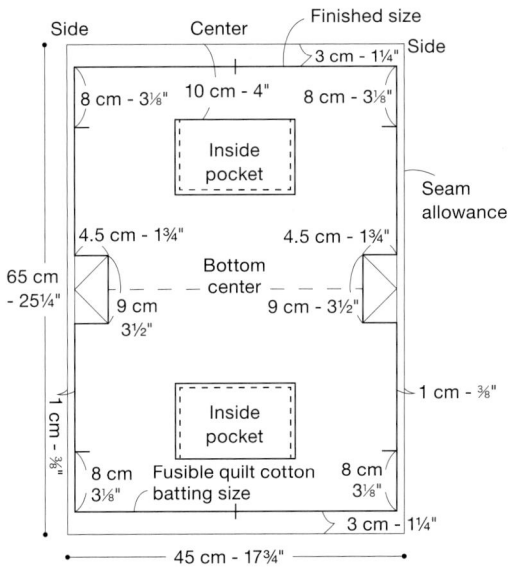

* Cut the fusible quilt batting to size (no seam allowance).

[How to Knit Leaf Decoration] Crochet hook: 5/0, 3.00 mm, #1185

Inside pocket: 2 pieces

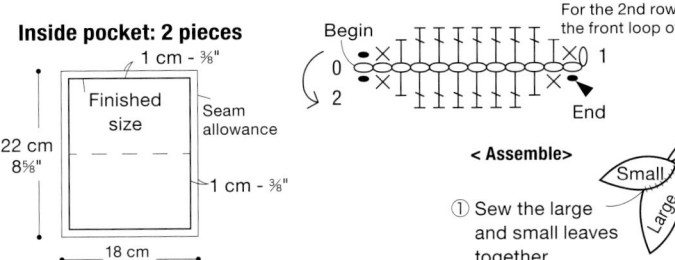

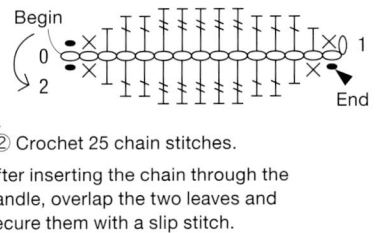

② Crochet 25 chain stitches.
③ After inserting the chain through the handle, overlap the two leaves and secure them with a slip stitch.

141

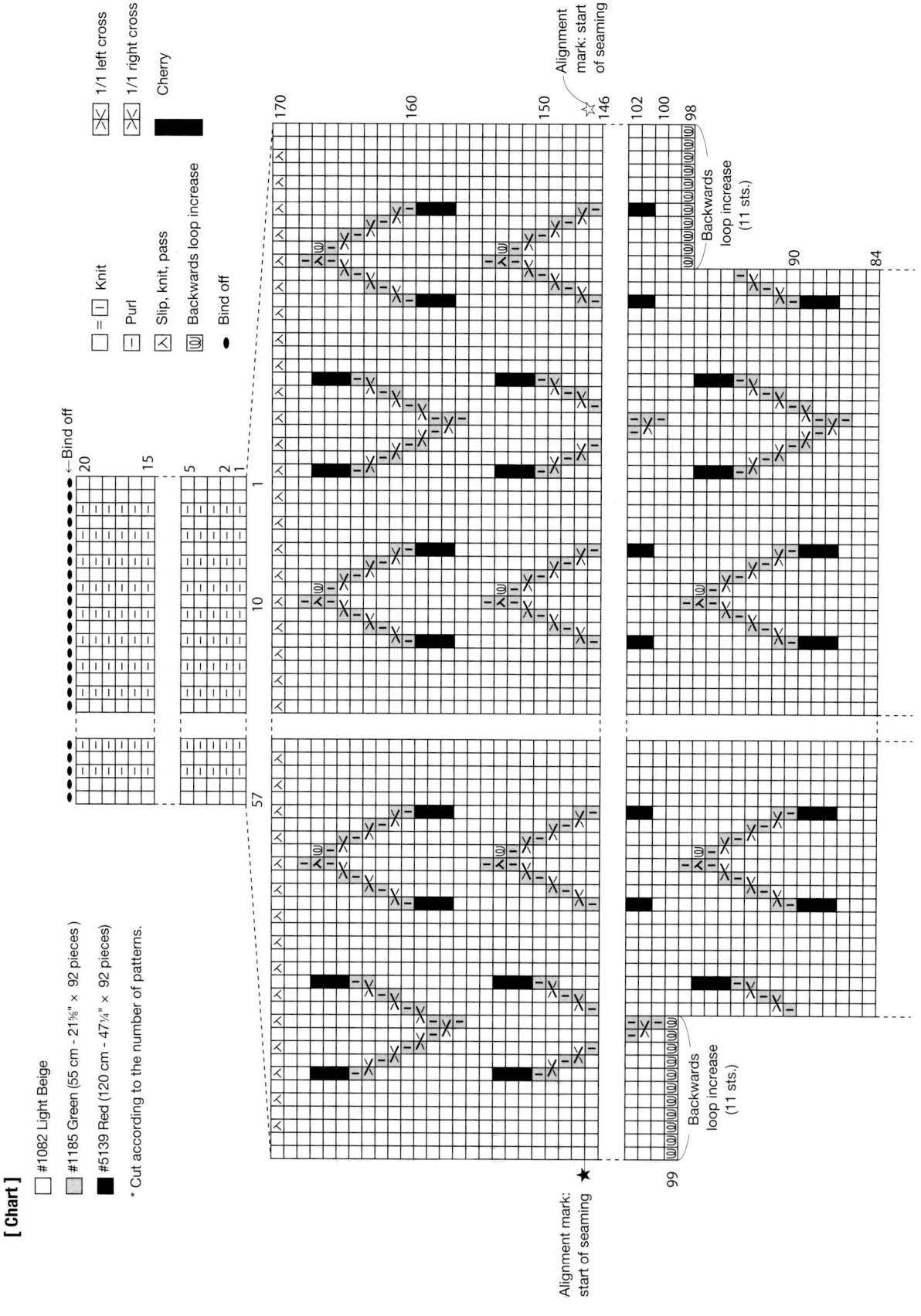

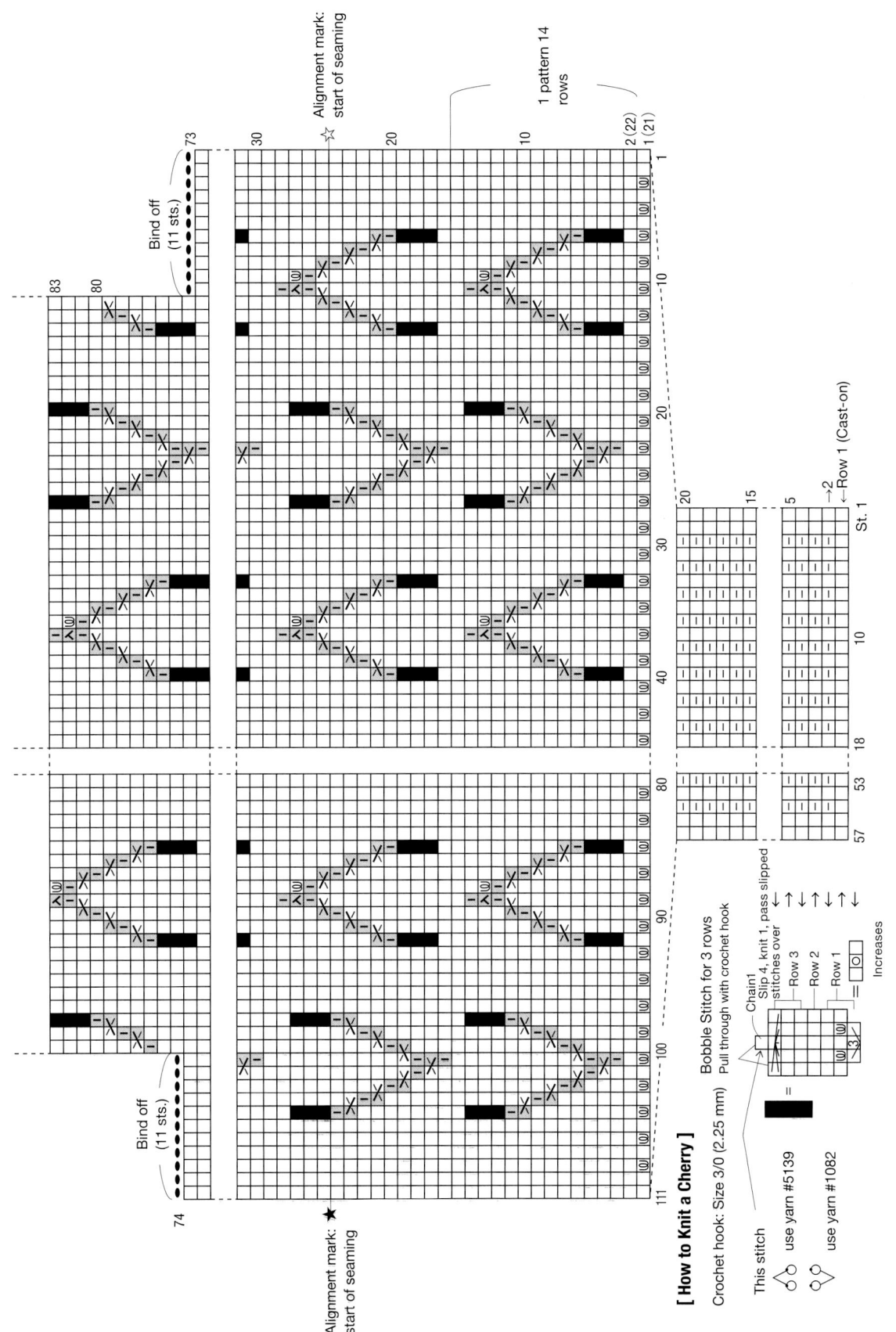

[How to Assemble the Bag]

②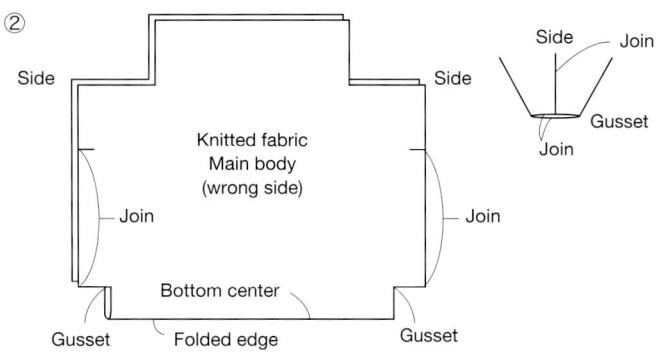

③ **< Pocket >**

① With the right sides facing each other, sew the edges, leaving an opening for turning. Trim the corners.

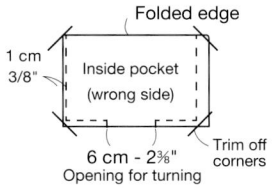

② Turn it right side out, press with an iron to smooth, and sew it to the lining, aligning the folded edge at the top. Trim the corners.

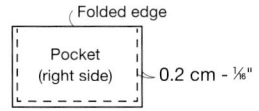

< Lining >

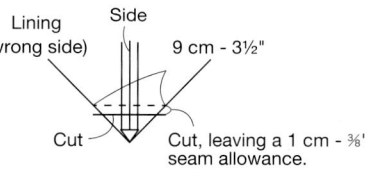

③ Attach the fusible quilt batting.

Make the inside pocket, sew it to the lining, and sew the lining into the bag.

④ With the right sides facing each other, sew both sides up to the start of the seaming.

⑤ Press the seam allowances open and sew the gusset.

⑥ Fold the 1 cm - ⅜" seam allowances on both sides and the 3 cm - 1¼" opening, then sew.

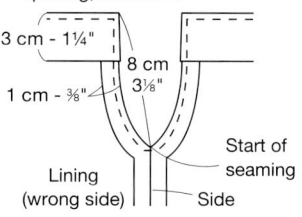

④ ① Insert the lining into the main body, aligning the bottom and sides, and sew from the opening to the start of the seaming. Trim the corners.

② Gather the opening of the lining with a running stitch and pull it tight.

③ Sew it onto the first row of the ribbing.

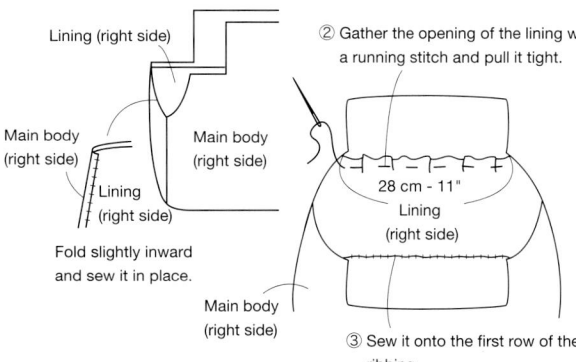

⑤ ① Wrap quilt batting around the handle and secure the edges with stitches.

② Place the handle on the front side of the main body and wrap it with the handle slot.

③ Using an up-and-down motion, bring the needle through to the back and sew, being careful not to stitch over the knitted stitches with the thread.

④ Sew both sides down 1.5 cm - ⅝" from the bottom edge.

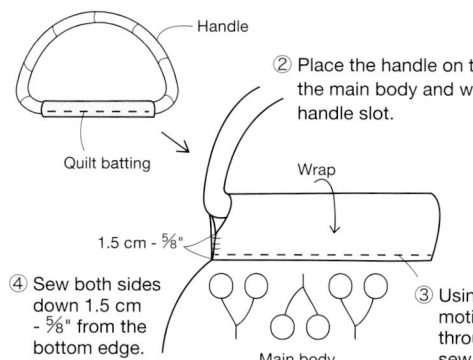

⑥ ① Crochet double chain
Crochet hook: Size 5/0, 3.00 mm, #1082

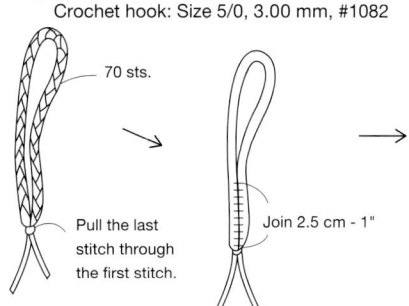

② Secure the double chain at the center of the inside opening, ensuring it is facing downward.

③ Place the grosgrain ribbon over the gathered area, folding both ends inward by 1 cm - ⅜", and sew the top and bottom edges with blind stitches.

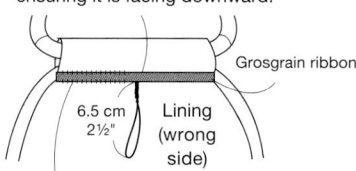

④ Sew the bamboo button to the center of the ribbing on the opposite side of the opening.

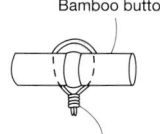

Add a loop of background color yarn (#1082) and wrap the yarn around the base of the loop behind the button to create space.

Page 116 Lady's Mantle

Finished Dimensions: Length 40 cm - 15¾", Width from cuff to cuff 104 cm - 41"

▶ **Tools and Materials**

Yarn

Puppy New2PLY
#260 Yellow 95g / 3.3 oz.

Puppy Kid Mohair Fine
#51 Lemon Yellow 95g / 3.3 oz.

Puppy British Fine
#086 Neon Yellow 3g / 0.1 oz.
Yarn for provisional chain stitch as needed

* For the lace chart, see page 105; for smocking stitch, see page 111.

Needles

80 cm - 31½" circular needle
Size 5 (3.50 mm)

60 cm - 33⅝" circular needle
Size 4 (3.25 mm, UK Size 10)
Size 5 (3.50 mm)

Straight Needles:
Size 4 (3.25 mm, UK Size 10)
Size 5 (3.50 mm)

Crochet Hook:
Size 4/0 (2.50 mm, UK Size 12)
6/0 (3.50 mm, UK Size 9)
(for a provisional chain)

Cable needle

▶ **Gauge**

20 sts. 29 rows

▶ **Knitting and Assembly Instructions**

① Start from a provisional chain and knit the body according to the chart for 86 rows. From row 87, divide the work into left and right sections with 80 stitches each, and knit both sides according to the chart until row 156. After that, rejoin and knit both sides together following the chart.

② Continue to knit the first cuff and bind off. For the second cuff, unravel the provisional chain, place the stitches onto the needle, knit according to the chart, and bind off.

③ Pick up 160 stitches around the neckline and knit the collar following the chart. Weave in the yarn ends and steam block.

④ Embroider the cuffs and collar as indicated.

⑤ With the right sides facing each other, join using the New 2PLY yarn and a 4/0 (2.50 mm) crochet hook with a slip stitch.

⑥ Steam block to shape.

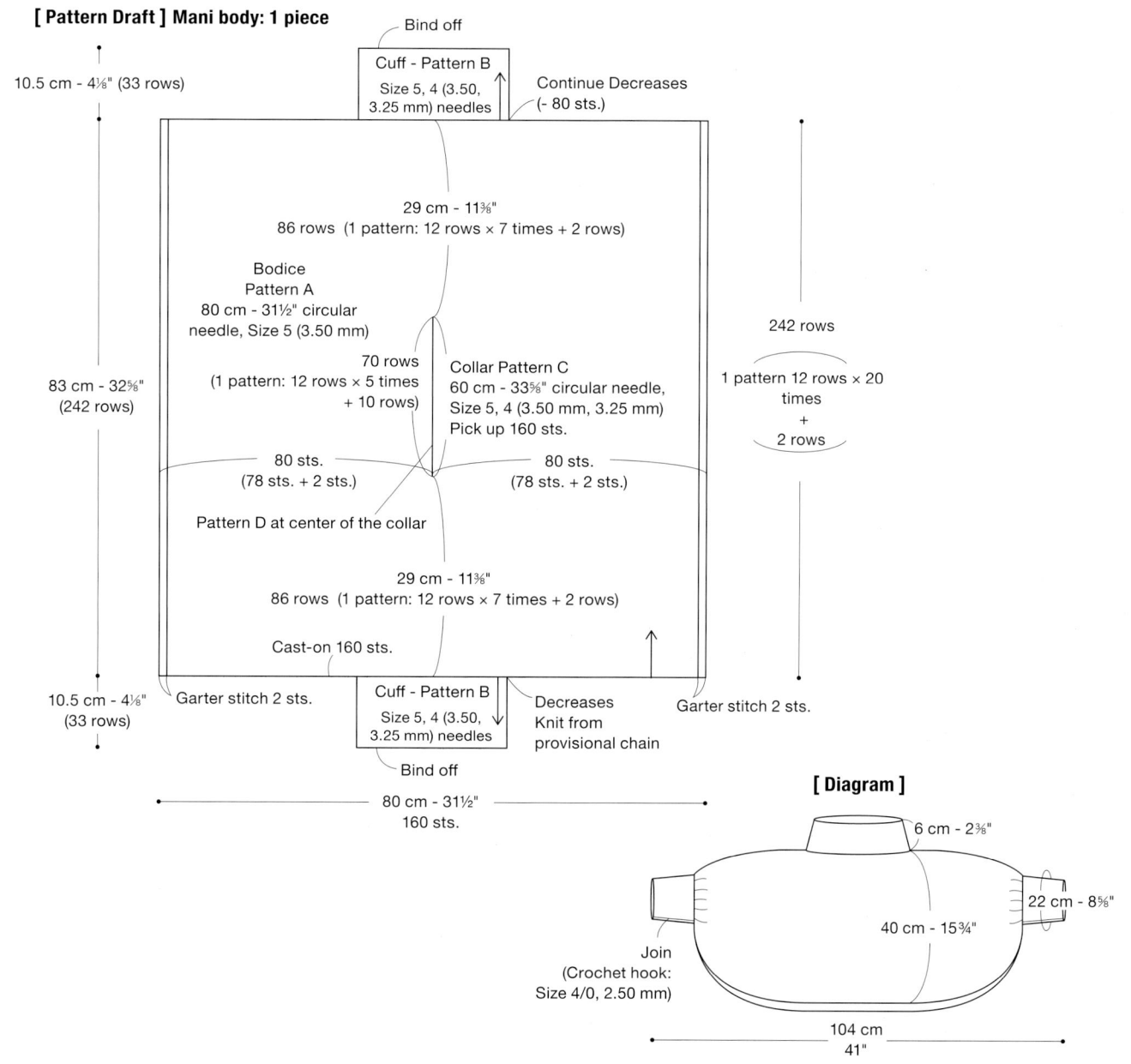

[Pattern A Chart: Bodice] 80 cm - 31½" circular needle, Size 5 (3.50 mm)

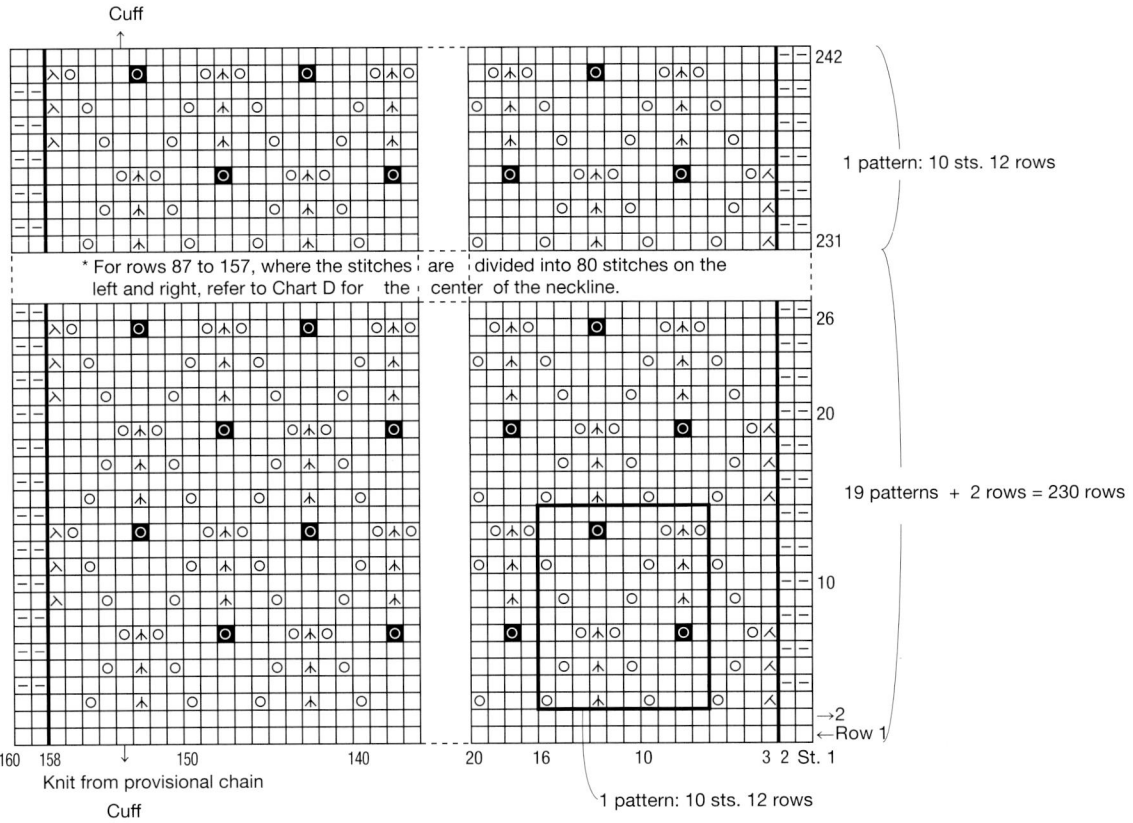

[Pattern B Chart: Cuff] Size 5, 4 (3.50 mm, 3.25 mm) needles, cable needle

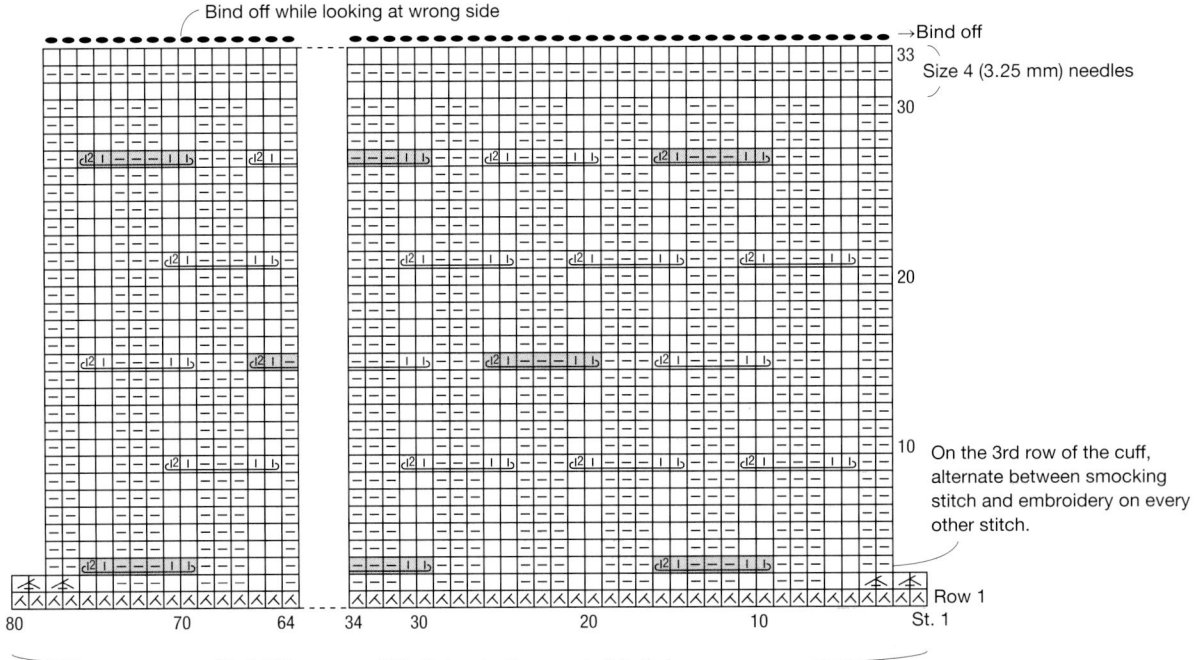

Work k2tog across 160 stitches to decrease to 80 stitches.
On Row 2, decrease 2 stitches at both the beginning and end of the row, reducing the total to 76 stitches.

[Pattern C Chart: Collar]

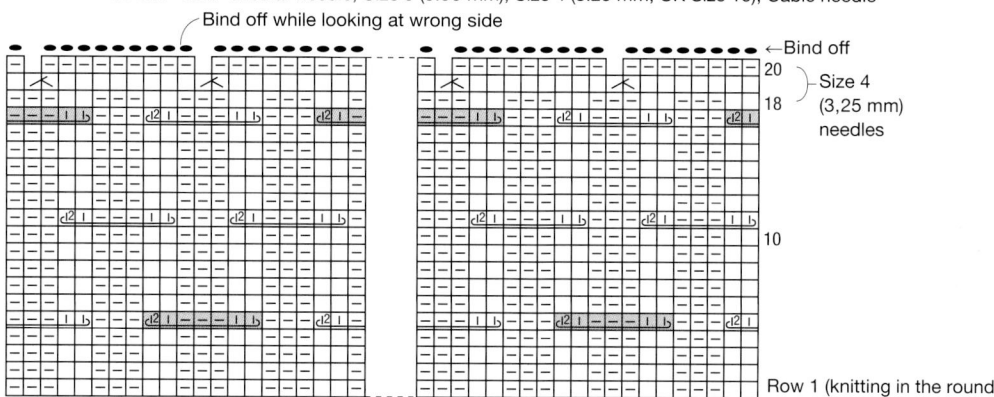

[Pattern D Chart: Neckline Center]

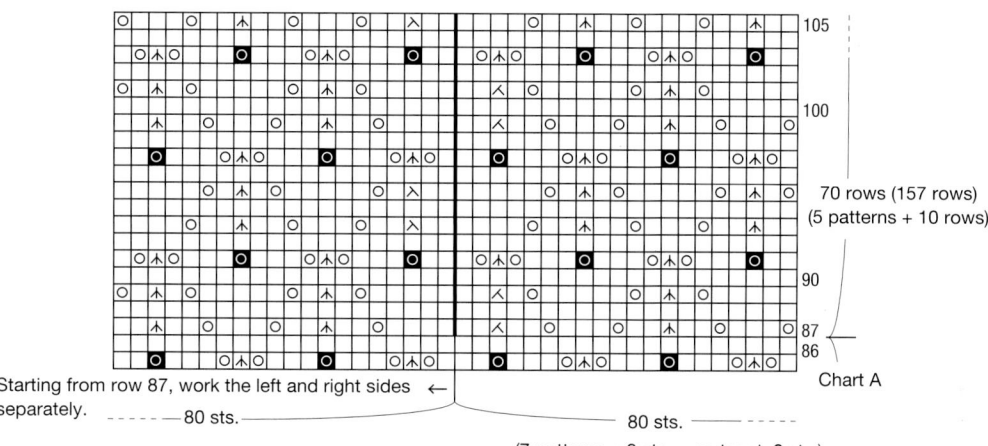

- □ = ① Knit
- ⊟ Purl
- ⼈ Slip, knit, pass
- ⼊ Knit 2 together
- ○ Yarn over
- ⼈ Slip 2, knit 1, pass 2 slipped stitches over
- ⼊ Purl 2 together (purl side)

● Knitting bobble stitch for 1 row

Pull through with crochet hook
Chain 1
Slip 6, knit 1, pass slipped stitches over
= ○○○ ○○○ ○○○
Slip stitch into the increase
Increases

Smocking stitch: wrap twice

Smocking stitch: wrap twice + embroidery

Work 5 French knots (wrap twice) using British Fine #086 on smocking stitch.

Page 98 Tea Cozy and Coaster

Finished Dimensions: Tea Cozy Height 17 cm - 6¾", Circumference 41 cm - 16⅛", Mat: 13 cm - 5⅛" x 14 cm - 5½"

▶ **Tools and Materials**

Yarn

• **Tea Cozy**

Jamieson's Spindrift
- #104 Natural White 10g / 0.14 oz.
- #259 Leprechaun 5g / 0.15 oz.
- #665 Bluebell 6g / 0.2 oz.
- #655 China Blue 6g / 0.2 oz.
- #880 Coffee 4g / 0.14 oz.
- #188 Sherbet 3g / 0.1 oz.

• **Coaster**

Jamieson's Spindrift
- #104 Natural White 3g / 0.1 oz.
- #259 Leprechaun 4g / 0.14 oz.
- #665 Bluebell 1g / 0.03 oz.
- #880 Coffee 1g / 0.03 oz.
- #188 Sherbet 2g / 0.07 oz.

Other Materials
- 15 x 15 cm - 5⅞" x 5⅞" square felt
- 35 mm - 1⅜" diameter pompom maker

Needles
- Straight Needles: Size 5 (3.50 mm)
- 40 cm - 15¾" long circular needle Size 5 (3.50 mm)
- Crochet Hook: Size 3/0 (2.25 mm, UK Size 13)

▶ **Gauge**

26 sts. 30 rows

* Refer to page 91 for the chart.

▶ **Knitting and Assembly Instructions**

• **Tea Cozy**

① Cast on the required number of stitches and knit two separate pieces according to the chart up to row 24. From row 25, overlap the first and last 3 stitches of both pieces and continue knitting according to the pattern. Pass the yarn through the remaining 10 stitches and pull tight to gather stitches. Weave in the yarn tail and steam block.

② Seam the 8 rows of the hem on both sides using the ladder stitch from the right side. At row 5, fold the edges inwards and blind stitch to secure.

③ Make a pompom and sew it to the top, then add embroidery.

④ Weave in all remaining yarn ends. Wet block and let dry completely.

• **Coaster**

① Cast on required number of stitches and knit according to the charts. Then, bind off.

② Cut a piece of felt to match the size of the knitted fabric. Place the felt behind the knitting and sew them together using a backstitch.

③ Work the blanket stitch around the edges.

④ Wet block and let dry.

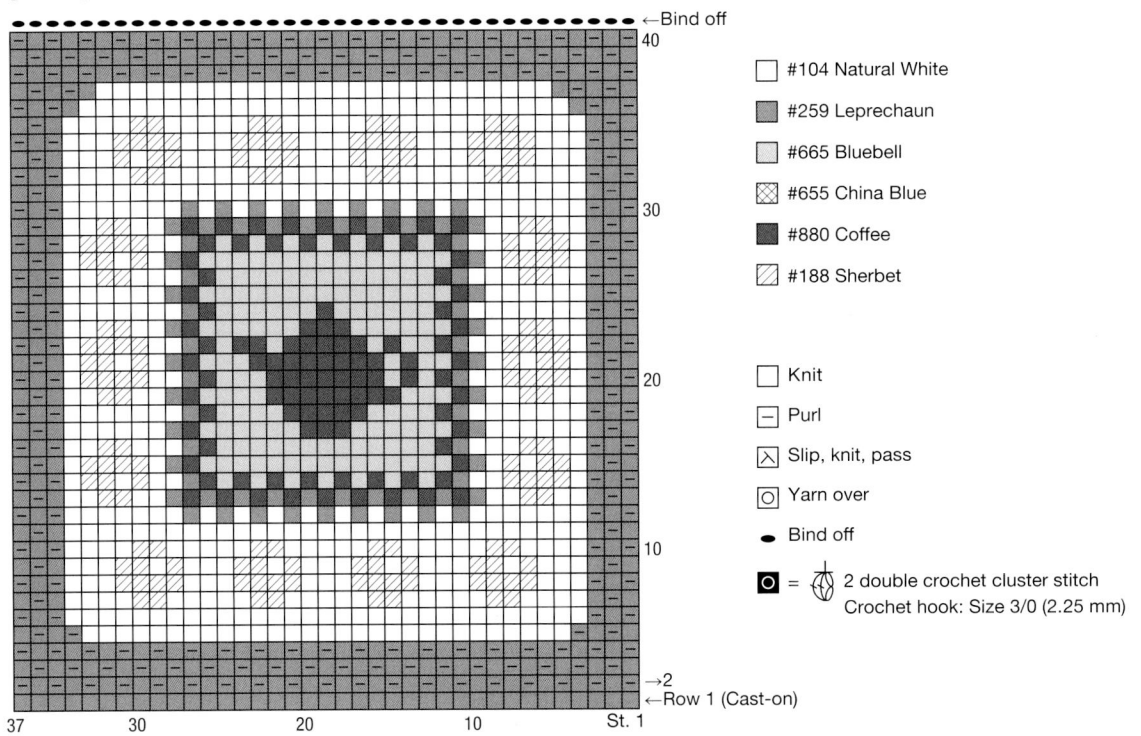

[Chart] Coaster

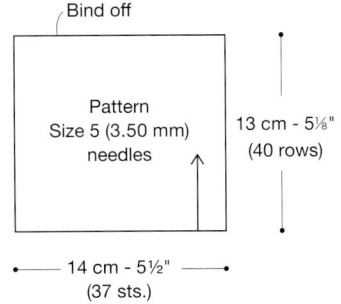

[Pattern Draft]

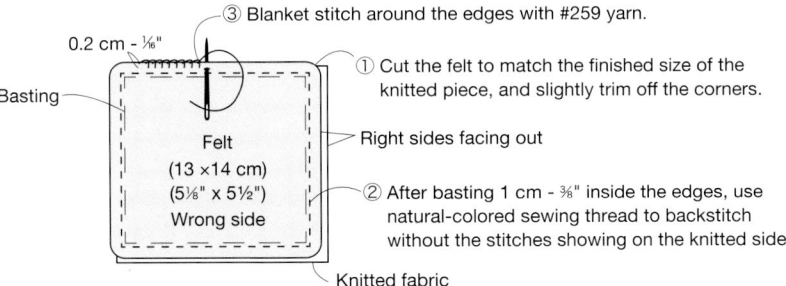

[Finishing]

[Chart] Tea Cozy

[Pattern Draft]

[Knitting · Finishing]

On row 25, begin working in the round by overlapping 3 stitches from the beginning and end of pieces A1 and A2.

This will result in a total of 90 stitches (48 stitches x 2 - 3 stitches x 2).

Continue knitting Pattern B in the round.

Slip stitch along 8 rows of the side seams. At Row 5, fold the bottom edge inward and secure it with a blind stitch using green yarn.

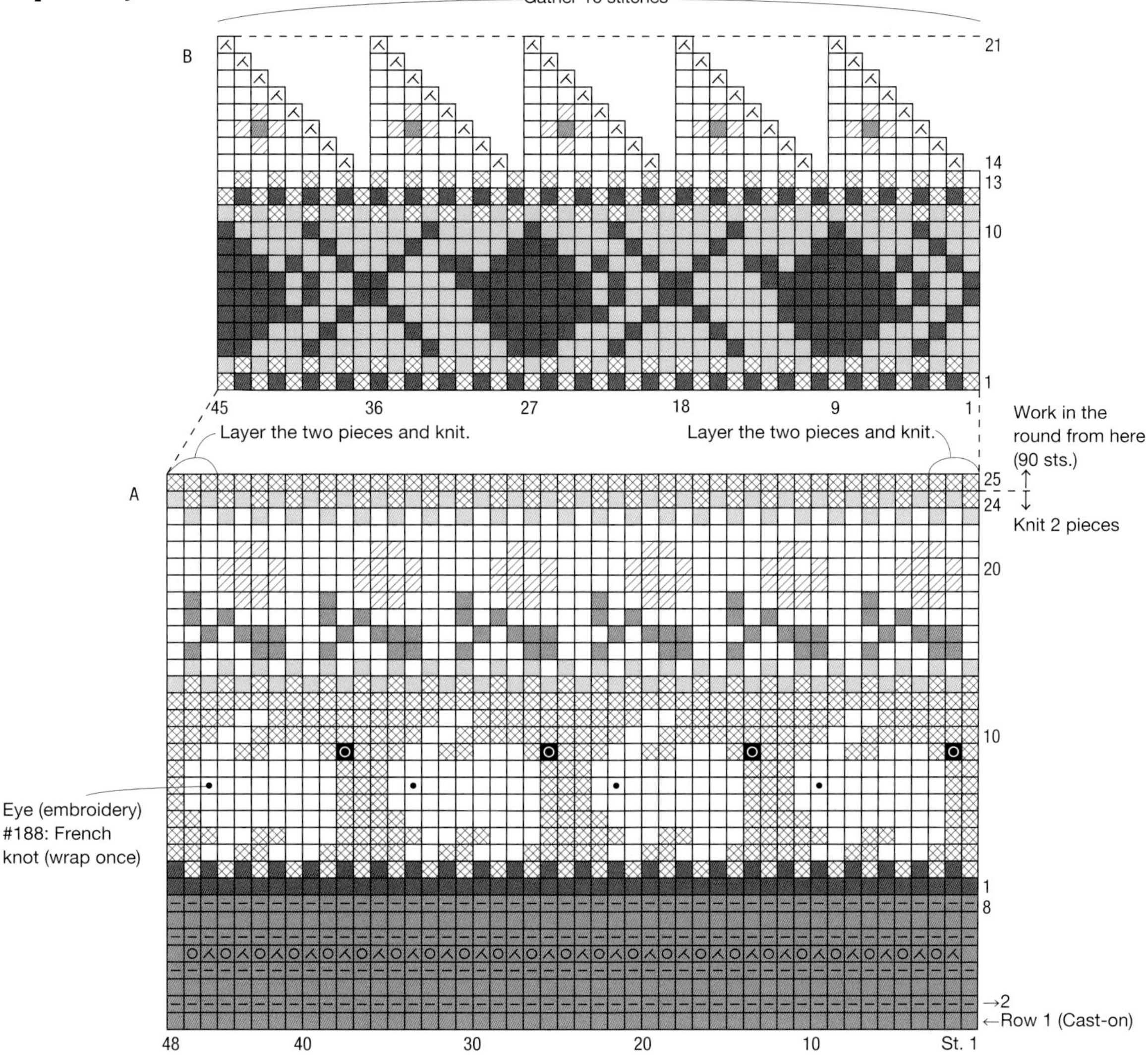

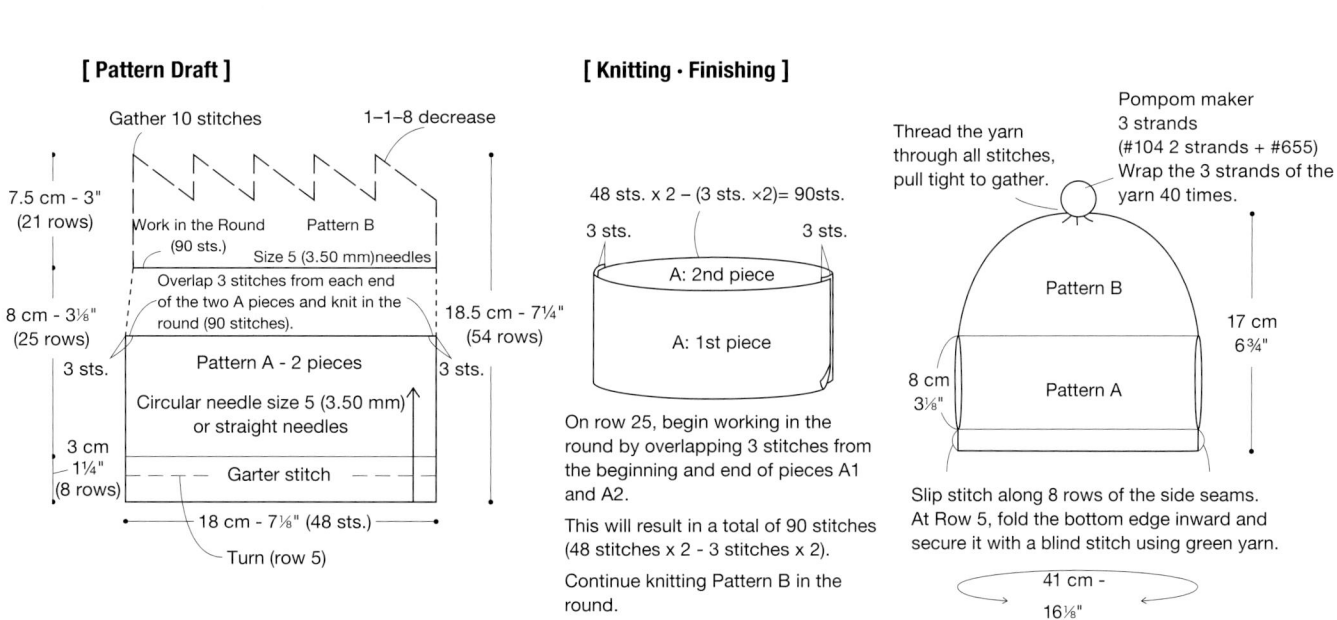

Page 99 Wrist Warmer

Finished Dimensions: Wrist circumference 21.5 cm - 8½" x Length 10 cm - 4"

▶ **Tools and Materials**

Yarn

- **Mushrooms**

Jamieson's Spindrift

#103 Sholmit 10g / 0.3 oz.

#500 Scarlet 4g / 0.1 oz.

#104 Natural White 4g / 0.1 oz.

- **Violets**

Jamieson's Spindrift

#105 Eesit 5g / 0.17 oz.

#788 Leaf 1g / 0.03 oz.

#410 Cornfield 2g / 0.07 oz.

#720 Dewdrop 3g / 0.1 oz.

#665 Bluebell 1g / 0.03 oz.

#616 Anemone 2g / 0.07 oz.

#600 Violet 1g / 0.03 oz.

Needles

Mini-circular needles Size 3 (3.00 mm)

▶ Gauge

32 sts. 36 rows

* For the charts, see page 17 for the Mushrooms and page 87 for the Violets.

▶ Knitting and Assembly Instructions

① Cast on the required number of stitches and knit according to the charts. Weave in the yarn tails and steam block.

② Wet block and let dry.

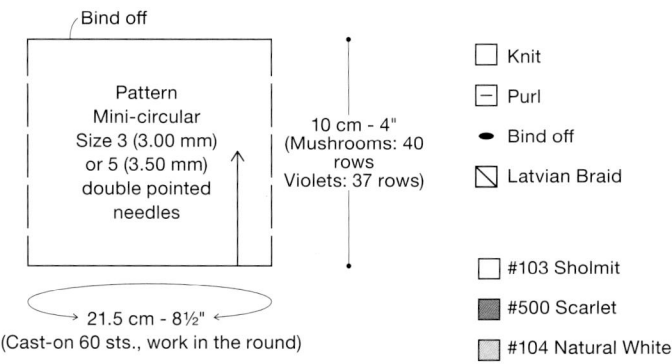

[Pattern Draft] Main body

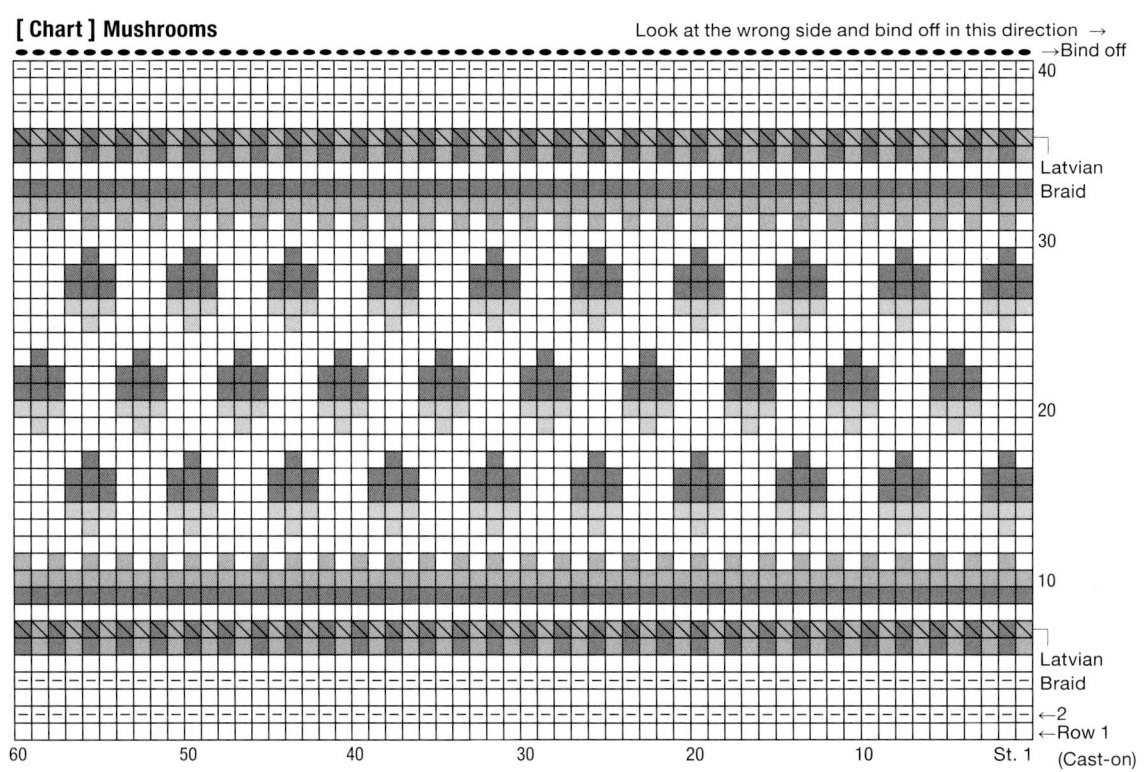

Latvian Braid

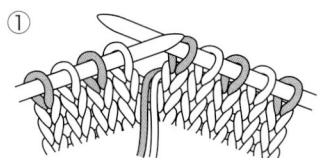

For the base of your braid, knit a row alternating two colors, and at the end of the row, bring both yarns to front.

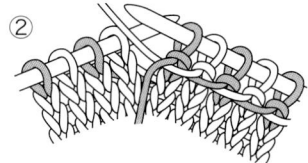

In the next row (Latvian braid), bring the yarn for the next color up from under the previous stitch, and purl.

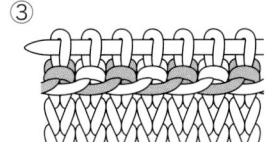

[Chart]
Violets

- ☐ #105 Eesit
- ■ #788 Leaf
- ■ #665 Bluebell
- ☐ #720 Dewdrop
- ☐ #410 Cornfield
- ▨ #616 Anemone
- ▩ #600 Violet

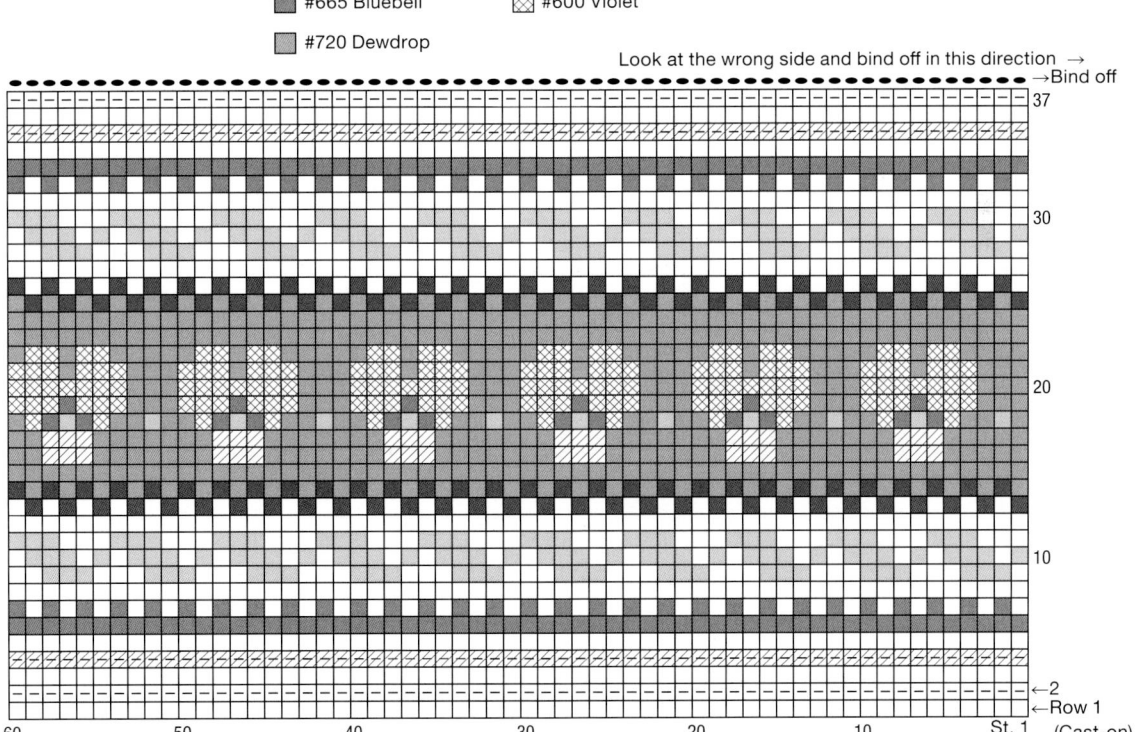

Page 114 Long Hand Warmer

Finished Dimensions: Wrist circumference 20 cm - 7⅞" x Length 24.5 cm - 9⅝"

▶ Tools and Materials

Yarn
ROWAN Kidsilk Haze
#712 Ultra 16g / 0.5 oz.

* Refer to page 101 for the chart.

Needles
Mini-circular needle Size 3 (3.00 mm)
Crochet Hook: Size 3/0
(2.25 mm, UK Size 13)

▶ Gauge
30 sts. 36 rows

▶ Knitting and Assembly Instructions

① Cast on the required number of stitches and knit according to the charts. Bind off, weave in the yarn tails, and steam block.

[Pattern Draft] Main body: 2 pieces

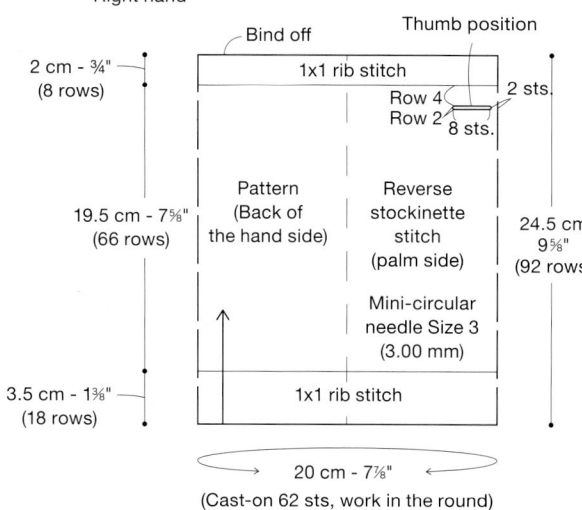

* If the bind-off is too loose, it may spread out, so it's better to bind off a bit tighter.

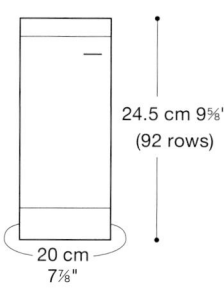

- □ Knit
- ⊟ Purl
- ⊠ Slip, knit, pass
- ⊠ Knit 2 together
- Backwards loop increase
- ○ Yarn over
- • Bind off
- ● Knit bobble stitch for 1 row
  Pull through with crochet hook

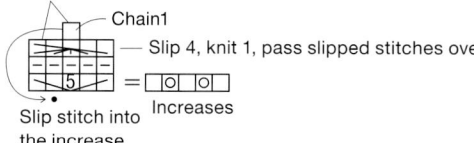

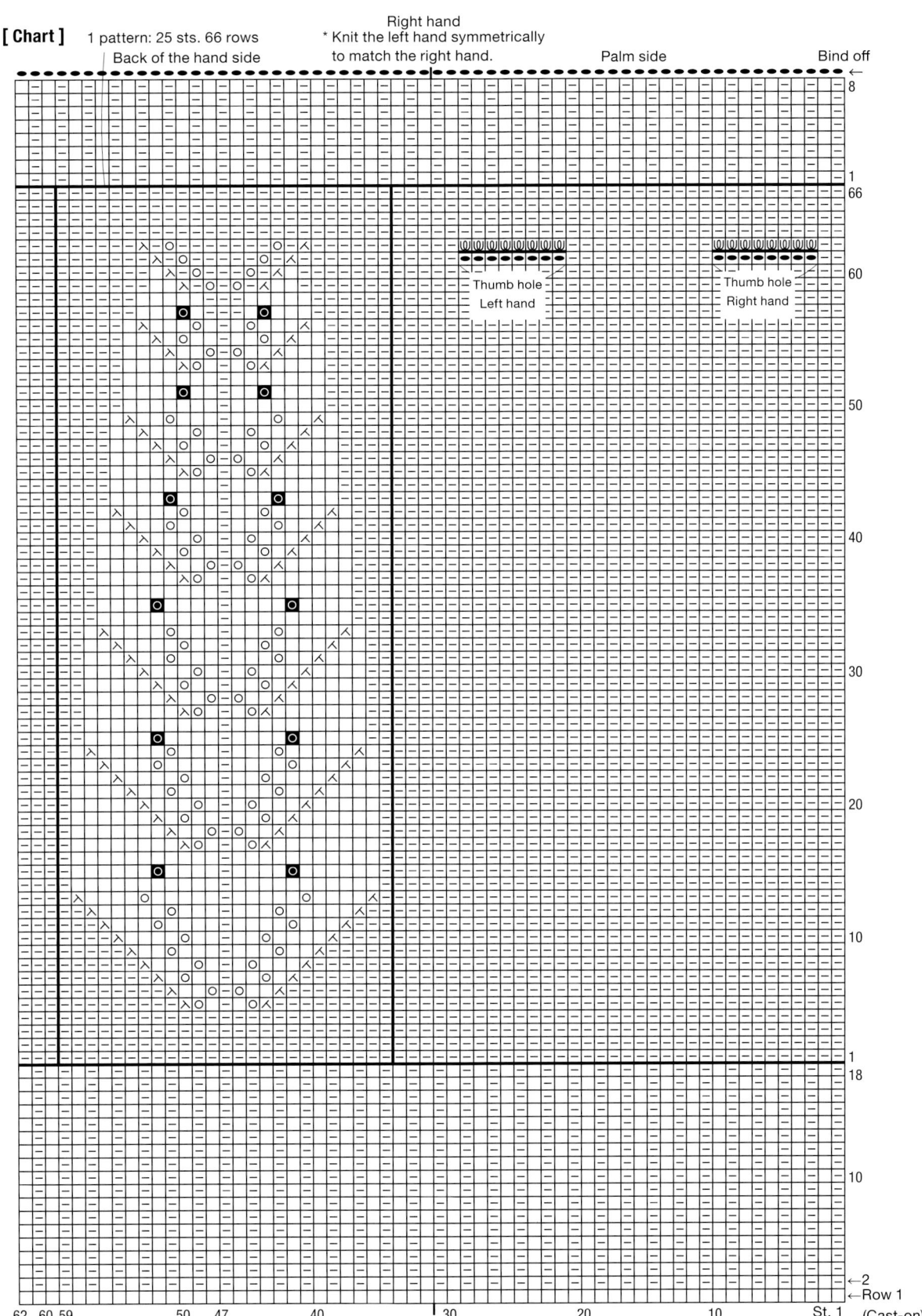

Page 118 Brooches

Finished Dimensions: Poppy diameter 7.5 cm - 3", Blue flower 5 x 6 cm - 2" x 2⅜", Pansy diameter 5.2 cm - 2".

▶ Tools and Materials

Yarn

• Poppy
Jamieson's Spindrift
#180 Mist 2g / 0.07 oz.
#259 Leprechaun 1g / 0.03 oz.
#500 Scarlet 1g / 0.03 oz.
#585 Plum 1g / 0.03 oz.
#999 Black 1g / 0.03 oz.
#780 Lime 1g / 0.03 oz.

• Blue Flower
Puppy British Fine
#034 Dark Green 1g / 0.03 oz.
#092 Turquoise as needed
#035 Mustard as needed
#086 Neon Yellow as needed

• Pansy
Jamieson's Spindrift
#769 Willow 1g / 0.03 oz.
#390 Daffodil as needed
#104 Natural White as needed
#780 Lime as needed
#600 Violet as needed
#410 Cornfield as needed

* For the charts, refer to page 49 for the Poppy, page 55 for the blue flower, and page 53 for the violet.

Other Materials (shared)
One button for each:
Diameter 7 cm - 2.8",
Oval 4.5 cm - ¾" x 6 cm - 2⅜",
Diameter 5 cm - 2" each
10 x 10 cm - 4" x 4" quilt batting
10 x 10 cm - 4" x 4" thick felt
10 x 10 cm - 4" x 4" thick paper (cardstock)
One 3.5 cm - 1⅜" long brooch pin

Needles
Straight Needles:
Size 2 (2.50 mm) – Poppy, Pansy.
Size 4 (3.25 mm, UK Size 10) – Blue Flower

▶ Gauge

32 sts. 34 rows

▶ Knitting and Assembly Instructions

① Cast on the required number of stitches and knit according to the charts. Bind off, weave in the yarn ends, and steam block.
② Embroider, then wet block the poppy and pansy and let them dry.
③ Layer the knitted fabric with quilt batting, baste stitch around the edges, pull tight to fit the button, and tie a knot at the thread end.
④ Attach the brooch pin to the felt.
⑤ Glue the thick paper to the back, layer the felt, and glue it down. Blind stitch the edges of the felt onto the knitted fabric.

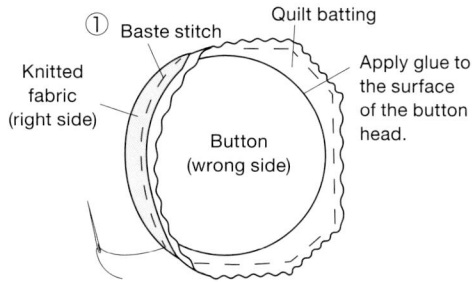

Layer the knitted fabric with the quilt batting and baste stitch around the edges.
Place it over the button head, pull the basting stitch tight to fit the knitted fabric around the button, and tie a knot to secure.

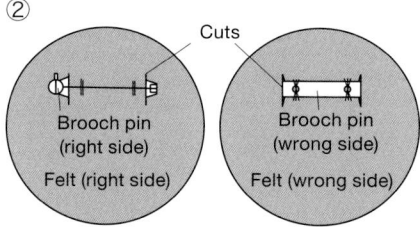

Make small cuts in the felt, pass the brooch pin through, and sew it in place.

* Cut the quilt batting 1.5 cm - ⅝" larger than the button all around, the thick paper two sizes smaller, and the felt one size smaller.

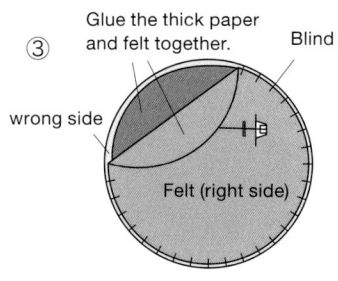

Glue the thick paper to the back of piece 1, then glue the felt on top, ensuring it is positioned according to the design.
Blind stitch the edges of the felt onto the knitted fabric.

Pansy

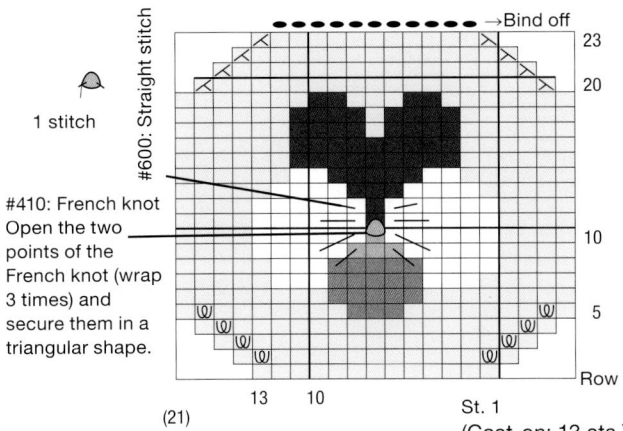

1 stitch

#600: Straight stitch

#410: French knot
Open the two points of the French knot (wrap 3 times) and secure them in a triangular shape.

→Bind off

Row 1
St. 1
(Cast-on: 13 sts.)

- ☐ #769 Willow
- ▨ #390 Daffodil
- ☐ #104 Natural White
- ▨ #780 Lime
- ■ #600 Violet
- —
- ◉ #410 Cornfield

Blue Flower

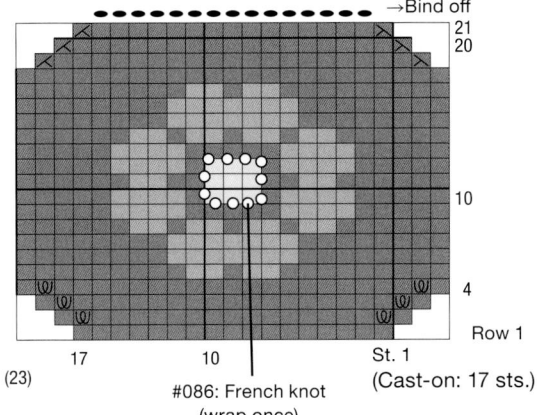

→Bind off

#086: French knot (wrap once)

Row 1
St. 1
(Cast-on: 17 sts.)

- ▨ #034 Dark Green
- ▨ #092 Turquoise
- ☐ #035 Mustard
- ☐ #086 Neon Yellow

- ☐ Knit
- ⍵ Backwards loop increase
- ⊠ Slip, knit, pass
- ⊠ Knit 2 together
- ● Bind off

Poppy

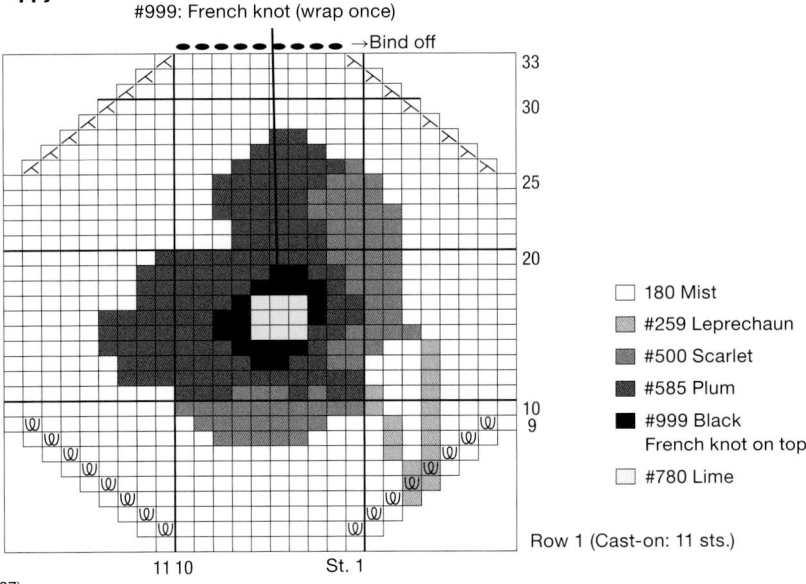

#999: French knot (wrap once)

→Bind off

Row 1 (Cast-on: 11 sts.)

- ☐ 180 Mist
- ▨ #259 Leprechaun
- ▨ #500 Scarlet
- ▨ #585 Plum
- ■ #999 Black
  French knot on top
- ☐ #780 Lime

Page 118 Coaster

Finished Dimensions: 10.5 x 10.5 cm - 4⅛" x 4⅛"

▶ **Tools and Materials**

Yarn
Jamieson's Spindrift
#268 Dog Rose 3g / 0.1 oz.
#599 Zodiac as needed
#780 Lime 1g / 0.03 oz.
#788 Leaf 1g / 0.03 oz.
#578 Rust 1g / 0.03 oz.

* Refer to page 91 for the chart.

Other Materials (shared)
15 x 15 cm - 5 ⅞" x 5 ⅞" gray thick felt
No. 25 embroidery floss in white and black, as needed

Needles
Straight Needles:
Size 4 (3.25 mm, UK Size 10)

▶ **Gauge**
27 sts. 30 rows

▶ **Knitting and Assembly Instructions**

① Cast on the required number of stitches and knit according to the charts. Bind off on the wrong side, weave in the yarn ends, and steam block.
② Embroider the acorn cap and the squirrel's tail.
③ Wet block and lightly felt by hand, then allow to dry. Embroider the squirrel's eyes.
④ Align the knitted fabric and felt with the right sides facing out, then sew around the edges using a blanket stitch.

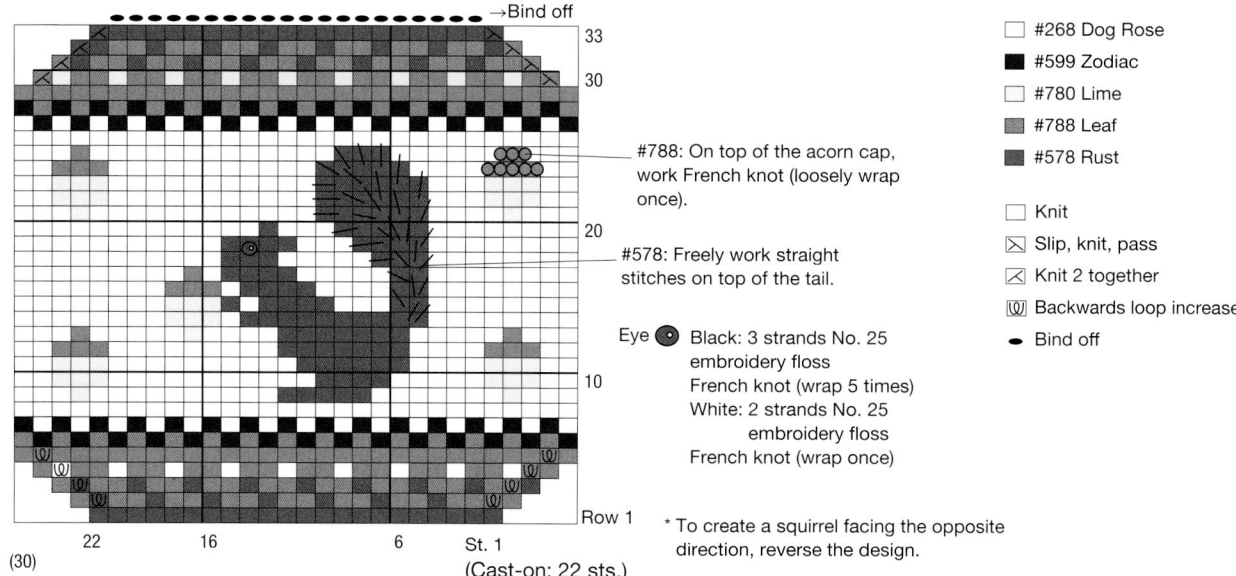

#788: On top of the acorn cap, work French knot (loosely wrap once).

#578: Freely work straight stitches on top of the tail.

Eye
Black: 3 strands No. 25 embroidery floss French knot (wrap 5 times)
White: 2 strands No. 25 embroidery floss French knot (wrap once)

* To create a squirrel facing the opposite direction, reverse the design.

- ☐ #268 Dog Rose
- ■ #599 Zodiac
- ☐ #780 Lime
- ▨ #788 Leaf
- ▨ #578 Rust

- ☐ Knit
- ⊠ Slip, knit, pass
- ⊠ Knit 2 together
- Ⓤ Backwards loop increase
- ● Bind off

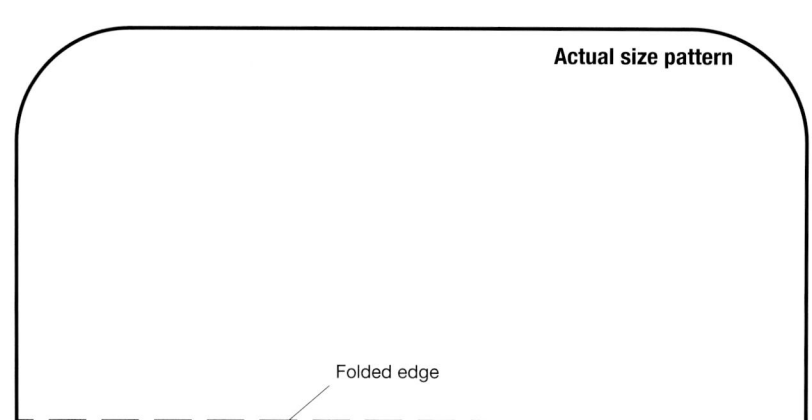

Actual size pattern

Folded edge

[Finishing]

Knitted fabric (wrong side)
0.3 cm - ⅛"
Blanket stitch (yarn)
Felt (right side)

Align the knitted fabric and felt right sides facing out and sew around the edges with a blanket stitch.

Page 119 Pin Cushion

Finished Dimensions: Rosebud diameter 8 cm - 3⅛", Small Roses diameter 8 cm - 3⅛"

▶ **Tools and Materials**

Yarn

• **Rosebud**
Puppy British Fine
#017 Navy Blue 3g / 0.1 oz.
#080 Yellow Green 1g / 0.03 oz.
#006 Red 1g / 0.03 oz.

• **Small Roses**
Puppy British Fine
#021 Light Beige 3g / 0.1 oz.
#068 Rose Pink 1g / 0.03 oz.
#080 Yellow Green 1g / 0.03 oz.
#031 Pink as needed

* For the chart, see page 51 for the Rosebud and page 11 for the Small Roses.

Other Materials (shared)
15 x 15 cm - 5⅞" x 5⅞" back fabric
8 x 8 cm - 3⅛" × 3⅛" felt
Wool: 10 g / 0.3 oz.
One preferred container:
Diameter 8 ~ 10 cm - 3⅛" ~ 4"

Needles
Straight Needles:
Size 4 (3.25 mm, UK Size 10)

▶ **Gauge**
Rosebud: 26 sts. 40 rows
Small Roses: 28 sts. 32 rows

▶ **Knitting and Assembly Instructions**

① Cast on the required number of stitches and knit according to the charts. Bind off, weave in the yarn ends, and steam block.

② Cut the felt into a circle with a diameter of 8 cm - 3⅛", and wet block it along with the knitted fabric. Then, let dry.

③ Align the knitted fabric and the backing fabric with the right sides together. Sew around the edges and turn right side out through the opening.

④ Place the felt and wool inside, then baste stitch the opening closed and pull tight.

⑤ Place the finished piece into your preferred container.

☐ #017 Dark Navy
▨ #081 Yellow Green
■ #006 Red

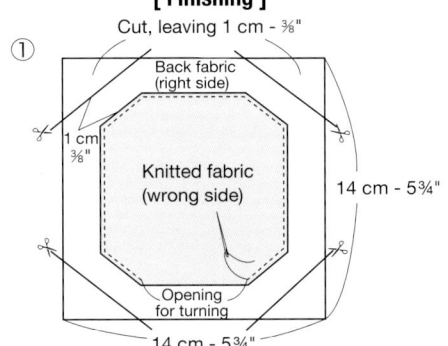

Align the knitted fabric and the backing fabric with the right sides together, leaving an opening, and sew around the edges.

Layer the felt on the back of the knitted fabric.

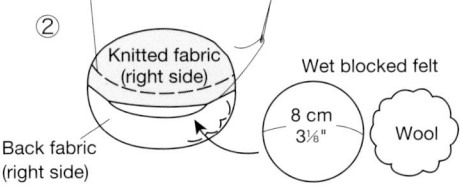

Turn right side out through the opening, place the felt on the back of the knitted fabric, and pack the wool into a round shape inside.

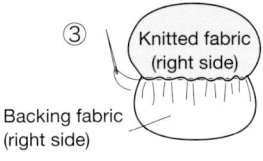

Using the reserved needle and thread, fold in the seam allowance at the opening, baste stitch it, and gather it to fit the size of the container, then tie a knot to secure.

☐ Knit
ω Backwards loop increase
⊠ Slip, knit, pass
⊠ Knit 2 together
− Purl
● Bind off

☐ #021 Light Beige
■ #068 Rose Pink
▨ #080 Yellow Green
▨ #031 Pink

Rosebud

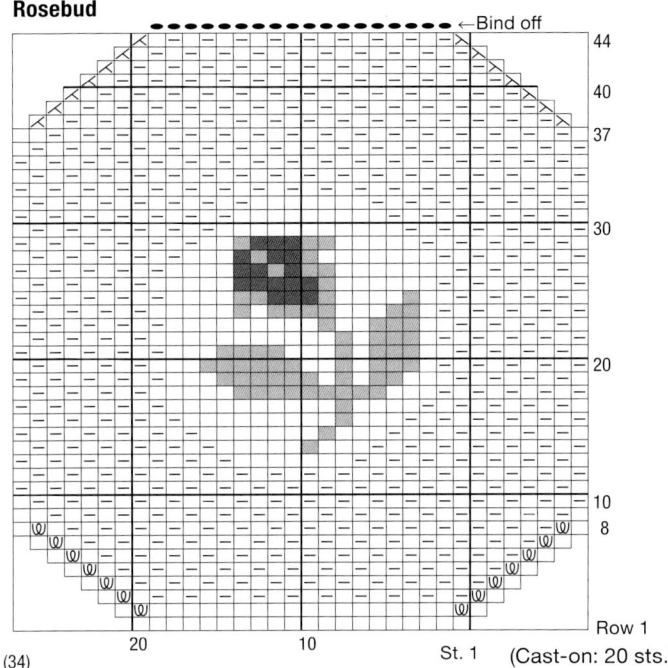

Small Roses

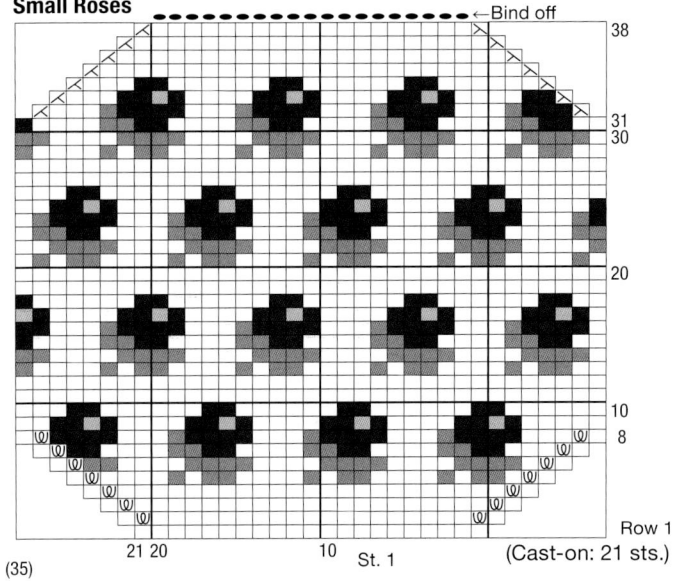

Page 119 Mini Frames

Finished Dimensions: Mimosa and Wild Rose inner diameter of 8.7 x 6.6 cm - 3⅜" x 2⅝", and Daisy inner diameter of 7.7 cm - 3"

▶ Tools and Materials

Yarn

• **Mimosa**
Jamieson's Spindrift
#764 Cloud 3g / 0.1 oz.
#772 Verdigris 1g / 0.03 oz.
#400 Mimosa 1g / 0.03 oz.
#616 Anemone 1g / 0.03 oz.

• **Pink Wild Rose**
Jamieson's Spindrift
#104 Natural White 3g / 0.1 oz.
#788 Leaf 1g / 0.03 oz.
#390 Daffodil as needed
#780 Lime as needed

• **Daisy**
Puppy British Fine
#055 Green 3g / 0.1 oz.
#080 Yellow Green as needed
#001 White as needed
#006 Red as needed
#086 Neon Yellow as needed

* Refer to the charts for the Mimosa on page 57, the Wild Rose on page 97, and the Daisy on page 53.

Other Materials (shared)
10 x 10 cm - 4" x 4" thick felt
15 x 15 cm - 5⅞" x 5⅞" fabric
Mini embroidery hoop:
oval with an inner diameter of
8.7 x 6.6 cm - 3⅜" x 2⅝" or
a round inner diameter of 7.7 cm - 3"

Needles
Straight Needles:
Size 2 (2.50 mm)
Crochet Hook:
Size 2/0 (2.00 mm, UK Size 14)

▶ Gauge
32 sts. 34 rows

▶ Knitting and Assembly Instructions

① Cast on the required number of stitches and knit according to the charts. Bind off, weave in the yarn ends, and steam block.
② Embroider on the wild rose. Wet block the mimosa and wild rose and let them dry.
③ Layer the knitted fabric and the backing fabric and embroider on the daisy.
④ Gather the edge of the knitted fabric with a running stitch, pulling it tight to fit the inner frame. Tie a knot at the thread end to hold everything in place.
⑤ Fit the outer frame and layer felt on the back, securing it with a blind stitch.

[Finishing]

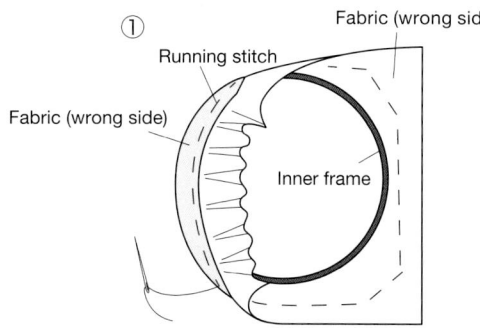

Layer the knitted fabric and the backing fabric together, then sew around the edge with a running stitch.
Align the inner frame while checking the position of the pattern, gather the running stitch tightly, and tie a knot. Trim off any excess fabric.

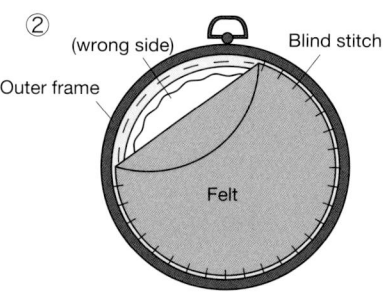

Fit the outer frame and layer the felt on the back, then sew it in place with a blind stitch.

- □ #104 Natural White
- ■ #788 Leaf
- ■ #188 Sherbet
- ■ #390 Daffodil
- ■ #780 Lime

Wild Rose

- □ #764 Cloud
- ■ #772 Verdigris
- ◙ #400 Mimosa
- ■ #616 Anemone

◙ = 2 half double crochet cluster stitch
Crochet hook: Size 2/0 (2.00 mm)

Mimosa

Daisy

[How to Embroider Daisy]

Work the blanket stitch around the eyelet edges, and then add another blanket stitch in red along the outer edge.
Make French knot in the center.
Before embroidering, layer the fabric and knitted piece together.

- □ #055 Green
- ■ #080 Yellow Green
- ● #006 Red
- — #001 White
- ○ #086 Neon Yellow

- □ Knit
- Backwards loop increase
- Slip, knit, pass
- Knit 2 together
- Yarn over
- • Bind off

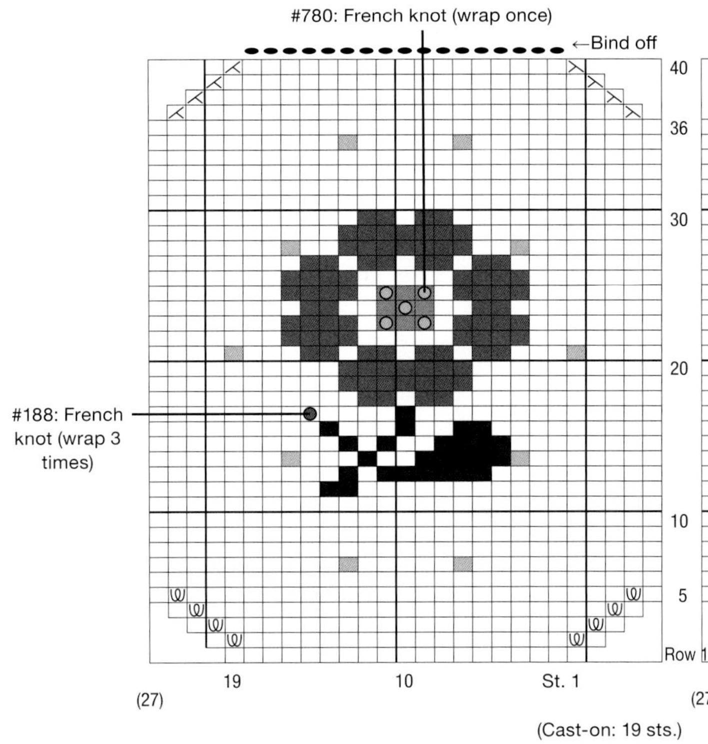

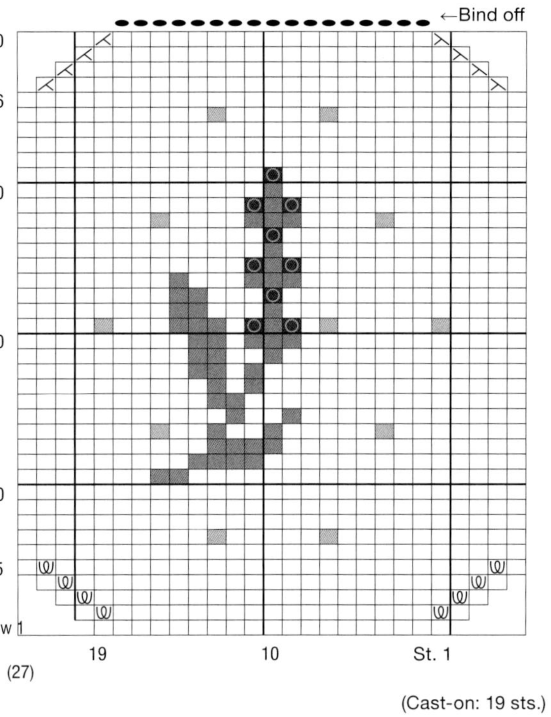

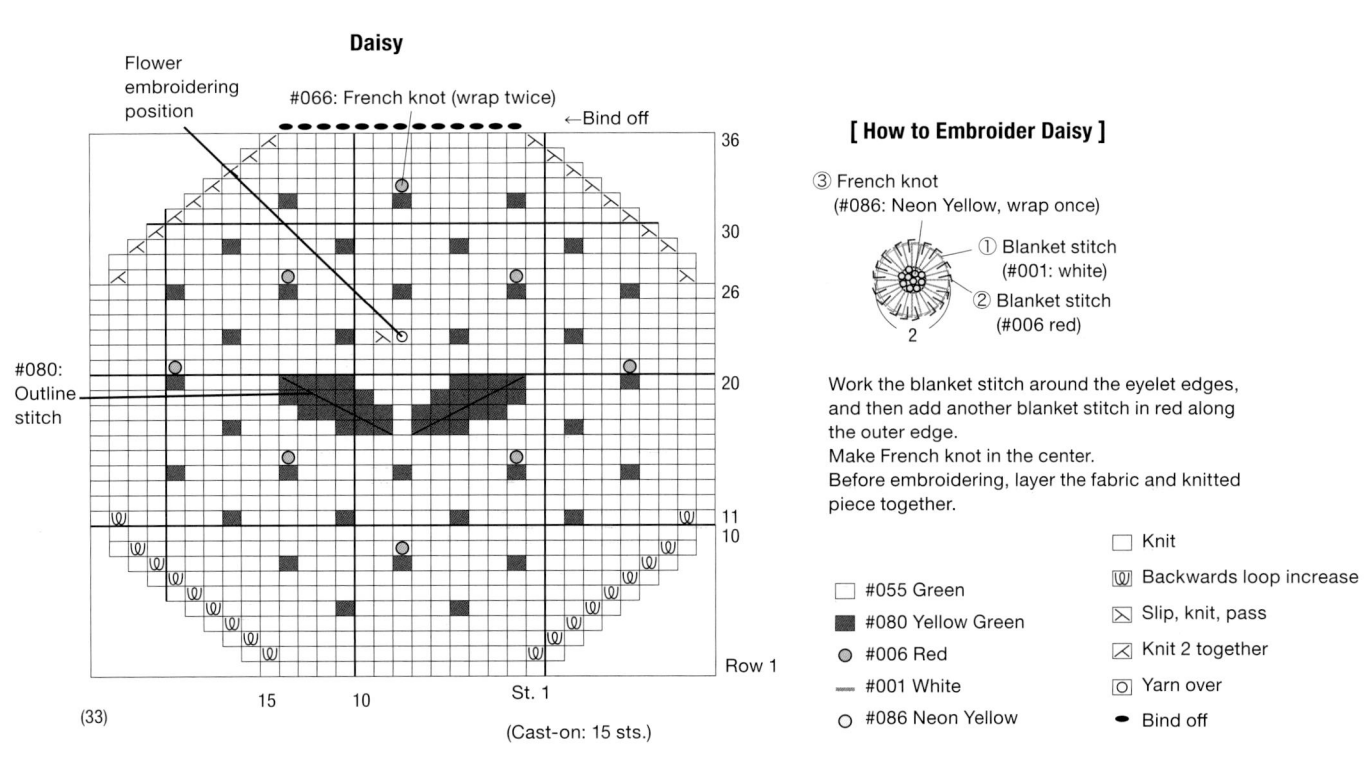

Page 115 Lily-of-the-Valley Hooded Shawl

Finished Dimensions: 51 x 128 cm - 20" x 50⅜"

▶ Tools and Materials

Yarn

ROWAN Kidsilk Haze

#634 Cream 200g / 7 oz.

* For the chart, see page 109.

Needles

Straight Needles
Size 3 (3.00 mm, UK Size 11)

80 cm - 31½" circular needle,
Size 3 (3.00 mm, UK Size 11)

Crochet Hook: Size 2/0
(2.00 mm, UK Size 14)

▶ Gauge

26 sts. 32 rows

▶ Knitting and Assembly Instructions

① From the cast on stitches, knit the left side of the main body according to the chart up to Row 246 and set it aside. Knit the right side of the main body in the same way, making fifteen backwards loop increases at the end of Row 247, and then continue knitting with the left side.

② Knit the hood section according to the chart for 120 rows. From Row 121, divide into left, center, and right sections, and seam them together with the right side facing. Steam block to shape.

③ Knit the border. Steam block to shape.

[Pattern Draft]

Main body: 1 piece

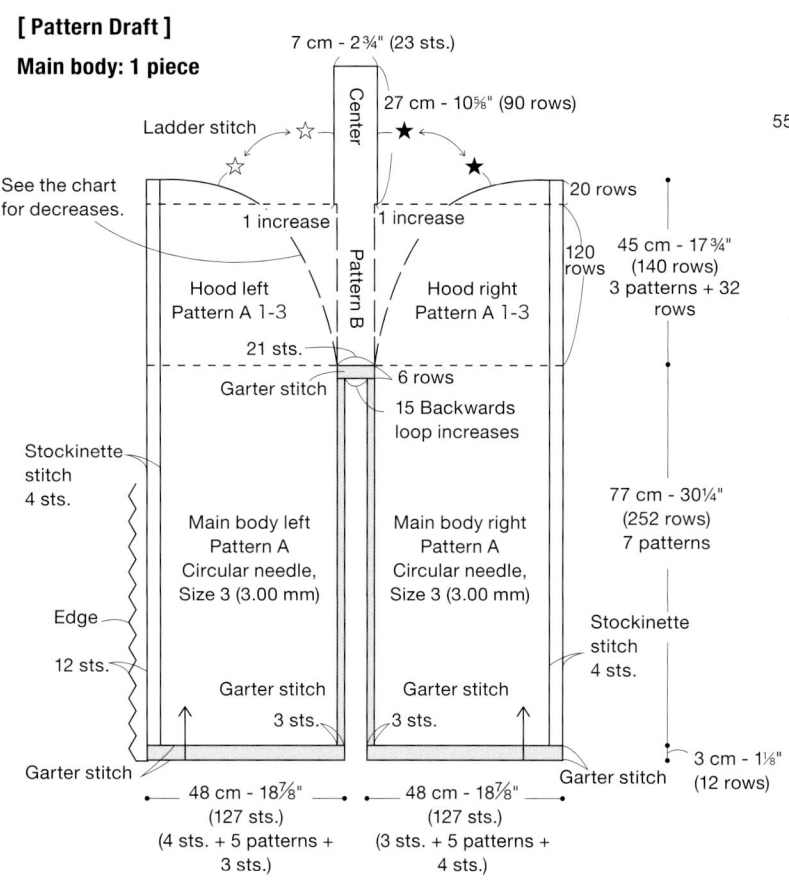

[Diagram]

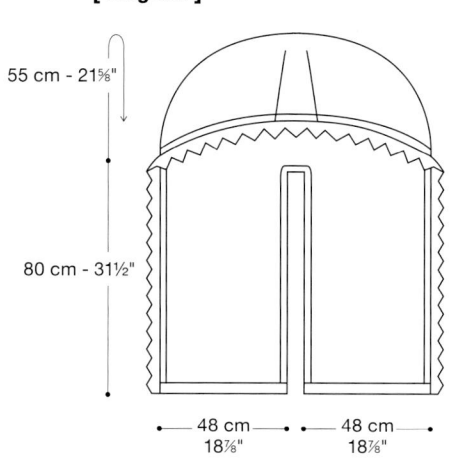

[How to Knit Edge]

Straight needles Size 3 (3.00 mm)

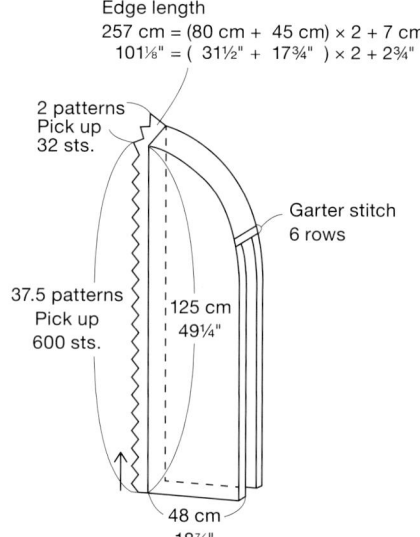

* Pick up stitches from 3 rows of the main body, skipping every 4th row.

Knit the left side of the main body up to Row 246 and place the stitches on hold. Repeat for the right side up to Row 246. At the end of Row 247, create fifteen backward loop increases, then continue knitting with the held stitches from the left side.

Work the increase section in garter stitch for 6 rows.

When knitting the main body, it may be helpful to place stitch markers every four stockinette stitches, every twenty-four pattern stitches, and every three garter stitches.

For the hood section, use pattern chart B to knit the twenty-one stitches that form the central part, consisting of three garter stitches from both the left and right sides of the main body, plus the fifteen increased stitches. Knit 120 rows as shown in the chart. From Row 121, divide into the left, center, and right sections of the hood. When finished, seam the edges together with the right side facing.

For the edge, cast on eight stitches and attach it to the main body as you knit.

[Pattern Chart]

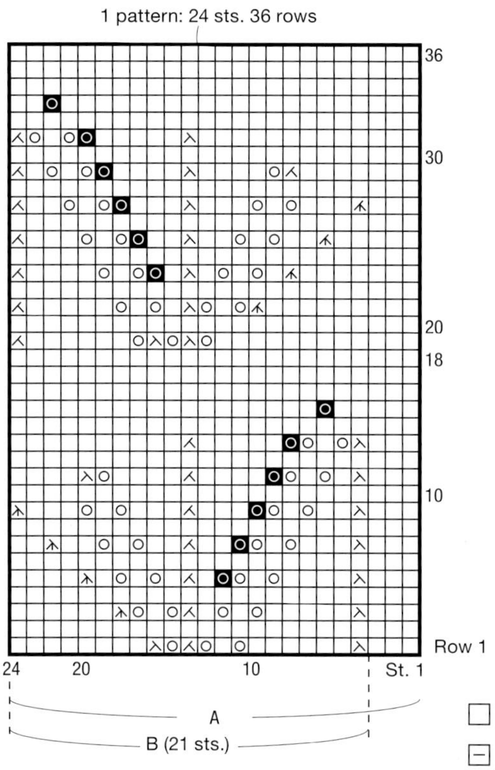

1 pattern: 24 sts. 36 rows
36
30
20
18
10
Row 1
24
20
10
St. 1
A
B (21 sts.)

[Pattern B Chart: Center]

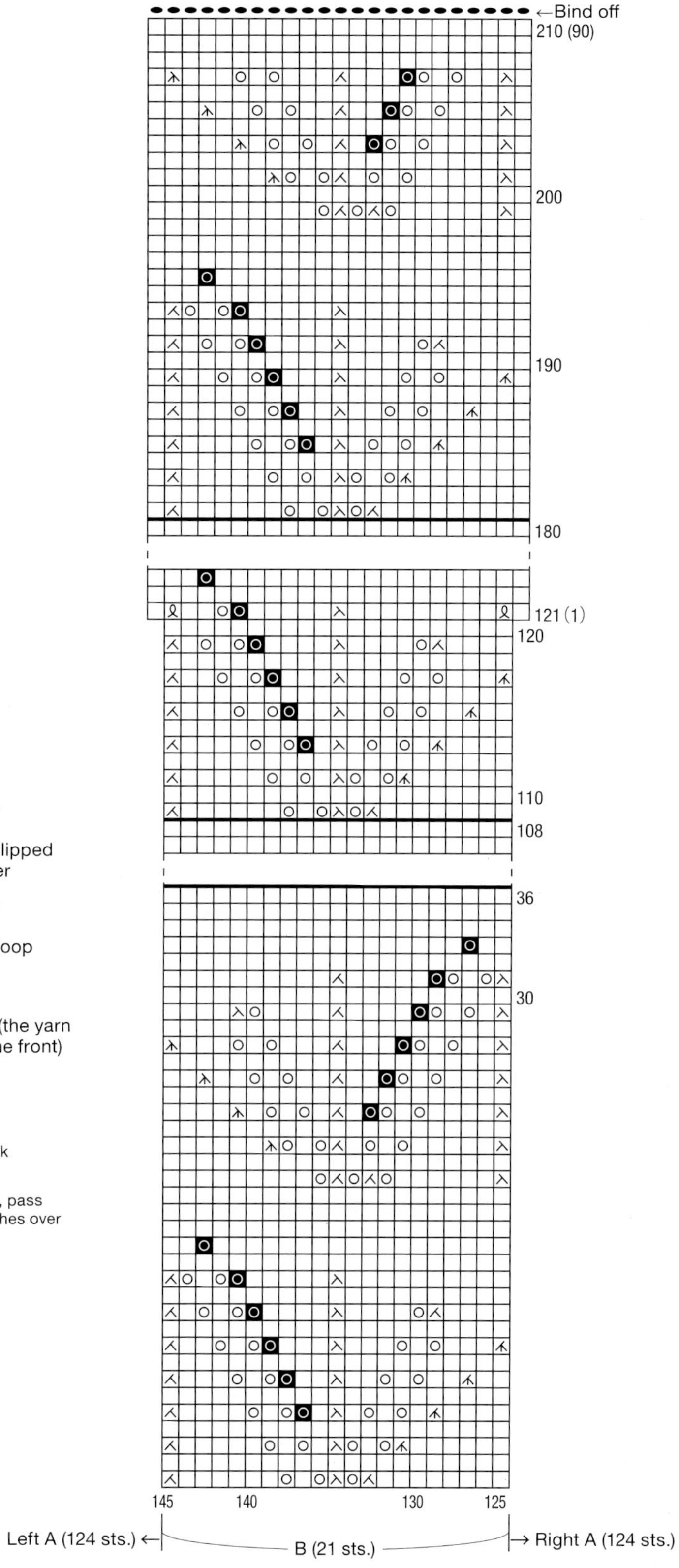

←Bind off
210 (90)
200
190
180
121 (1)
120
110
108
36
30
145
140
130
125
Left A (124 sts.)
B (21 sts.)
Right A (124 sts.)

- Knit
- Purl
- Slip, knit, pass
- Knit 2 together
- Slip, slip, knit slipped stiches together
- Knit 3 together
- Through back loop
- Yarn over
- Floating stitch (the yarn crosses over the front)
- Bind off

Knit bobble stitch for 1 row

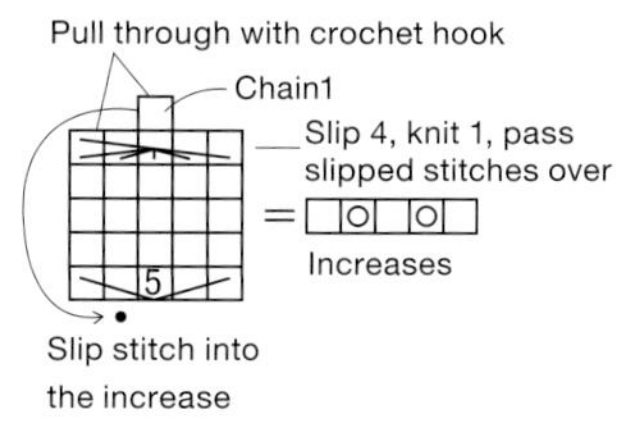

Pull through with crochet hook
Chain1
Slip 4, knit 1, pass slipped stitches over
Increases
5
Slip stitch into the increase

[How to Knit the Edge]

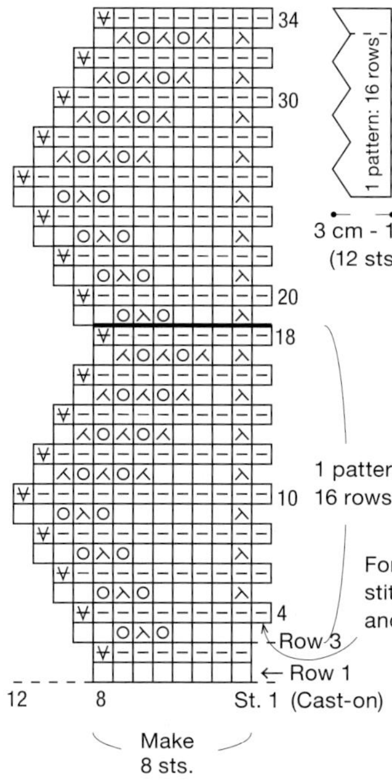

34
30
20
18
10
4
Row 3
Row 1
12
8
St. 1 (Cast-on)
Make 8 sts.
1 pattern: 16 rows

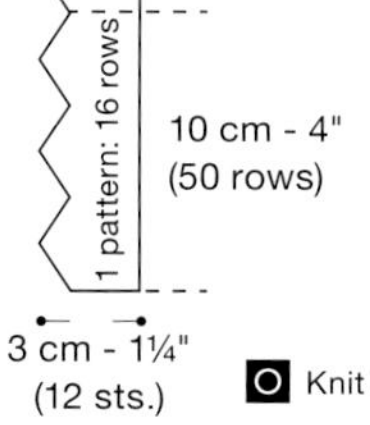

1 pattern: 16 rows
10 cm - 4" (50 rows)
3 cm - 1¼" (12 sts.)

For the edging, pick this stitch up on the main body and knit it vertically.

[**Pattern A Chart: Hood Left ③**]

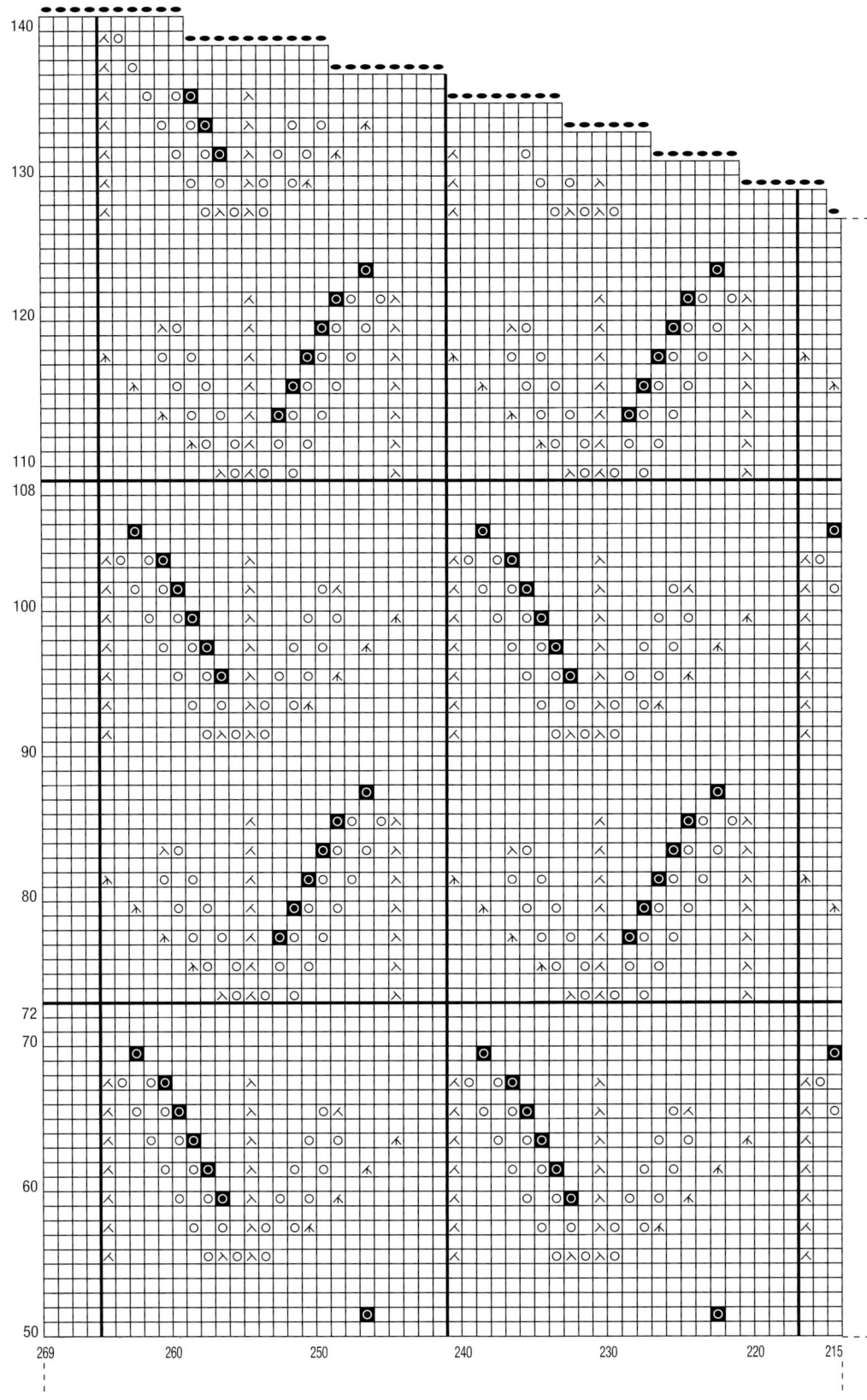

[Pattern A Chart: Hood Left ②]

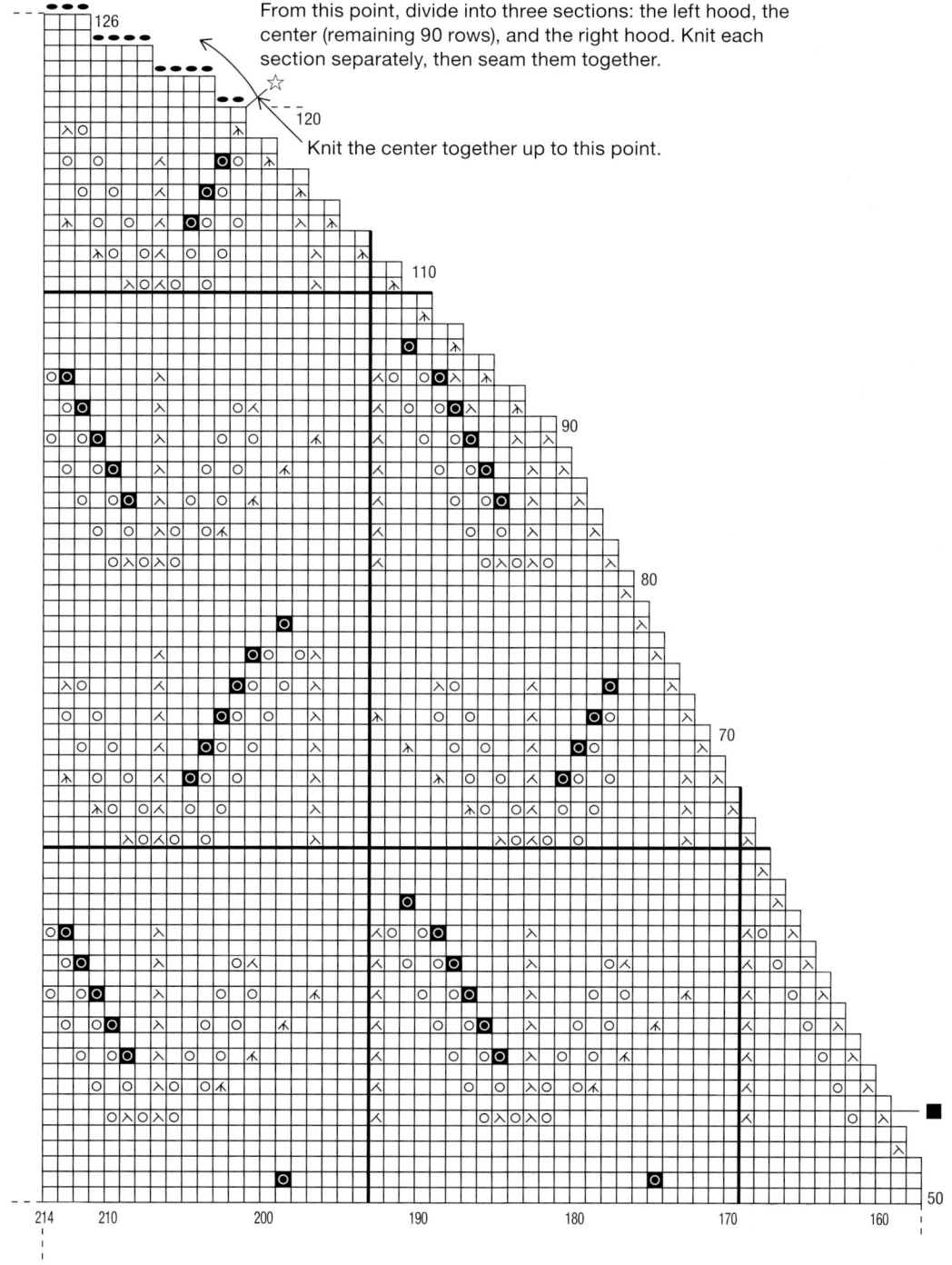

From this point, divide into three sections: the left hood, the center (remaining 90 rows), and the right hood. Knit each section separately, then seam them together.

Knit the center together up to this point.

[**Pattern A Chart: Hood Left ①**]

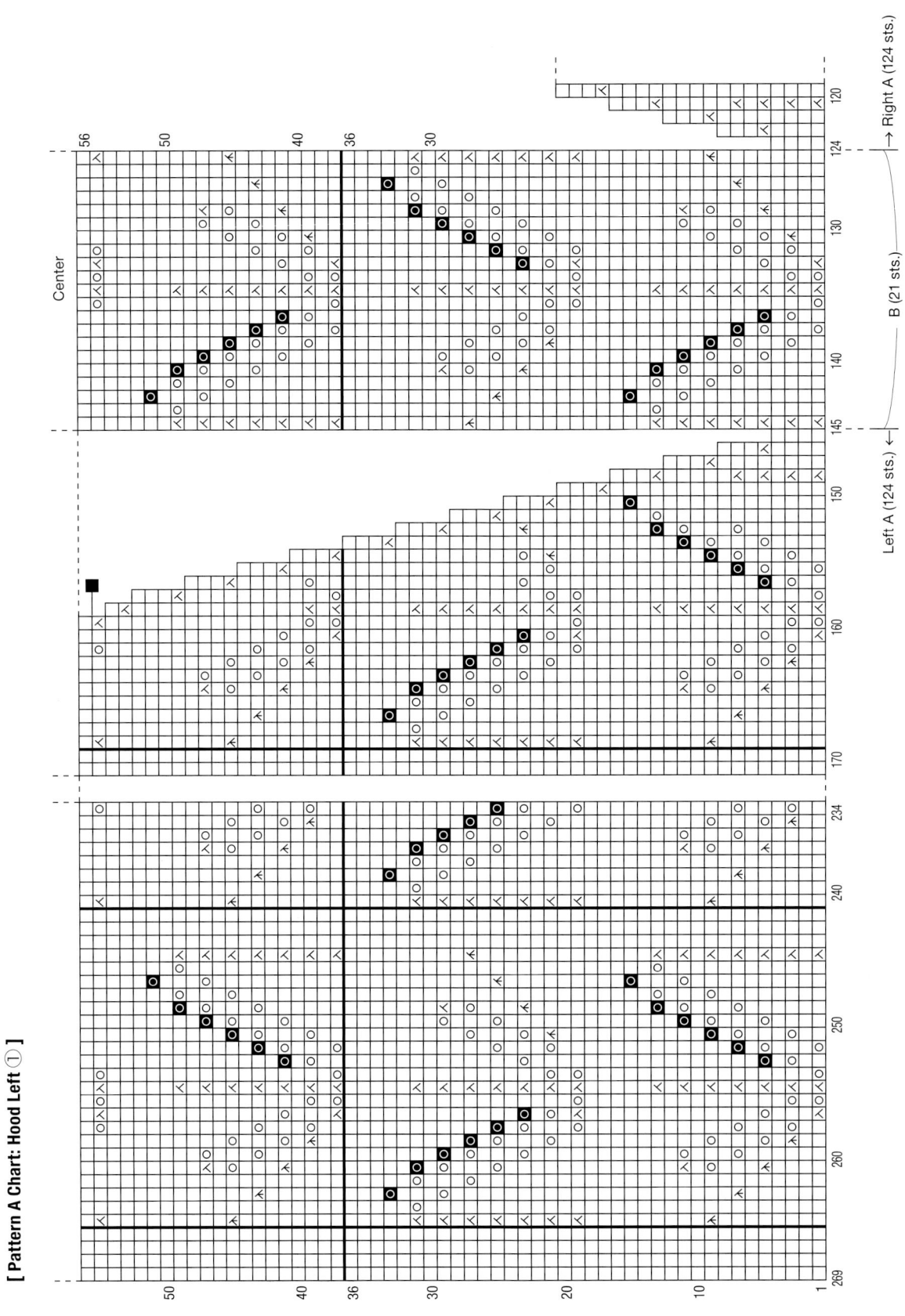

[Pattern A Chart: Hood Right ①]

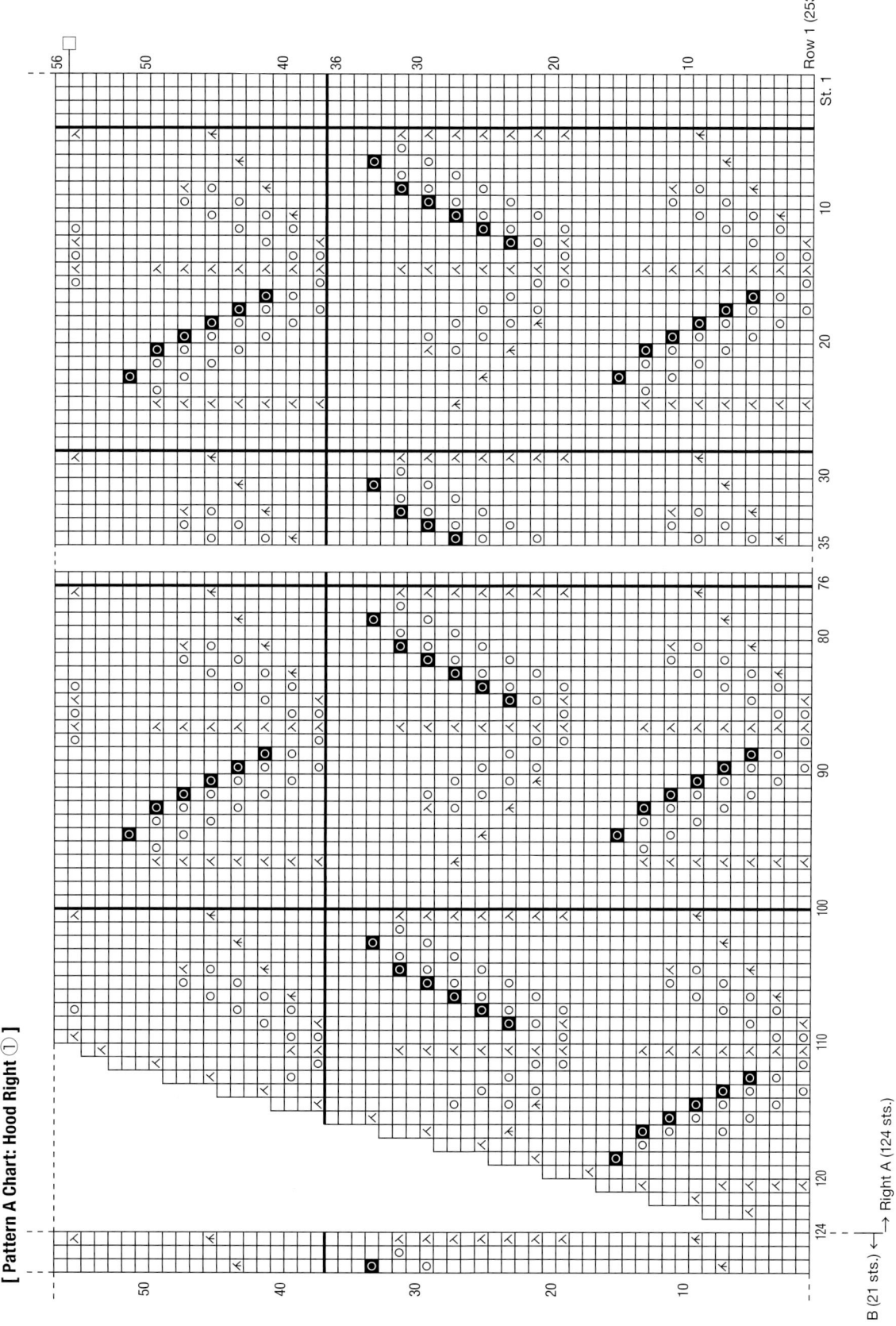

[Pattern A Chart: Hood Right ③]

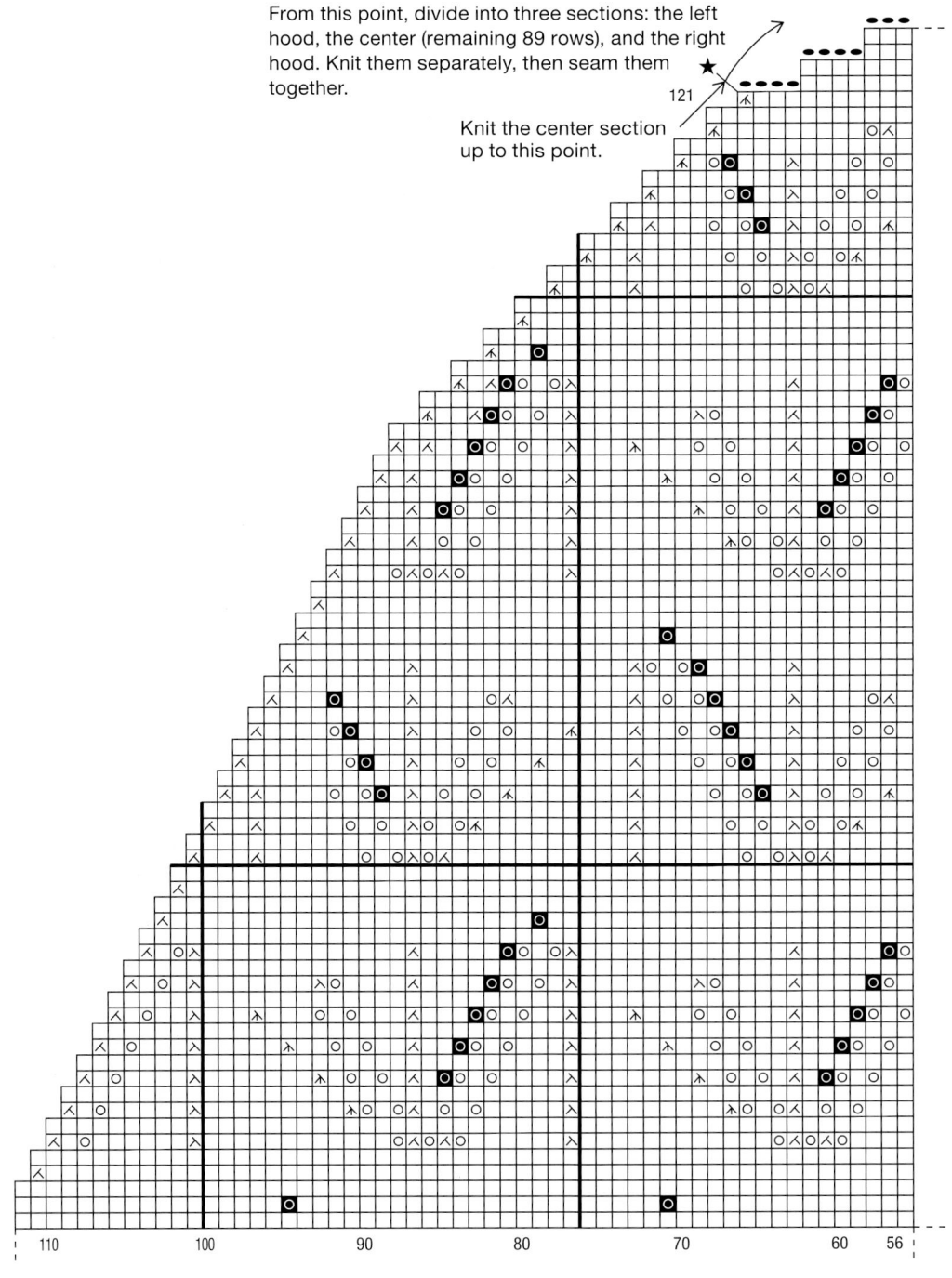

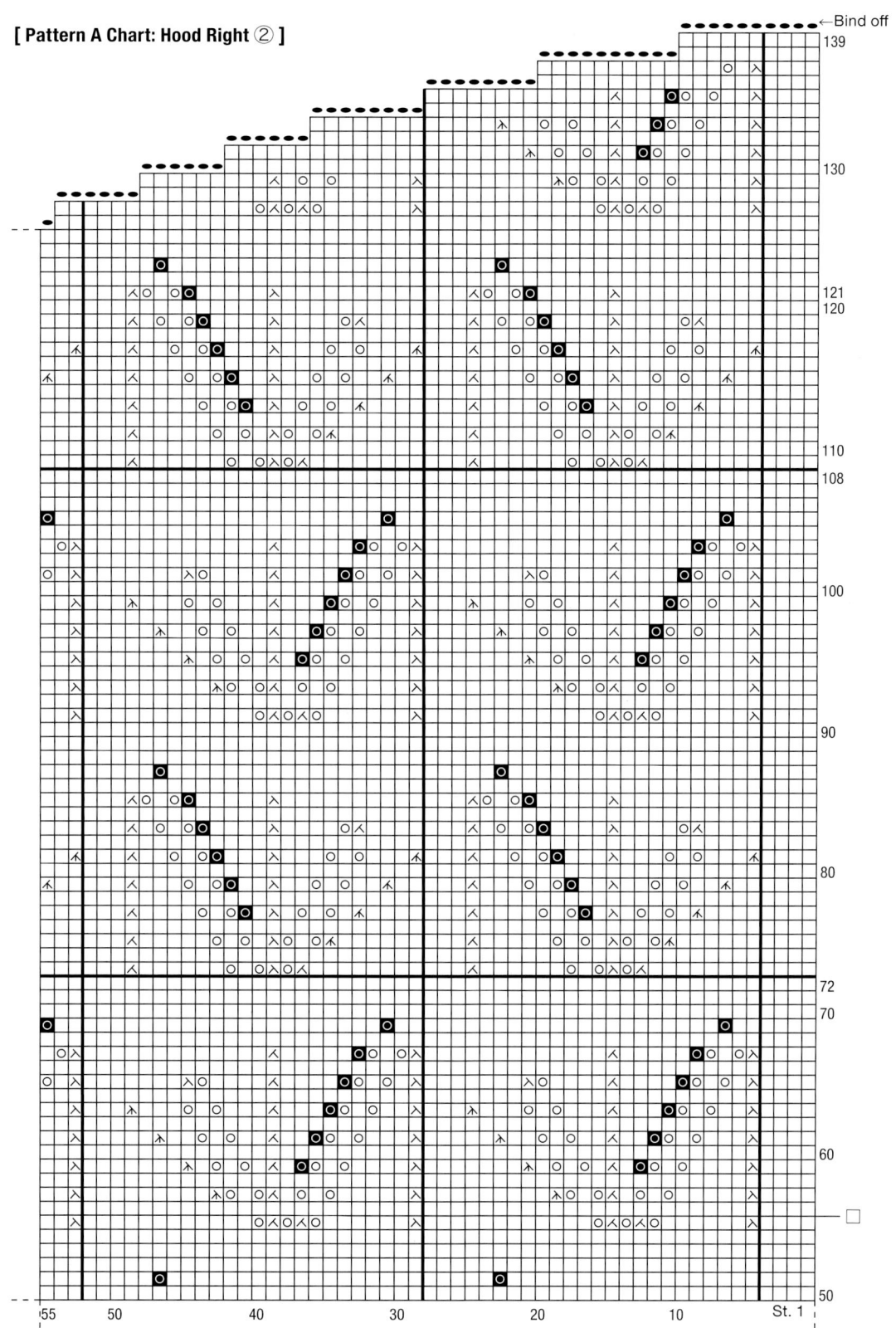

Page 120 Patchwork Bag

Finished Dimensions: Width 30 cm - 11¾" x Height 20 cm - 7⅞" x Depth 10 cm - 4"

▶ Tools and Materials

Yarn

Jamieson's Spindrift

Refer to the chart. Prepare the yarn as needed.

* Refer to the chart on each page. Knit with your favorite designs. The finished size of the swatch is approximately 11 cm - 4¼" square.

Other Materials

One commercially available canvas tote bag (Natural canvas, 20 cm - 7⅞" x 30 cm - 11¾" x 10 cm - 4", use without handles)

One set of handles (clip-on type)

30 x 50 cm - 11¾" x 19⅝" quilt batting

20 x 9 cm - 7⅞" x 3½" bottom board

30 x 30 cm - 11¾" x 11¾" linen fabric for inner pocket and bottom board

10 x 10 cm - 4" x 4" yellow felt

Needles

60 cm - 33⅝" circular needle, Size 3 (3.00 mm, UK Size 11)

Straight Needles: Size 4 (3.25 mm, UK Size 10)

Crochet Hook:
Size 2/0 (2.00 mm, UK Size 14),
Size 3/0 (2.25 mm, UK Size 13)

Cable needle

▶ Gauge

29 sts. 31 rows

▶ Knitting and Assembly Instructions

① Cast on the required number of stitches and knit thirteen swatches according to the charts, then bind off. Weave in the yarn ends and steam block.

② Embroider the swatches.

③ Divide the swatches into an upper and lower row and join them together using a slip stitch to form a circle. If the lengths do not match, adjust by pulling or easing, then baste and join. Repeat the same process for the upper and lower rows and attach the bottom. Steam block to shape.

④ Crochet the edging.

⑤ Make an inside pocket and sew it to the opening of the tote bag.

⑥ Wrap the bottom board in fabric and glue it on, then place it inside the tote bag.

⑦ Make a bag with quilt batting, cover the tote bag with it, and place it inside the knitted bag. Fold back the edging and sew it in place.

⑧ Attach the handles.

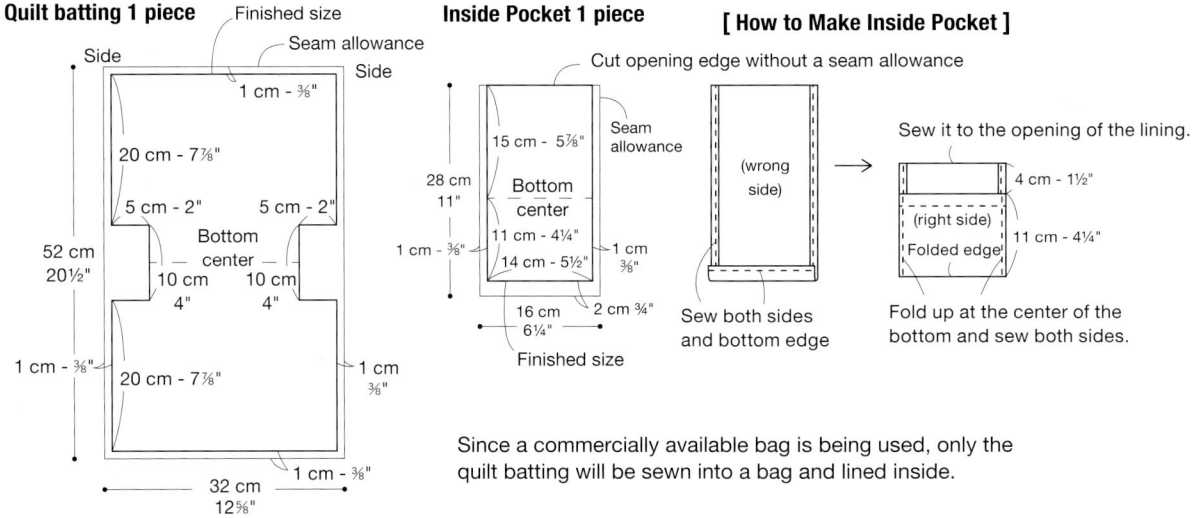

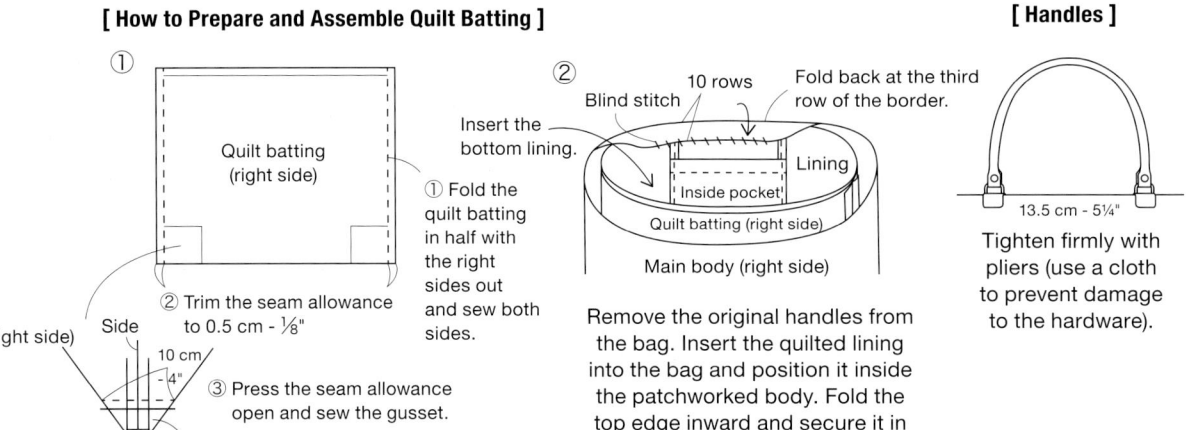

[**Swatch Layout**]

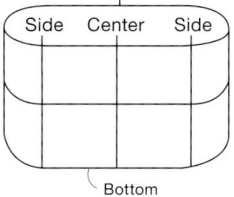

Join the pieces together to form the shape of a bag.

* To make joining swatches easier, bind off the edges on the wrong side using knit stitches (or a crochet hook).

[**Edging Chart**]

60 cm - 33⅝" circular needle Size 3 (3.00 mm) #343 Ivory
Pick up 25 stitches from each swatch.

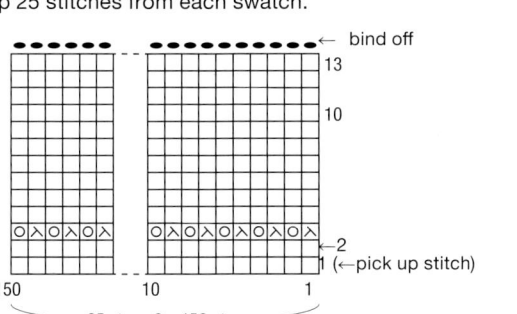

- ☐ Knit
- — Purl
- ⋋ Slip, knit, pass
- ⋌ Knit 2 together
- ○ Yarn over
- ℬ Through back loop
- ⋈ 1/1 left cross
- ⋈ 1/1 right cross
- ● Bind off

① **Smocking Flowers**

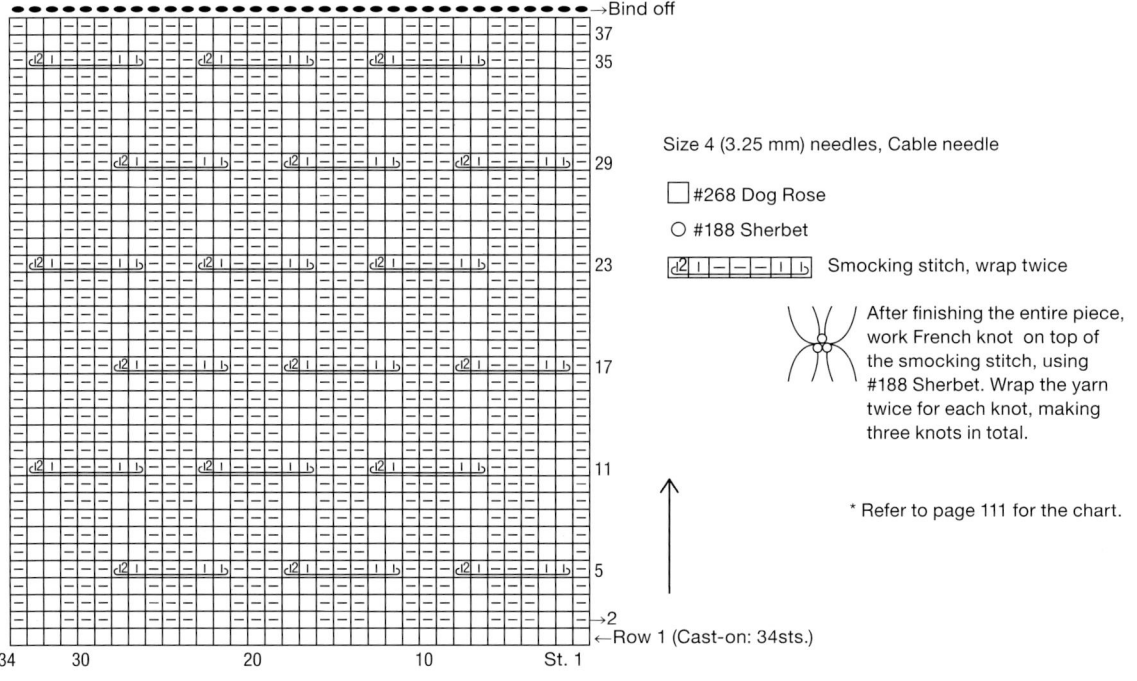

Size 4 (3.25 mm) needles, Cable needle

☐ #268 Dog Rose
○ #188 Sherbet

Smocking stitch, wrap twice

After finishing the entire piece, work French knot on top of the smocking stitch, using #188 Sherbet. Wrap the yarn twice for each knot, making three knots in total.

* Refer to page 111 for the chart.

② Violets

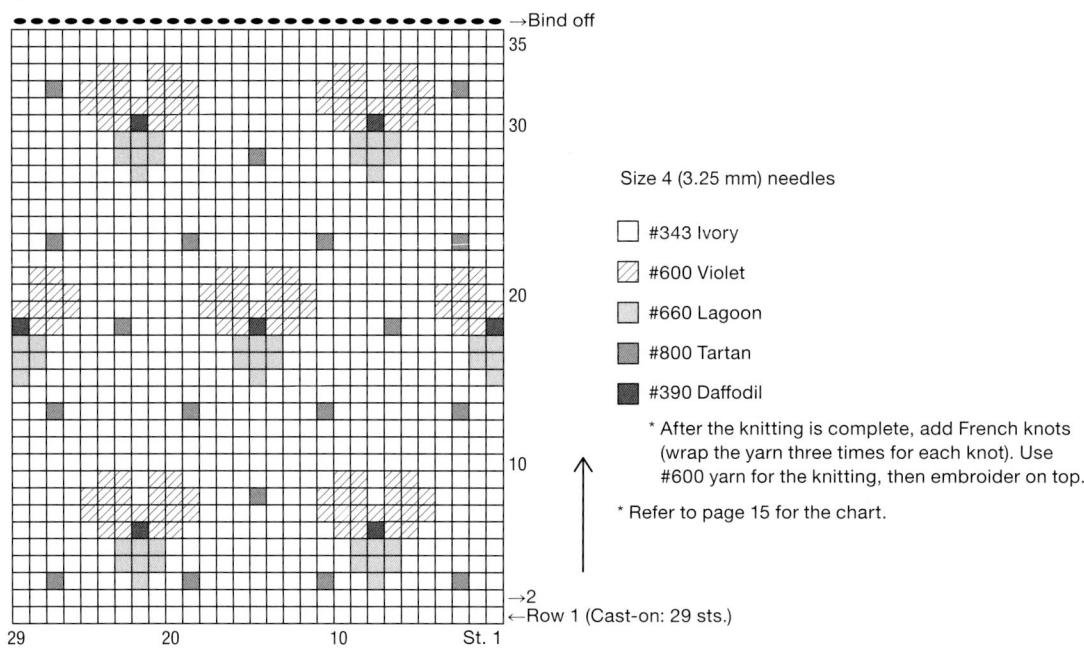

Size 4 (3.25 mm) needles

- ☐ #343 Ivory
- ▨ #600 Violet
- ▢ #660 Lagoon
- ▣ #800 Tartan
- ■ #390 Daffodil

* After the knitting is complete, add French knots (wrap the yarn three times for each knot). Use #600 yarn for the knitting, then embroider on top.

* Refer to page 15 for the chart.

③ Thistle

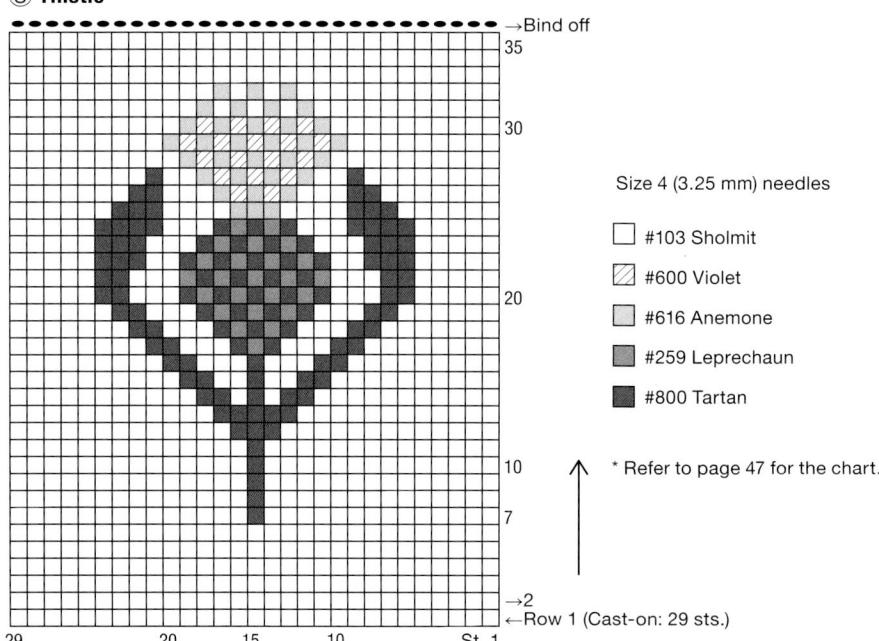

Size 4 (3.25 mm) needles

- ☐ #103 Sholmit
- ▨ #600 Violet
- ▢ #616 Anemone
- ▣ #259 Leprechaun
- ■ #800 Tartan

* Refer to page 47 for the chart.

④ **Berries**

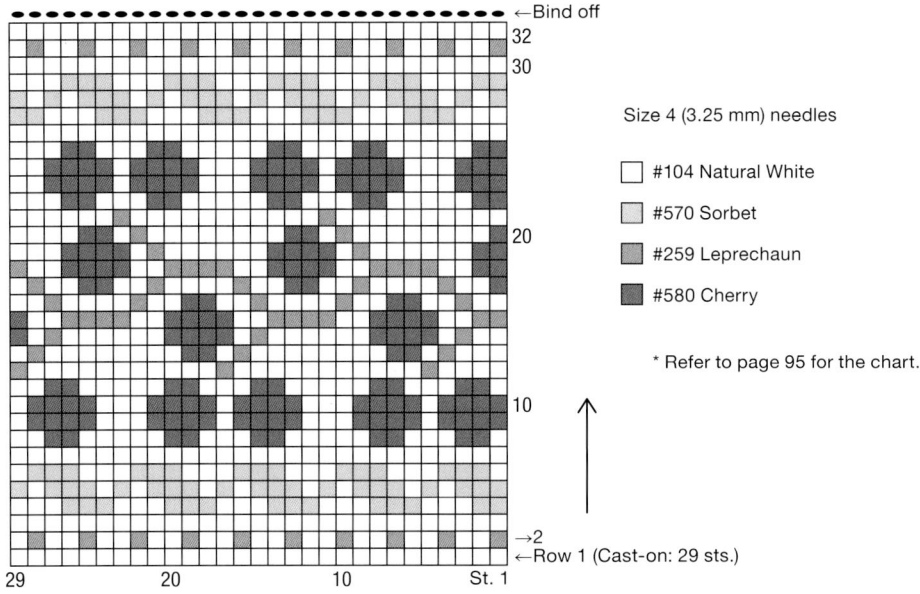

⑤ **Pansy**

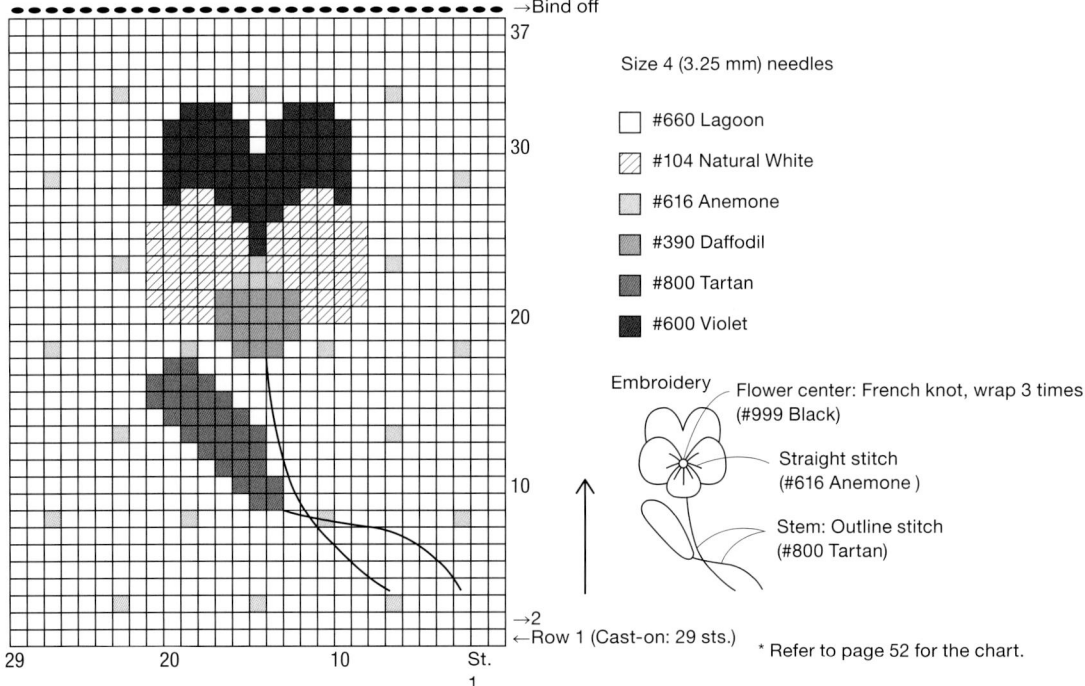

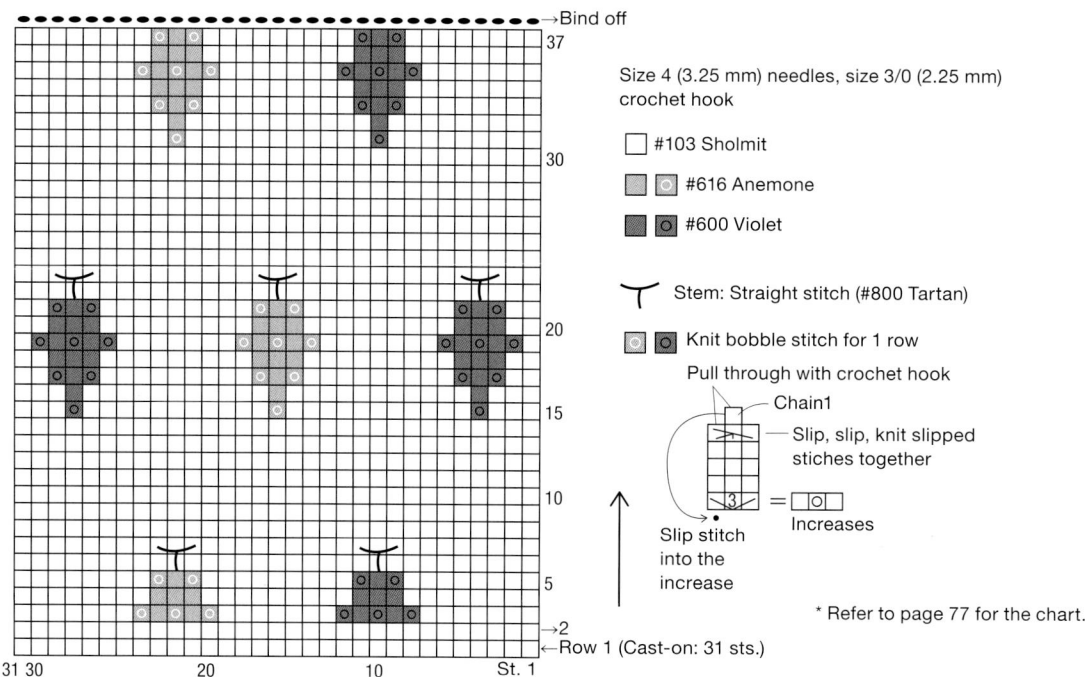

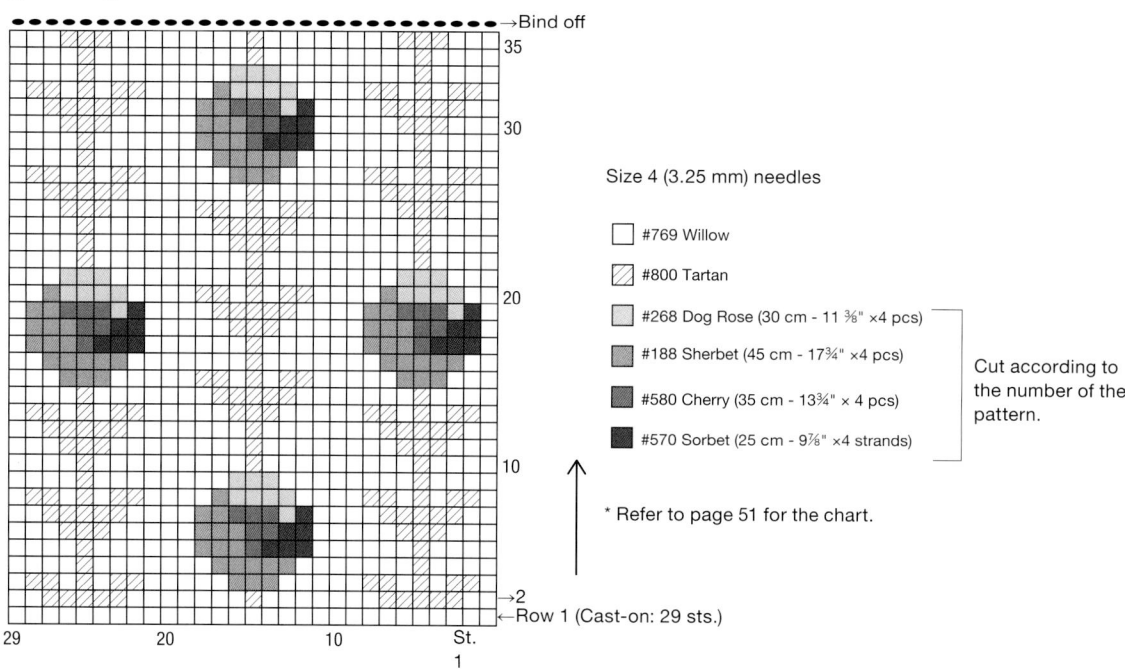

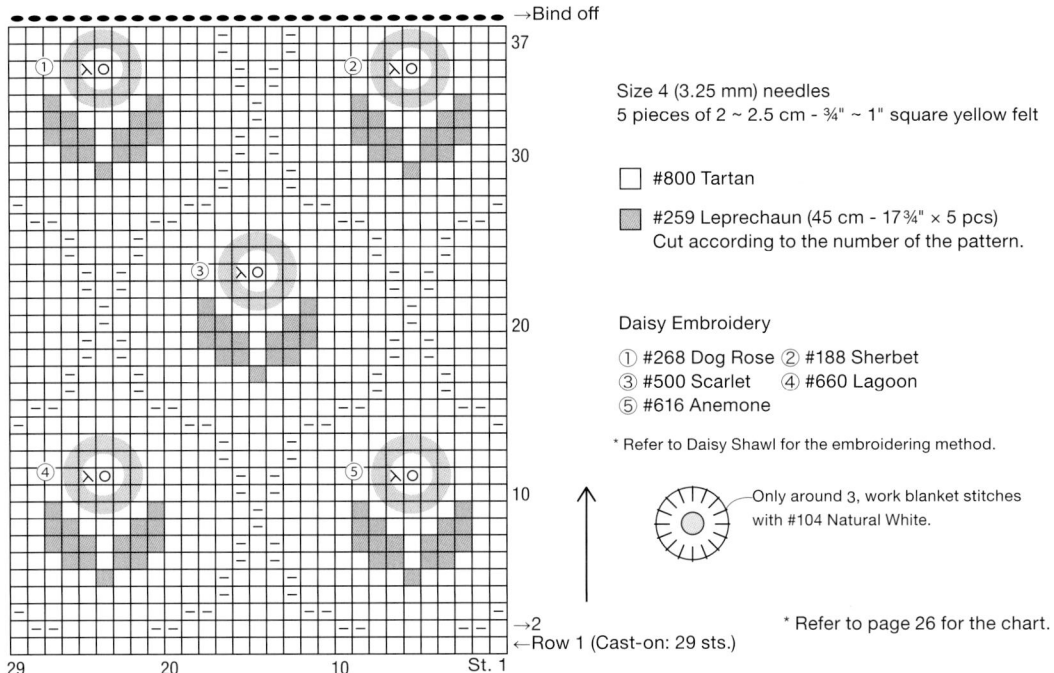

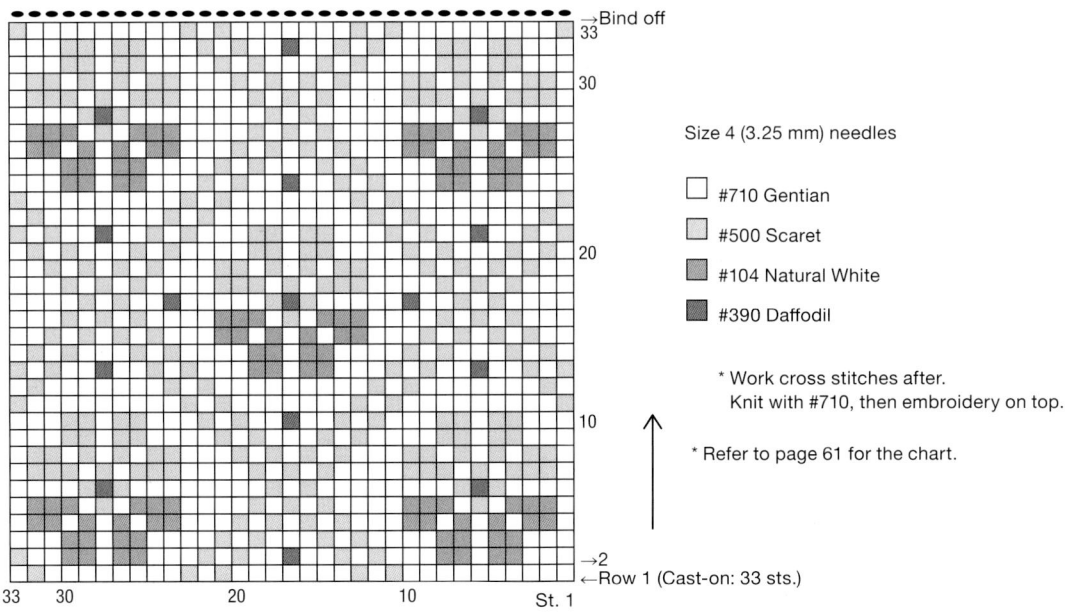

10 Dandelion

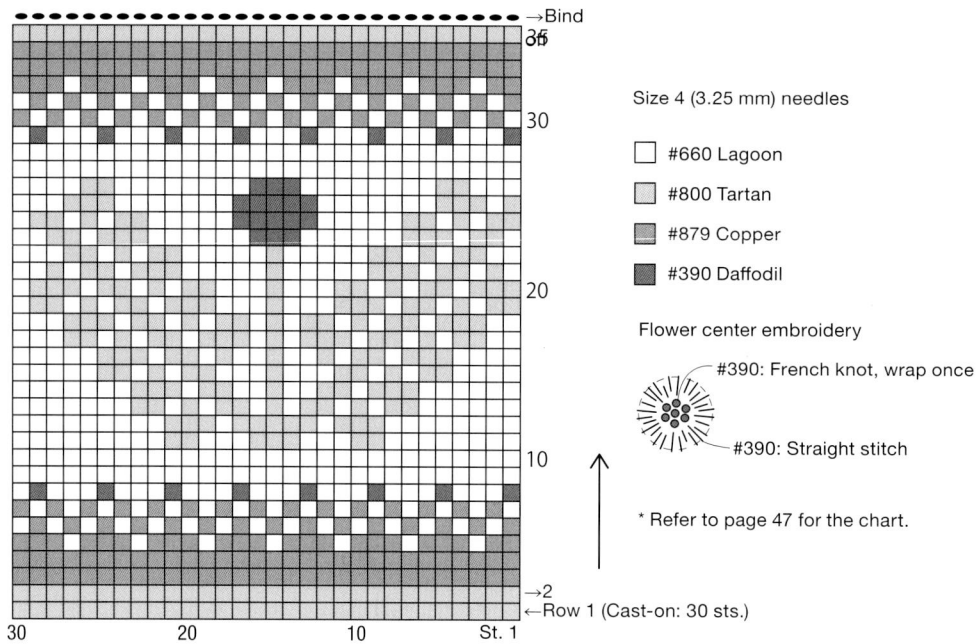

Size 4 (3.25 mm) needles

- ☐ #660 Lagoon
- ■ #800 Tartan
- ■ #879 Copper
- ■ #390 Daffodil

Flower center embroidery

#390: French knot, wrap once

#390: Straight stitch

* Refer to page 47 for the chart.

11 Up & Down Strawberries

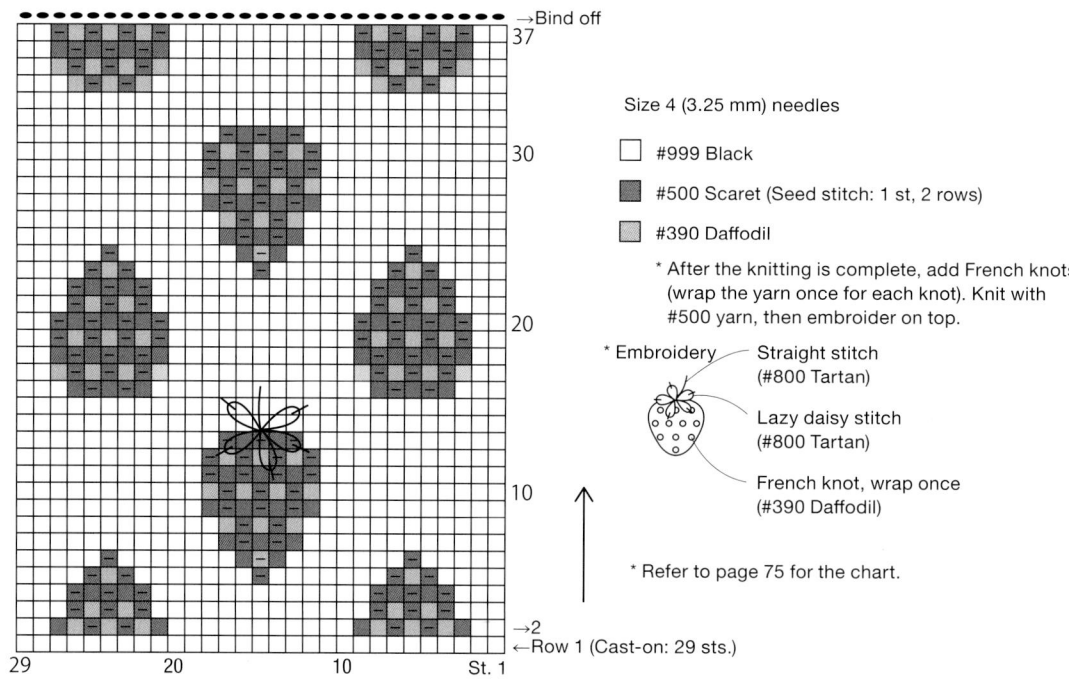

Size 4 (3.25 mm) needles

- ☐ #999 Black
- ■ #500 Scaret (Seed stitch: 1 st, 2 rows)
- ■ #390 Daffodil

* After the knitting is complete, add French knots (wrap the yarn once for each knot). Knit with #500 yarn, then embroider on top.

* Embroidery
  - Straight stitch (#800 Tartan)
  - Lazy daisy stitch (#800 Tartan)
  - French knot, wrap once (#390 Daffodil)

* Refer to page 75 for the chart.

12 Mistletoes

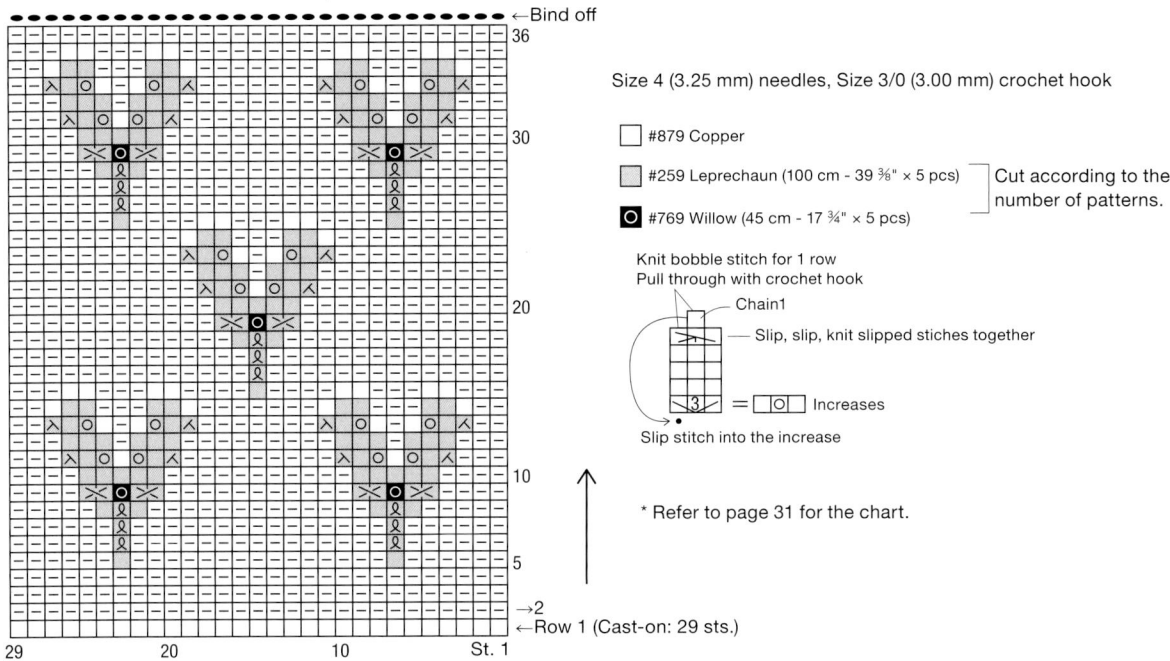

Size 4 (3.25 mm) needles, Size 3/0 (3.00 mm) crochet hook

☐ #879 Copper
▨ #259 Leprechaun (100 cm - 39 ⅜" × 5 pcs)
◉ #769 Willow (45 cm - 17 ¾" × 5 pcs)

Cut according to the number of patterns.

Knit bobble stitch for 1 row
Pull through with crochet hook
Chain1
Slip, slip, knit slipped stiches together
= Increases
Slip stitch into the increase

* Refer to page 31 for the chart.

13 Bag's Bottom – Berries

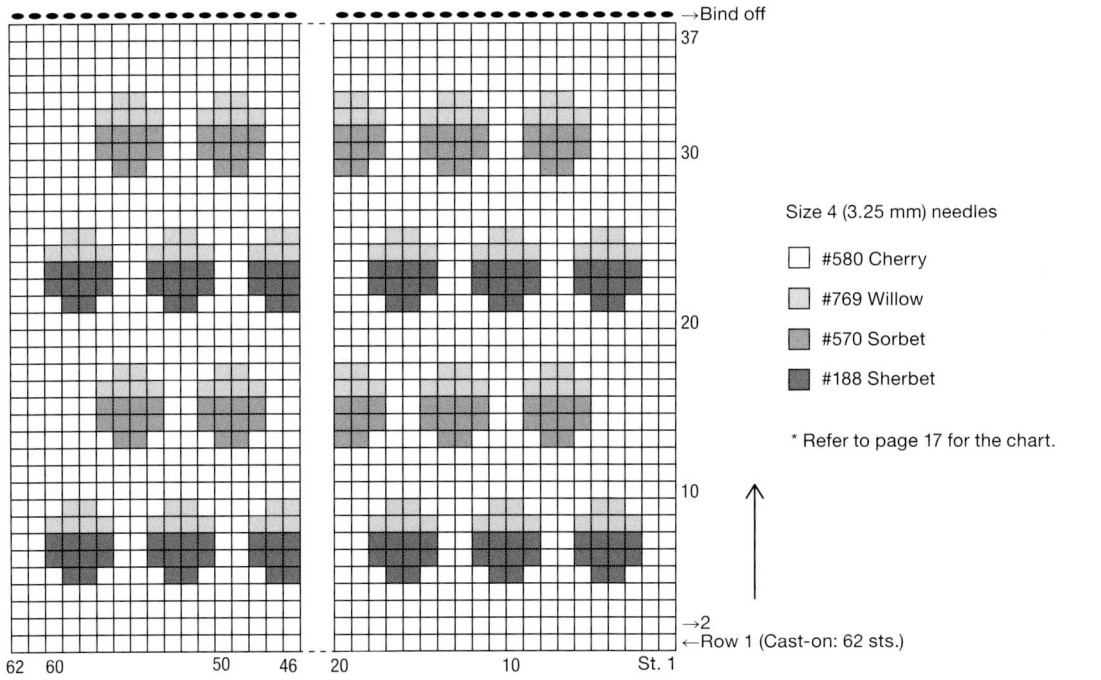

Size 4 (3.25 mm) needles

☐ #580 Cherry
▨ #769 Willow
▨ #570 Sorbet
▨ #188 Sherbet

* Refer to page 17 for the chart.

Page 121 Patchwork Shawl

Finished Dimensions: 54 x 128 cm - 21¼" x 50⅜"

▶ Tools and Materials

Yarn

Jamieson's Spindrift

* Refer to the chart. Prepare the yarn as needed.

* Refer to the chart on each page. Knit with your favorite designs.

Needles

Straight Needles:
Size 4 (3.25 mm, UK Size 10)

Crochet Hook:
Size 2/0 (2.00 mm, UK Size 14),
Size 3/0 (2.25 mm, UK Size 13)

▶ Gauge

26 sts. 32 rows

▶ Knitting and Assembly Instructions

① Cast on stitches using the thumb method and knit seven motifs according to the chart, then bind off. Weave in the yarn ends and steam block.

② Embroider the piece.

③ With the right sides facing each other, join the pieces in the following order: 4 and 5 → 6 → 3 → 2 → 1 → 7, using slip stitch. Steam block to shape.

④ Knit the edging. Wet block and let dry.

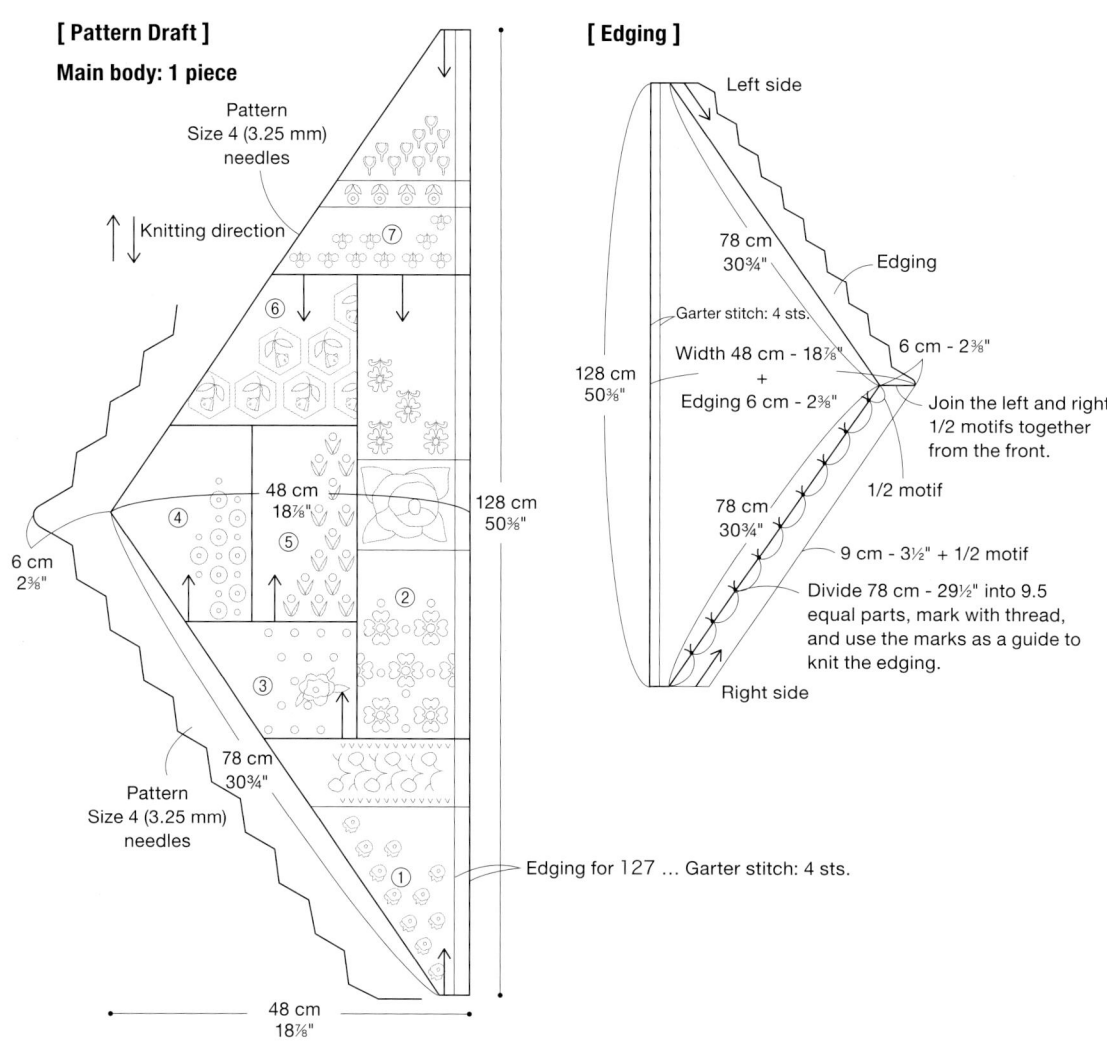

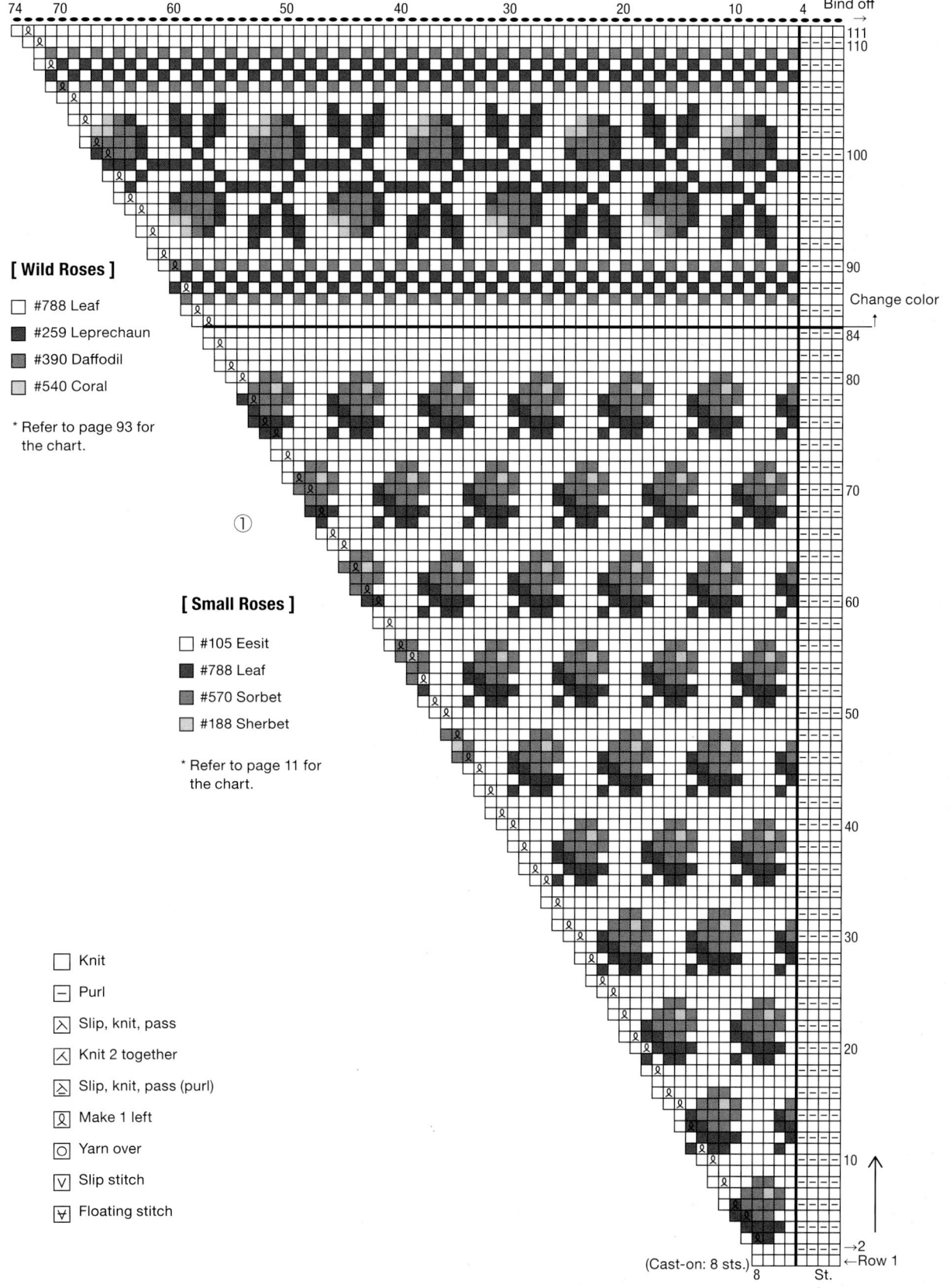

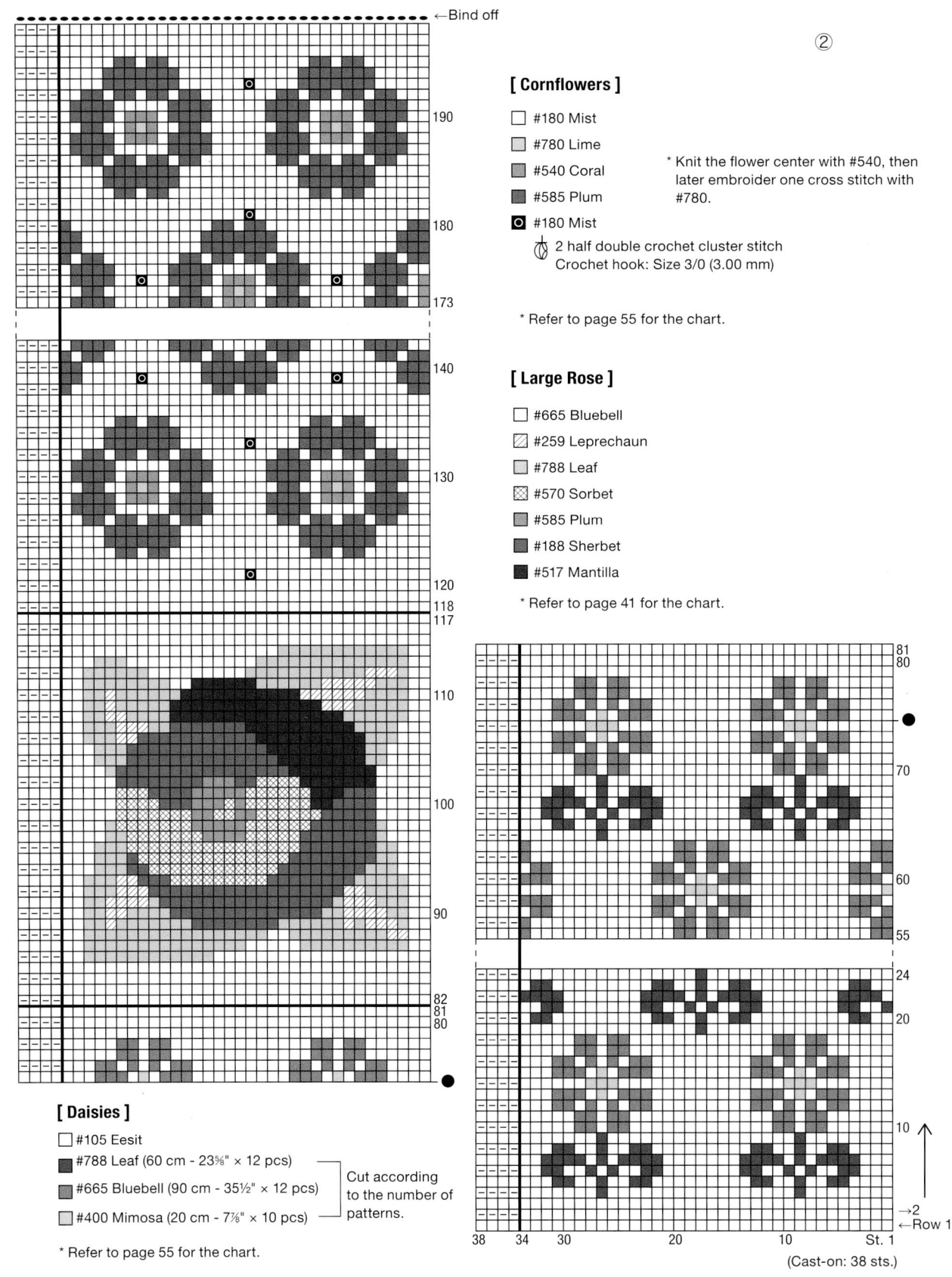

③

[Bobble Stitches and Rose]

- ☐ #127 Pebble
- ☐ #259 Leprechaun
- ▨ #188 Sherbet
- ■ #570 Sorbet
- ■ #517 Mantilla
- ■ #788 Leaf
- ◙ #127 Pebble
- 2 half double crochet cluster stitch
  Crochet hook: Size 2/0 (2.00 mm)

* Refer to page 59 for the chart.

* Embroider center of the rose
#390 Daffodil: Make 5 French knot,
wrap twice for each knot
Embroider with #390 on #570

[Chart: Edging]

Size 4 (3.25 mm) needles, #616 Anemone
Knit while attaching to the main body.

- ☐ Knit
- ⊟ Purl
- Slip, knit, pass
- Knit 2 together
- Slip, knit, pass (purl)
- Make 1 left
- Yarn over
- Slip stitch
- Floating stitch (the yarn crosses over the front)

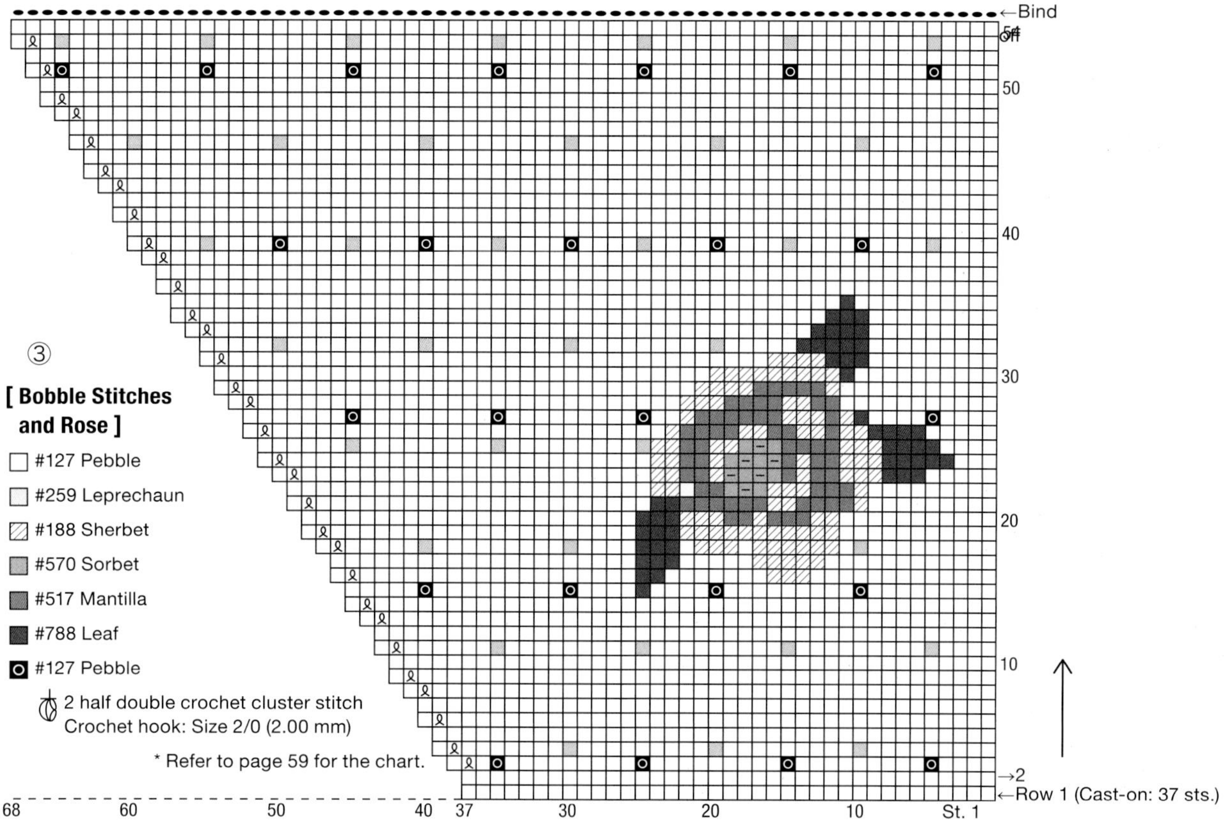

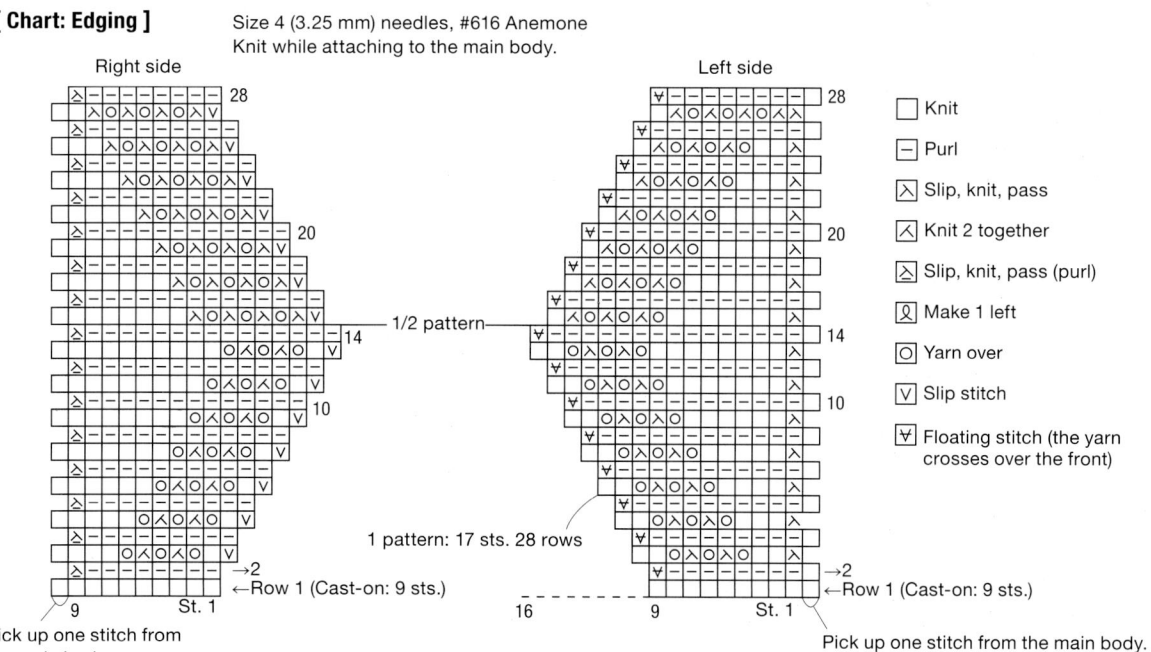

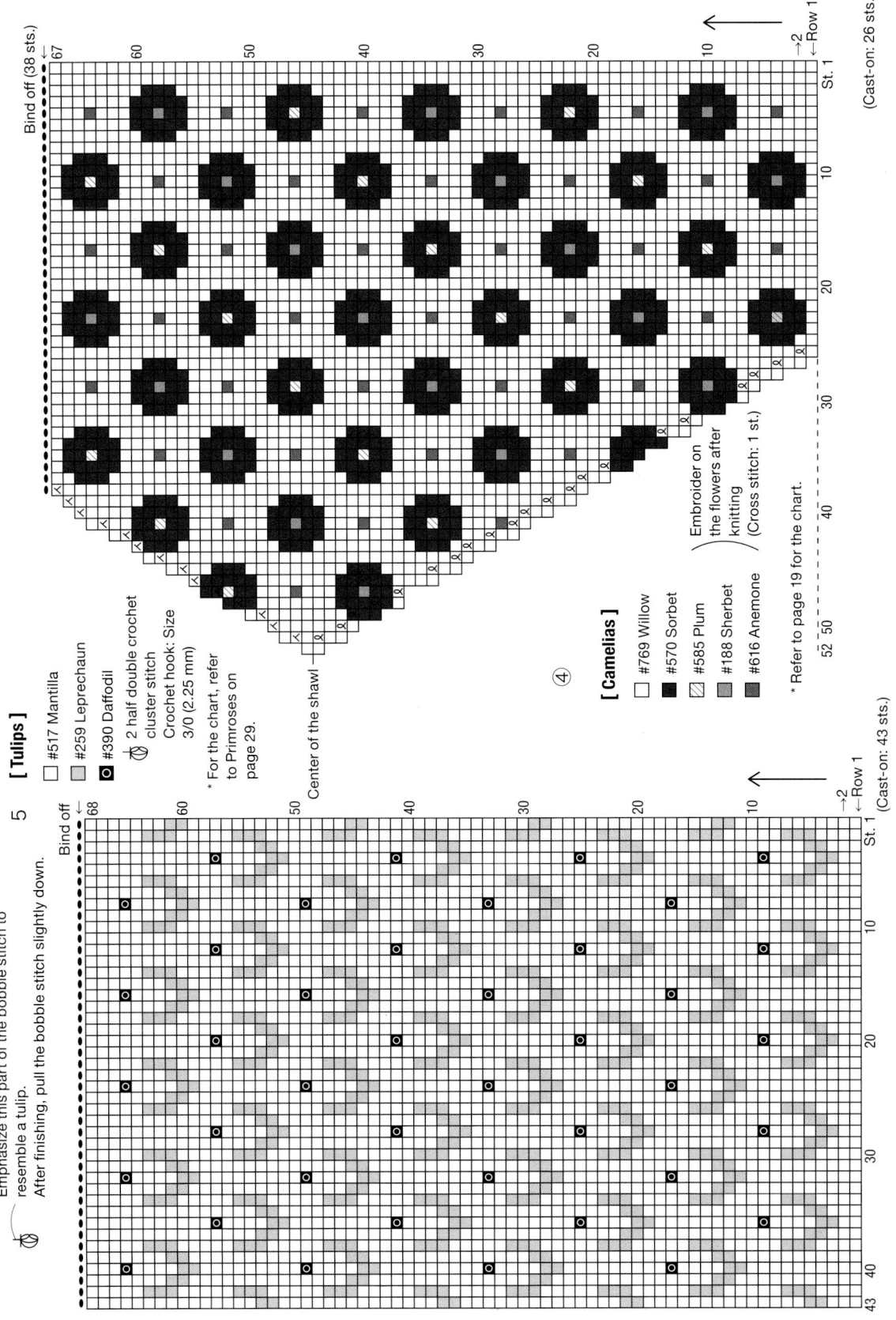

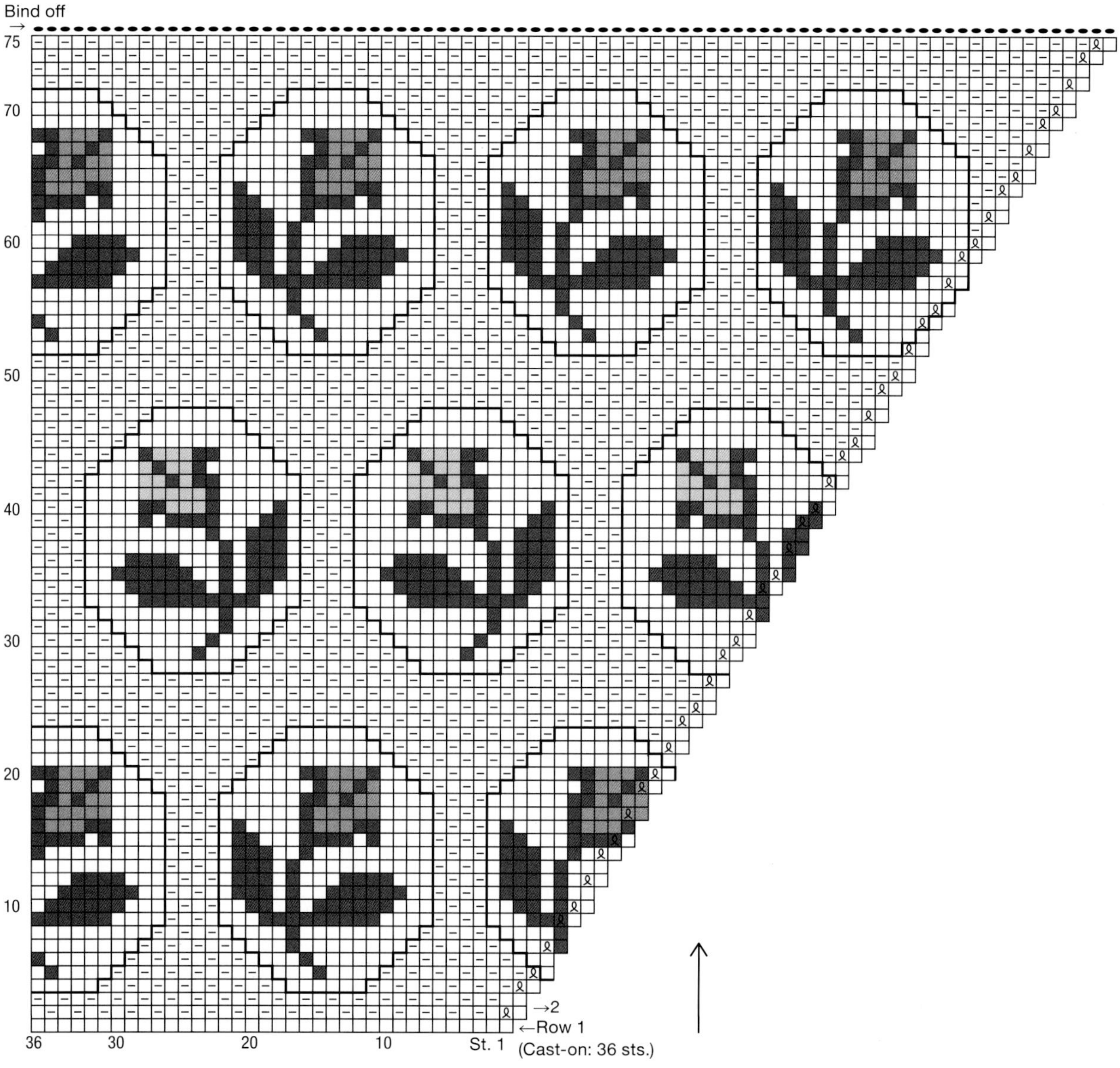

⑥ [Rosebuds]

- □ #655 China Blue
- #570 Sorbet (right facing rosebuds) (40 cm - 15¾" × 3 pcs)
- #585 Plum (left facing rosebuds) (40 cm - 15¾" ×7 pcs)
- ■ #780 Leaf (155 cm - 61" × 10 pcs)

Cut according to the number of the pattern.

* Refer to page 51 for the chart.

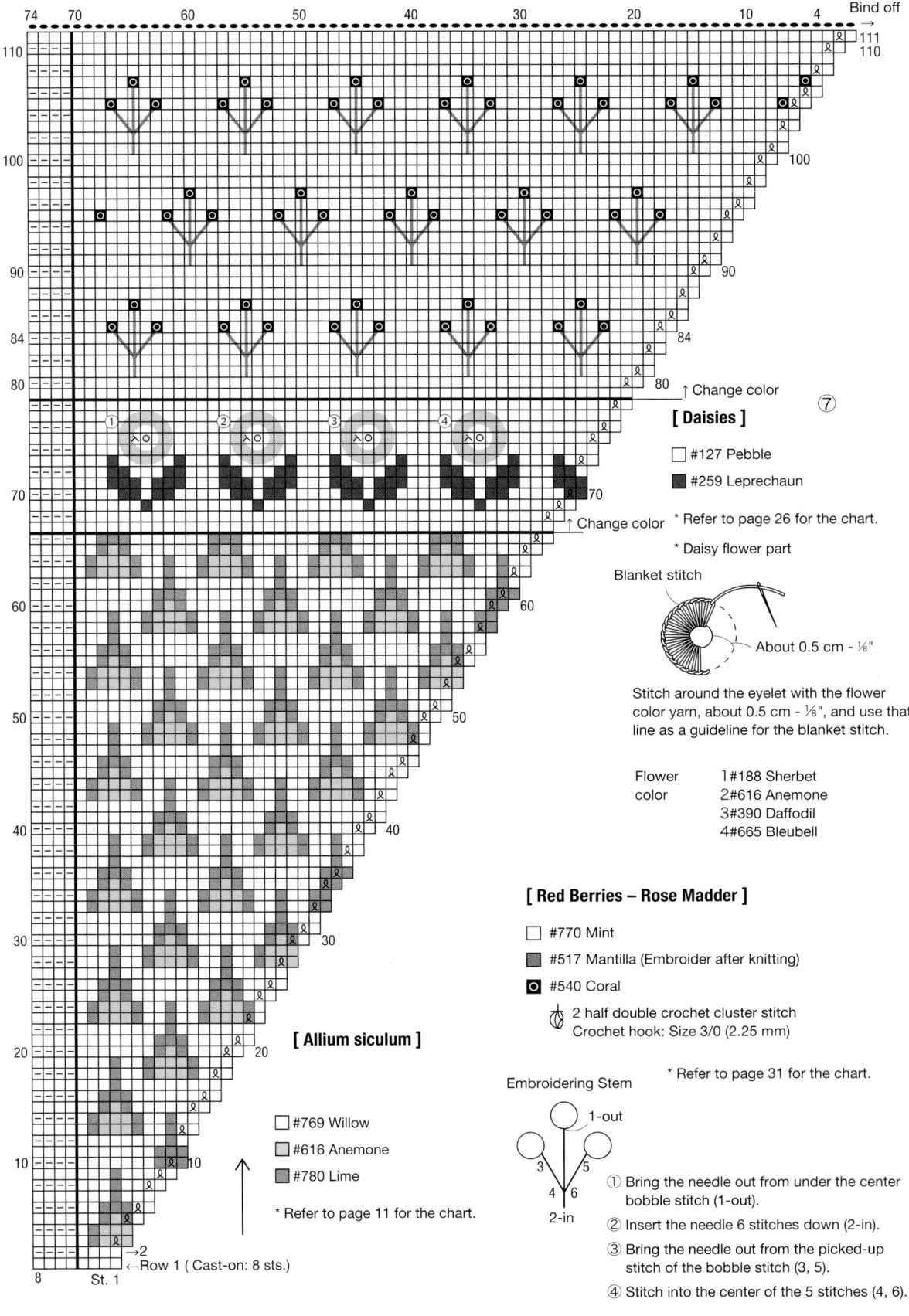

Basic Stitches

• Knitting
Casting On (Thumb Method)

* If your cast-on stitches are too loose, it's advisable to use just one needle.

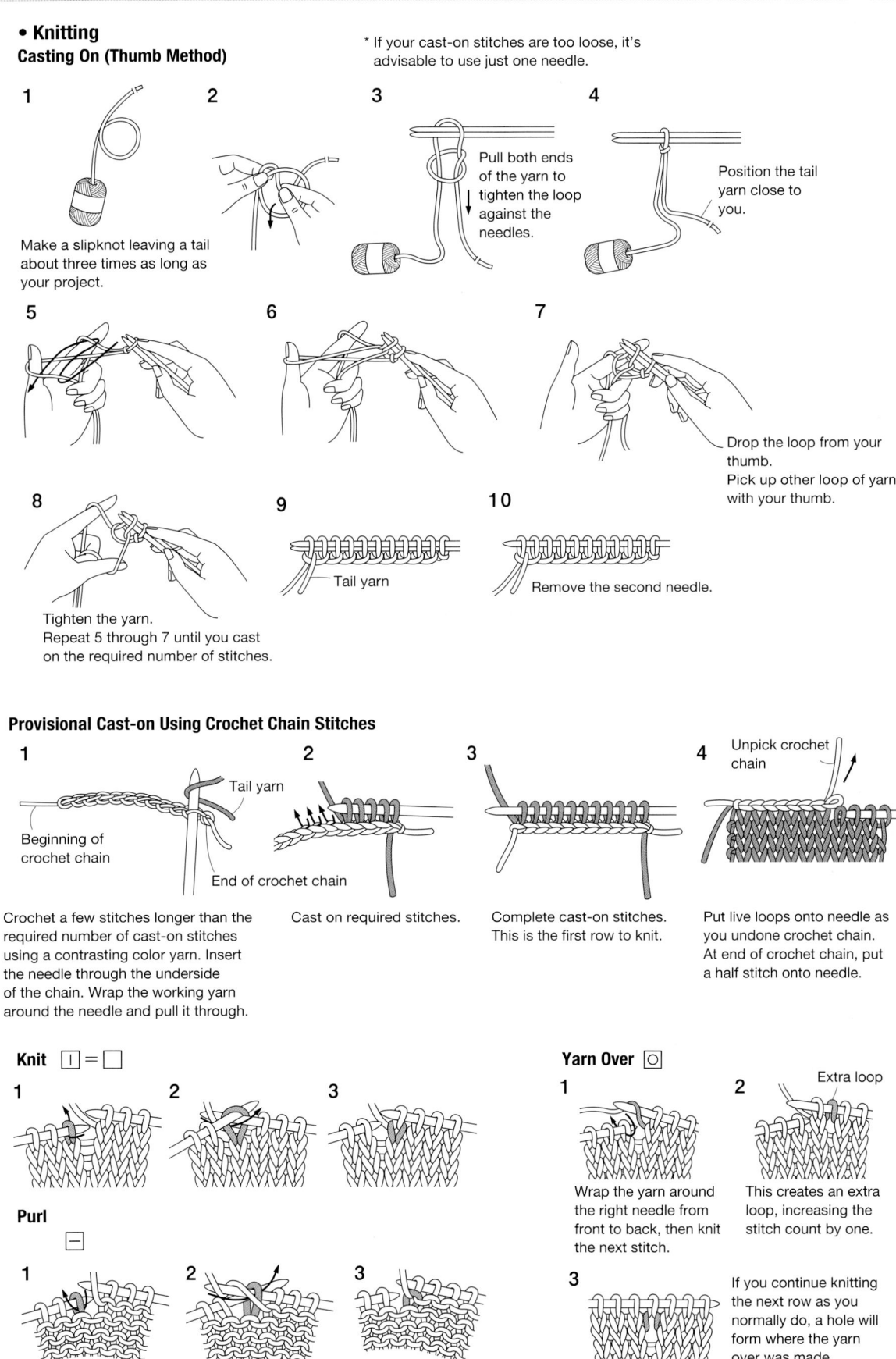

1 Make a slipknot leaving a tail about three times as long as your project.

3 Pull both ends of the yarn to tighten the loop against the needles.

4 Position the tail yarn close to you.

7 Drop the loop from your thumb. Pick up other loop of yarn with your thumb.

8 Tighten the yarn. Repeat 5 through 7 until you cast on the required number of stitches.

9 Tail yarn

10 Remove the second needle.

Provisional Cast-on Using Crochet Chain Stitches

1 Beginning of crochet chain / Tail yarn / End of crochet chain

Crochet a few stitches longer than the required number of cast-on stitches using a contrasting color yarn. Insert the needle through the underside of the chain. Wrap the working yarn around the needle and pull it through.

2 Cast on required stitches.

3 Complete cast-on stitches. This is the first row to knit.

4 Unpick crochet chain

Put live loops onto needle as you undone crochet chain. At end of crochet chain, put a half stitch onto needle.

Knit | = □

Purl −

Yarn Over ○

1 Wrap the yarn around the right needle from front to back, then knit the next stitch.

2 Extra loop

This creates an extra loop, increasing the stitch count by one.

3 If you continue knitting the next row as you normally do, a hole will form where the yarn over was made.

183

Through Back Loop

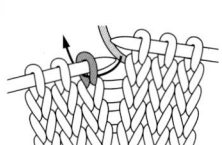

Through Back Loop on Purl Side

Insert the right needle in the direction of the arrow and purl.

Make 1 Left

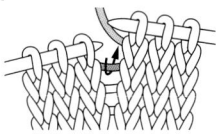
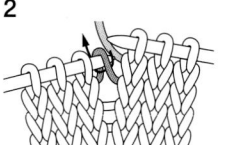

Pick up the strand between two stitches.

Insert the right needle into the lifted strand from left to right, and knit.

Backward Loop Increase

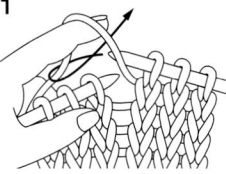
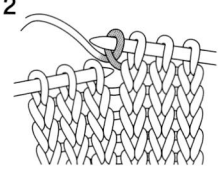
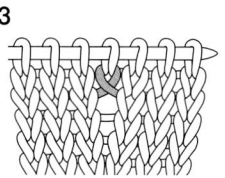

As shown above, wrap the working yarn around the right needle.

The yarn wrapped around the right needle creates an increase.

Worked on this row and next row.

Slip Stitch

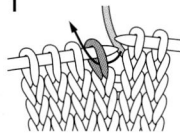
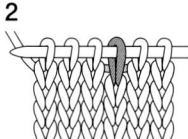

Place the working yarn at the back of your project and transfer next stitch to the right needle.

Continue knitting the following stitch. When slipping a stitch for two consecutive rows, slip the stitch purlwise on the next row.

Slip Stitch with Yarn in Front (one row)

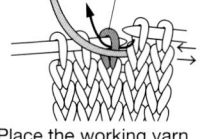
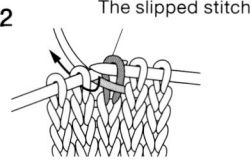

Transfer to the right needle

The slipped stitch

Place the working yarn in front of the next stitch, transfer the next stitch to the right needle.

Knit the next stitch.

Binding Off

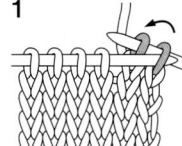
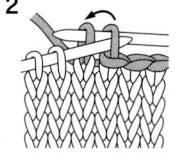

Pull the tailing yarn through to tighten.

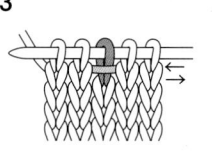
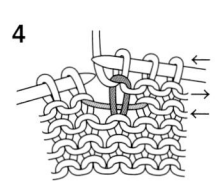

Knit two stitches, then lift the first stitch over the second.
Repeat this process until one stitch remaining on the right needle.

Slipping stitch with yarn in front complete.

Purl next row.

Binding Off (Purl Side)

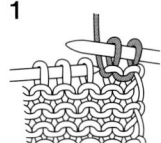
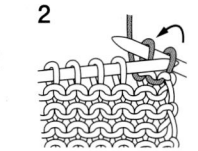
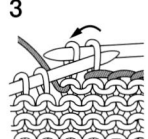
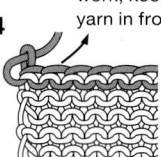

* On the wrong side of your work, keep the working yarn in front.

Purl the outermost two stitches, then lift the first stitch over to the second.

Repeat this process, purling and lifting the stitch.

Pull the tail yarn through the last stitch to tighten.

Slip, Knit, Lift

1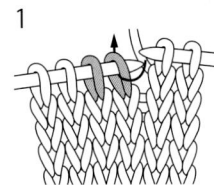
Transfer the next stitch to the right needle.

2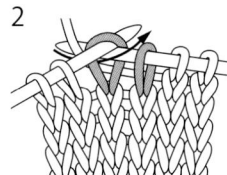
Knit the next stitch.

3

4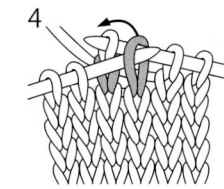
Lift the slipped stitch over.

5

Knit 2 Together

1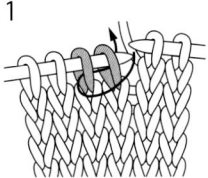
Knit the next two stitches together.

2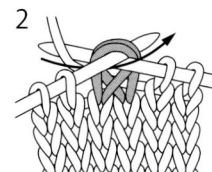

3

Slip, Slip, Purl (purl side)

1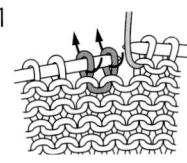
Transfer the first two stitches to the right needle.

2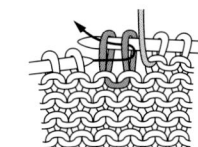
Insert the left needle into the two stitches on the right needle from right side.

3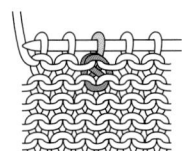
Purl the two stitches together.

Purl 2 Together (Purl Side)

1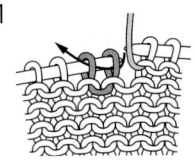
Insert the right needle in the direction of the arrow.

2
Wrap the working yarn around the needle and purl the two stitches together.

3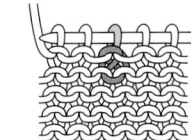

Knit 3 Together

1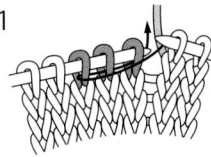
Knit the next three stitches together.

2

Slip, Knit 2 Together, Pass Slip Stitch Over

1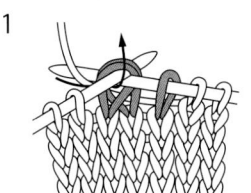
Without knitting the first stitch, insert the needle from the front and slip it onto the right needle. Then, knit the next two stitches together.

2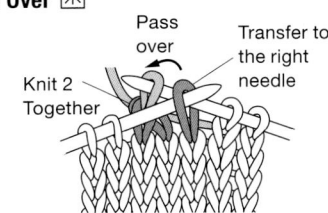
Pass over
Transfer to the right needle
Knit 2 Together
Pass the slipped stitch over the knitted stitch.

3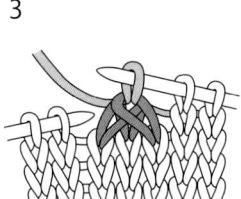

Slip 2, Knit 1, Pass 2 Slip Stitch Over

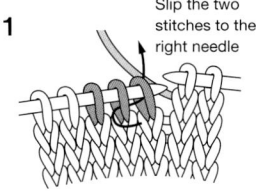
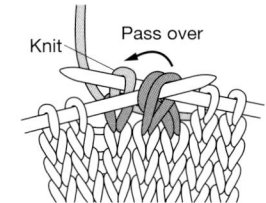
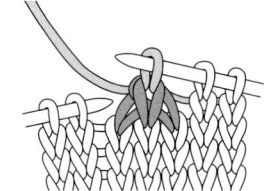

1. Insert the right needle into the next two stitches from the left side and slip them without knitting.

2. Knit the next stitch, and pass the slipped stitches over the one you just knit.

1/1 Left Cross

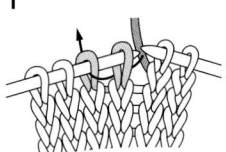
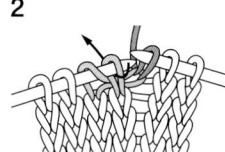
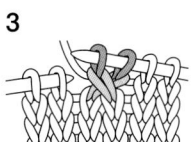

1. Pass the right needle behind the next stitch to skip one stitch. Then, insert the right needle into the next stitch in the direction of the arrow and knit.

2. Knit the skipped stitch.

3. Drop both stitches from the left needle.

1/1 Right Cross

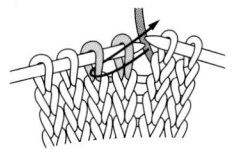
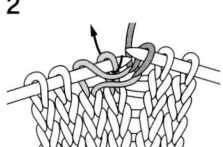
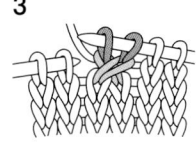

1. Pass the right needle in front of the next stitch to skip one stitch. Then, insert the right needle into the next stitch in the direction of the arrow and knit.

2. Knit the skipped stitch.

3. Drop both stitches from the left needle.

2/1 Right Cross (2nd Stitch Purl)

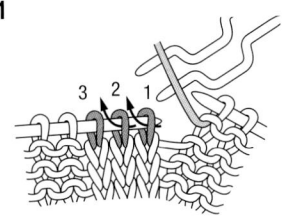
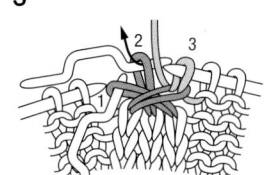
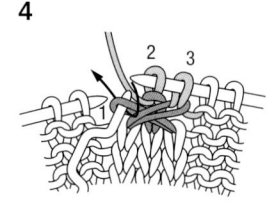

1. Slip stitches 1, and 2 onto a separate cable needle and hold them at back of your work.

2. Knit stitch 3.

3. Purl stitch 2 behind stitch 1.

4. Knit stitch 1.

2/2 Left Cross

1

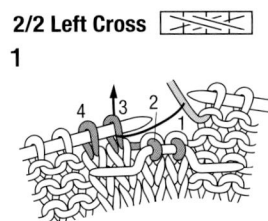

Place two stitches onto a cable needle and hold it in front of your work. Then, knit the next two stitches.

2

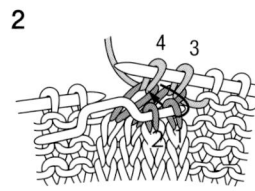

Knit the stitches on the cable needle.

3

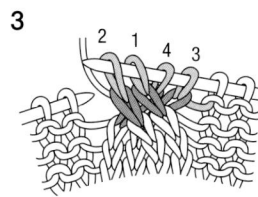

2/2 Right Cross

1

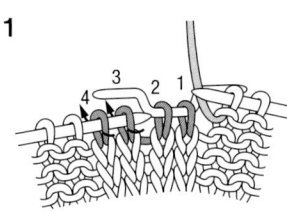

Place two stitches onto a cable needle and hold it at the back of your work. Then, knit the next two stitches.

2

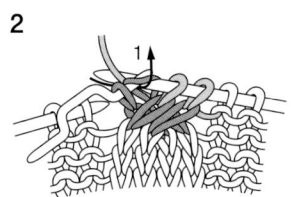

Knit the stitches on the cable needle.

3

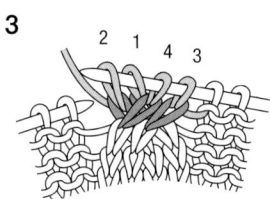

3/3 Left Cross

1

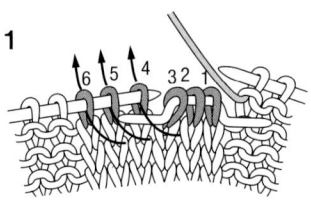

Place the next three stitches onto a cable needle and hold it in front of your work. Then, knit stitches 4, 5, and 6.

2

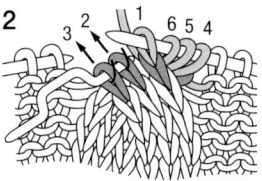

Knit the stitches from the cable needle in the order of stitches 1, 2, and 3.

3

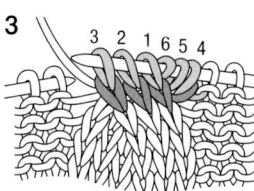

3/3 Right Cross

1

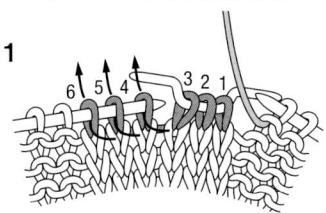

Place the next three stitches onto a cable needle and hold it behind your work. Then, knit the next three stitches: 4, 5, and 6.

2

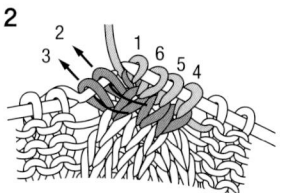

Knit the stitches from the cable needle in the order of stitches 1, 2, and 3.

3

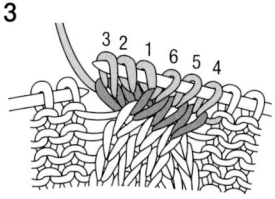

3/1 Left Cross

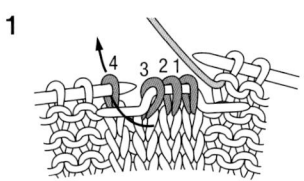

1. Transfer next three stitches onto a cable needle and hold it in front of your work. Then, knit the next stitch (stitch 4).

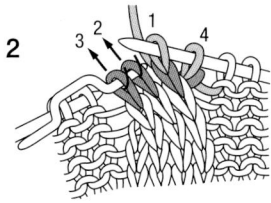

2. Knit the stitches from the cable needle in the order of stitches 1, 2, and 3.

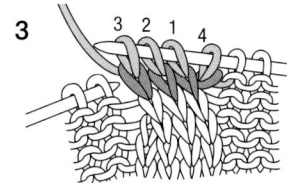

3.

3/1 Right Cross

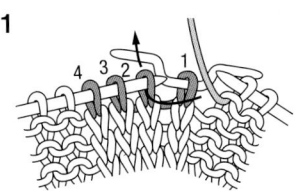

1. Transfer the next stitch onto a cable needle and hold it at the back of your work. Then, knit the next three stitches (stitches 2, 3, and 4).

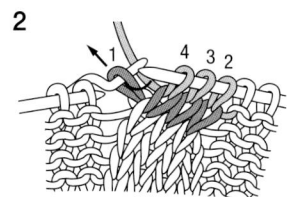

2. Knit the stitch from the cable needle.

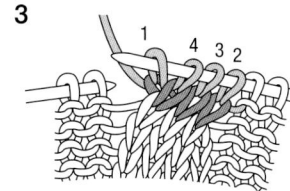

3.

1/3 Left Cross

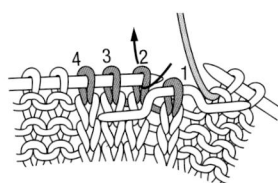

1. Transfer the next stitch onto a cable needle and hold it in front of your work. Then, knit the next three stitches (stitch 2, 3, and 4).

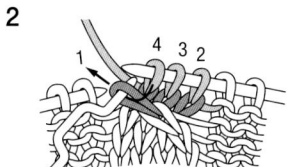

2. Knit the stitch from the cable needle.

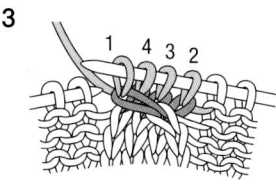

3.

1/3 Right Cross

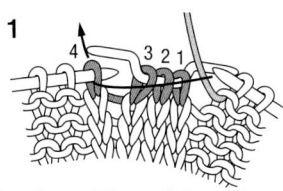

1. Transfer next three stitches onto a cable needle and hold it at the back of your work. Then, knit the next stitch (stitch 4).

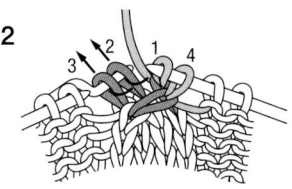

2. Knit the stitches from the cable needle (stitch 1, 2, and 3).

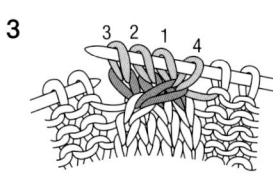

3.

1/1 Left Purl Cross

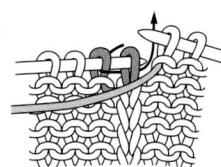

1. Insert the right needle as indicated by the arrow and pull it out.

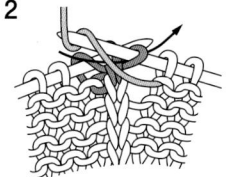

2. Wrap the yarn around the right needle and pull it out as shown by the arrow, then purl.

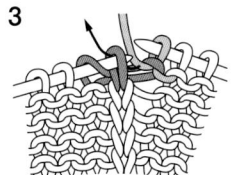

3. Insert the right needle as shown by the arrow and knit through the back loop.

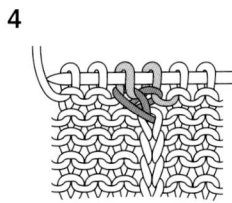

4.

1/1 Right Purl Cross

1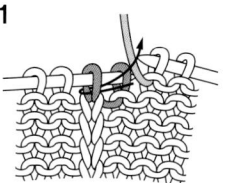
Insert the right needle as indicated by the arrow and pull it out.

2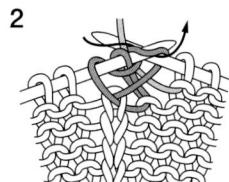
Wrap the yarn around the right needle and pull it out as shown by the arrow, then knit through back loop.

3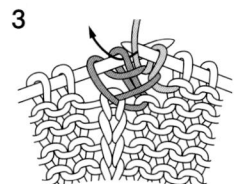
Insert the right needle as shown by the arrow, and purl.

4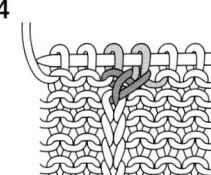

Latvian Braid

1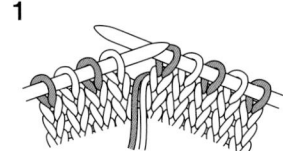
To create the base of your braid, knit a row alternating two colors. At the end of the row, bring both yarns to the front.

2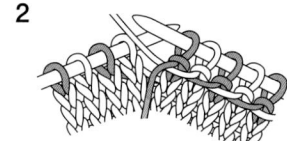
In the next row (for the Latvian braid), bring the yarn for the next color up from under the previous stitch and purl.

3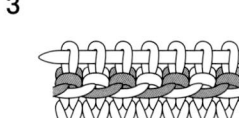

Latvian Braid (flat knitting)

*As you knit the Latvian braid, the two yarns will twist together, so be sure to occasionally untwist them as you go.

1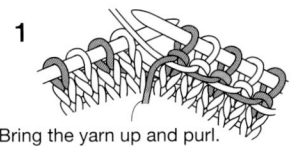
Bring the yarn up and purl.

Work the Latvian braid.

2 Bring the yarn up and knit.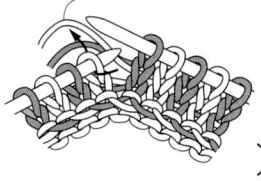

In the next row, work in flat knitting. With the yarn kept at the front of the work, bring the yarn up and knit.

 When viewed from the front, the pattern will resemble the illustration on the left.

Sewing Up Seams (Ladder Stitch)

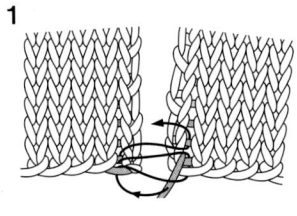

1 **2**

Grafting Two Sets of Live Stitches

1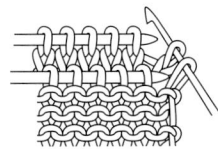
With the right sides facing each other, insert the crochet hook into the outermost stitches on both needles.

2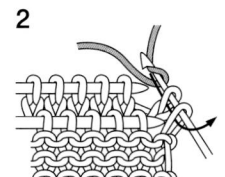
Place the yarn for joining the knit pieces at the far edge of your work, yarn over, and pull through the two stitches together.

3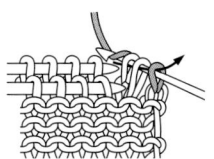
Next, insert the crochet hook into both the front and back stitches, yarn over, and pull through all three stitches at once.

4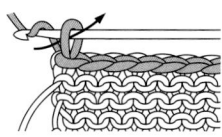
Seam the last stitch, pull the yarn through the remaining stitch on the crochet hook, and then cut the yarn.

• Crochet
How to Make a Magic Ring

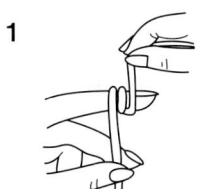
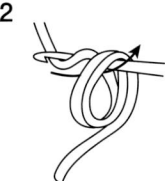
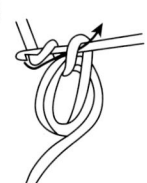

Wrap the yarn loosely twice around your left index finger.

Remove the loop from your finger. As you insert the crochet hook into center of the ring, make the required number of stitches.

Chain Stitch ⌒

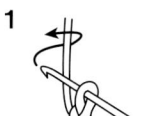
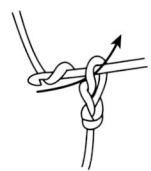

Wrap the yarn around the crochet hook as shown by the arrow.

Pull the yarn through the loop on the crochet hook to make the first chain.

Yarn over and pull the yarn through the loop on the crochet hook to make the second chain.

Single Crochet ×

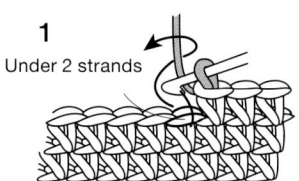

Under 2 strands

Insert the needle into the previous row and yarn over

Pull the yarn through to the front to make a loop.

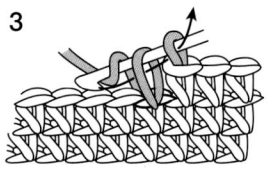

Yarn over again and pull through both loops on the hook.

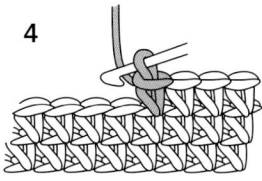

One single crochet stitch is complete.

Half Double Crochet ⊤

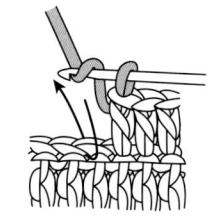

Yarn over, insert the crochet hook into the chain of the previous row, and pull the yarn through to make a loop.

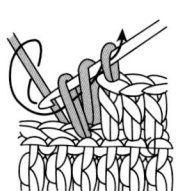

Yarn over again and pull through all three loops on the hook.

Double Crochet ⊤

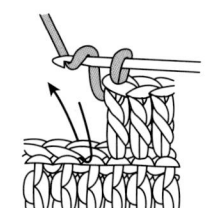

Yarn over, insert the crochet hook into the chain of the previous row, and pull the yarn through to make a loop.

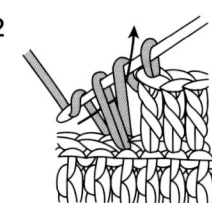

Yarn over and pull through the first two loops on the crochet hook.
* The cluster stitch ends here.

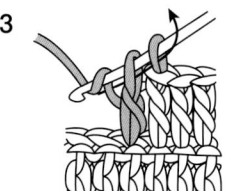

Yarn over once more and pull through the remaining loops.

Triple Crochet

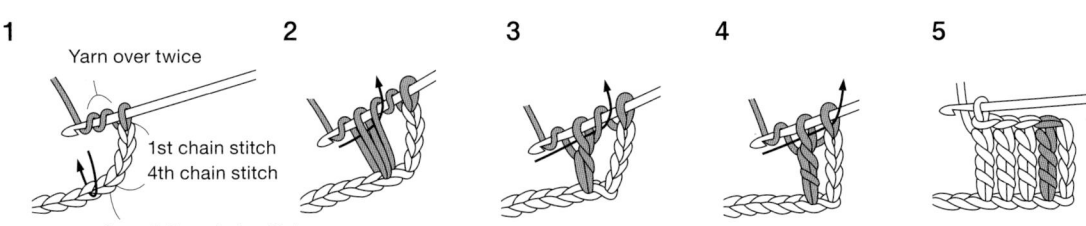

Yarn over twice and insert the hook under the two strands of the previous row.

Yarn over and pull through the first loop on your crochet hook. Adjust the loop so that it is two chain stitches tall. Yarn over and pull through the first two loops on your crochet hook. Yarn over and pull through the next two loops on your crochet hook. Finally, yarn over and pull through the remaining loop on your crochet hook.

2 Double Crochet Cluster

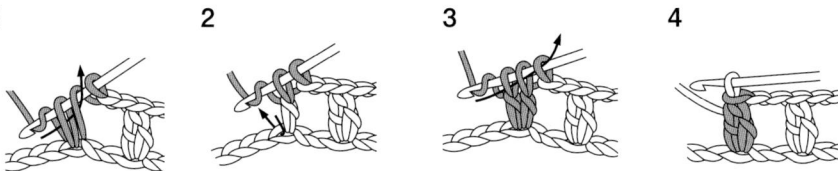

Work two unfinished double crochets into the same stitch of the previous row.

Pull through all the loops at once.

Working Chain Stitch on Foundation Chain

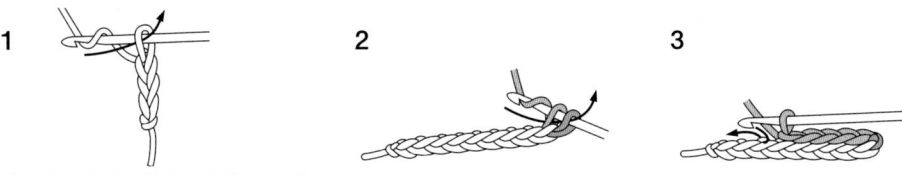

Crochet chain stitches to the required length.

* Note: If you choose to make slip stitches instead of chain stitches, the length will shrink slightly. Make the foundation row about 10% longer than needed.

Once you've crocheted the required length of chain stitches, insert your crochet hook into each chain stitch and work slip stitch.

• Embroidering Instructions

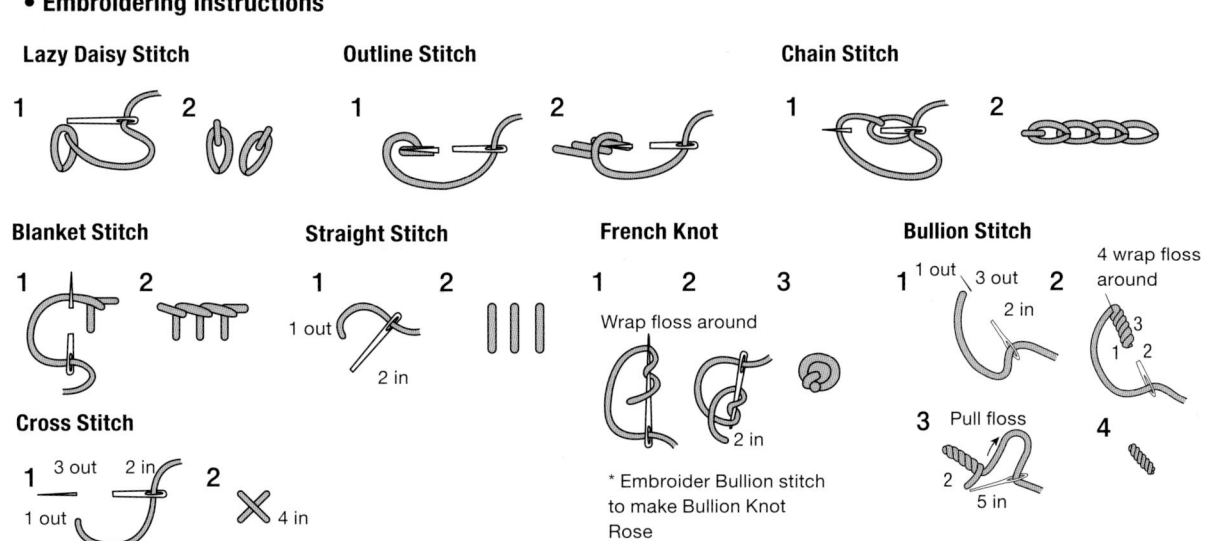

* Embroider Bullion stitch to make Bullion Knot Rose

Tuva Publishing
www.tuvapublishing.com

Address Merkez Mah. Cavusbasi Cad. No71 Cekmekoy - Istanbul 34782 / Türkiye Tel +9 0216 642 62 62

Flower Knitting

First Print 2025 / June

All Global Copyrights Belong to Tuva Tekstil ve Yayıncılık Ltd.

Content Knitting

Editor in Chief
Ayhan DEMİRPEHLİVAN

Project Editor
Kader DEMİRPEHLİVAN

Author
Hiroko IBUKI

Technical Editor
Leyla ARAS

Graphic Designers
Ömer ALP, Yunus GÜLDOĞAN
Abdullah BAYRAKÇI, Tarık TOKGÖZ

ISBN 978-605-7834-91-1

 TuvaPublishing

Hiroko Ibuki

A handicraft artist and knitting designer, she lived in London from the age of fourteen, where she became skilled in various crafts. After returning to Japan, she became a knitting instructor and has actively contributed to craft magazines. She is known for her delicate techniques and innovative color schemes. Since 1993, she has held solo exhibitions in Tokyo, Kyoto, and Shanghai. Additionally, she conducts workshops at her home studio, yarn specialty stores, and cultural centers. She has authored three knitting books, one book on rugs, and one book on amigurumi (knitted stuffed toys).

http://love-live-laugh.cocolog-nifty.com
Instagram: @hirokoibuki

The EEA authorised representative is Authorised Rep Compliance Ltd. Ground Floor, 71 Lower Baggot Street, Dublin, DO2 P593, Ireland (www.arccompliance.com)

FLOWER KNITTING
© 2023 Hiroko Ibuki
© 2023 Graphic-sha Publishing Co., Ltd.
This book was first designed and published in Japan in 2023 by Graphic-sha Publishing Co., Ltd.

This English edition is published in 2025 by Tuva Publishing
English translation rights arranged with GRAPHIC-SHA PUBLISHING CO., LTD. through Japan UNI Agency, Inc., Tokyo

Original edition creative staff
Photos: Yuko Fukui
Book design: Motoko Kitsukawa
Model: Tamako Miyazaki
Patterns: Mari Saito (ATELIER MARIRI)
Editor: Ayako Enaka (Graphic-sha Publishing Co., Ltd.)
Foreign Edition Production and Management: Takako Motoki, Yuki Yamaguchi (Graphic-sha Publishing Co., Ltd.)

Special thanks
DAIDOH FORWARD LTD. /
Puppy (http://www.puppyarn.com)
DMC [Dollfus Mieg & Cie, S.A.] (https://www.dmc.com)
Euro Japan Trading Co.
(https://www.eurojapantrading.com)
Chiharu Okahara, Miyuki Hayashi
BasketMoon (Instagram: @basketmoon_kagoami)